THE NEW PUBLIC SERVICE

FOURTH EDITION

The New Public Service: Serving, not Steering provides a framework for the many voices calling for the reaffirmation of democratic values, citizenship, and service in the public interest. It is organized around a set of seven core principles: (1) serve citizens, not customers; (2) seek the public interest; (3) value citizenship and public service above entrepreneurship; (4) think strategically, act democratically; (5) recognize that accountability isn't simple; (6) serve, rather than steer; and (7) value people, not just productivity.

The New Public Service asks us to think carefully and critically about what public service is, why it is important, and what values ought to guide what we do and how we do it. It celebrates what is distinctive, important, and meaningful about public service and considers how we might better live up to those ideals and values. The revised fourth edition includes a new chapter that examines how the role and significance of these New Public Service values have expanded in practice and research over the past 15 years.

Although the debate about governance will surely continue for many years, this compact, clearly written volume both provides an important framework for a public service based on citizen discourse and the public interest and demonstrates how these values have been put into practice. It is essential reading for students and serious practitioners in public administration and public policy.

Janet V. Denhardt is Chester A. Newland Professor of Public Administration and Director of the Price School Sacramento Center at the University of Southern California, USA.

Robert B. Denhardt is Professor and Director of Leadership Programs in the Price School of Public Policy at the University of Southern California, USA.

"The first edition of this book was published just after 9/11, a time when renewed attention to public service was exemplified by the firefighters and other volunteers who reminded us all what the true value of public service is. However, with the Great Recession government has been used to prop up markets and the Denhardts' call for renewed attention to serving the public is sorely needed. New Public Management's failure has been to equate government with market and substitute consumers for citizens. But, the Denhardts remind us that democracy, not consumer choice, must be the basis for government, and public service, not market service, is its primary function."

Mildred E. Warner, Cornell University, USA

"This book is a great read full of insights that challenge our status quo ways of thinking. It is a 'must read' for everyone who cares about building a better public service."

Rosemary O'Leary, Edwin O. Stene Distinguished Professor of Public Administration, University of Kansas, USA

THE NEW PUBLIC SERVICE

SERVING, NOT STEERING

FOURTH EDITION

JANET V. DENHARDT AND ROBERT B. DENHARDT

Routledge
Taylor & Francis Group

NEW YORK AND LONDON

First published 2015
by Routledge
711 Third Avenue, New York, NY 10017

and by Routledge
2 Park Square, Milton Park, Abingdon, Oxon OX14 4RN

Routledge is an imprint of the Taylor & Francis Group, an informa business

Library of Congress Cataloging in Publication Data
The new public service: serving, not steering/Janet V. Denhardt,
     Robert B. Denhardt.—Fourth edition.
     pages cm
     Includes bibliographical references and index.
     1. Public administration. 2. Public administration—United States.
     I. Denhardt, Robert B. II. Title.
     JF1351.D4495 2015
     351—dc23
     2014042776

ISBN: 978-1-138-89121-0 (hbk)
ISBN: 978-1-138-89125-8 (pbk)
ISBN: 978-1-315-70976-5 (ebk)

Typeset in Times New Roman
by Florence Production Ltd, Stoodleigh, Devon, UK

Printed and bound in the United States of America
by Edwards Brothers Malloy

To the women and men of the public service

Contents

Preface to the Fourth Edition

This book has two primary aims. The first is to synthesize some of the many ideas and voices that have called for a reaffirmation of democratic values, citizenship, and service in the public interest as the normative foundations for the field of public administration. The second is to provide a framework to organize those ideas around principles, giving them a name, a mantle, and a voice that we believe had been lacking. This book is a call to think about and act on our values. It is intended as a challenge for us to think carefully and critically about what public service is, why it is important, and what values ought to guide what we do and how we do it. We want to celebrate what is distinctive, important, and meaningful about public service and to consider how we might better live up to those ideals and values.

Two themes form both the theoretical core and the heart of this book: (1) to advance the dignity and worth of public service, and (2) to reassert the values of democracy, citizenship, and the public interest as the preeminent values of public administration. It is our hope that the ideas presented here may help us, not only to initiate more conversations, but also to look within ourselves for the soul of what we do. We want words such as "democracy" and "citizen" and "pride" to be more prevalent in both our speech and our behavior than words such as "market" and "competition" and "customers." *Public servants do not deliver customer service; they deliver democracy.*

These themes—the dignity and worth of public service and the values of democracy, citizenship, and the public interest—were the subject of two online articles we wrote for the American Society for Public Administration website following the September 11 attacks on the United States. In the first article, we expressed our grief and disbelief, along with our admiration for the brave public servants who went to the aid of those in need. The story of the police and firefighters running up the stairs of the World Trade Center as others struggled down was particularly compelling to us:

These people showed America, once again, that they stand apart. What makes them different is their quiet, often anonymous heroism. They are public servants. They serve their fellow citizens in a way that many people would find very difficult if not impossible to understand. . . . In a peculiar way, this ghastly act of terrorism reminds us of why we are in the public service. We care about our country, our community, and our neighbors. Each of us, whether we wear a uniform, a suit, a jacket, coveralls, or a hard hat, plays a role in improving the lives of others. Service to the public—helping people in trouble, making the world safer and cleaner, helping children learn and prosper, literally going where others would not go—is our job and our calling.

(Denhardt and Denhardt 2001a)

In the second article, we wrote about our continuing admiration for the many public servants who work tirelessly on our behalf and also about the importance of citizenship and our responsibility to promote citizens' active involvement in their government:

The spirit of public service extends beyond those formally working for government, those we think of as public servants. Ordinary citizens have also wished to contribute. However, the avenues through which they might bring their many talents to bear have been somewhat limited, in part, we think, because over the past several decades we have severely constrained the citizenship role, preferring to think of people as customers or consumers rather than citizens.

(Denhardt and Denhardt 2001b)

We were gratified and a little surprised at the response. Many people wrote to us and talked with us about what the articles meant to them and, most importantly, how much they wanted to hear and talk about the values, the soul, and the nobility of public service. In this book, we are trying to extend that discussion by grounding it in history and in the development of thought and practice in public administration. The ideas are not new, but they are beginning to have a clearer voice and spark a renewed interest. What happened to the ideals of public service, and when did we stop hearing about them? How have changes in management philosophy and theories about the proper role and identity of government altered how public servants act, think, and behave? What values of public service, especially those that give the field dignity, courage, and commitment, have been lost in the process? How can we rediscover and affirm them?

In the time since the first edition of *The New Public Service* was published, this discussion has continued. We have been grateful for the opportunity to visit with, and listen to the ideas of, those interested in the New Public Service in communities and organizations across the United States, as well as in Brazil, Sweden, the Netherlands, Italy, Korea, and China, where a Chinese translation of the book was published in 2004. The insights and ideas we gained from these discussions have reinforced our convictions and deepened our respect for the very difficult and important work of public servants in democratic governance. It reminds us of why we wrote this book in the first place—not to lay claim to a set of novel and original ideas, but rather to give voice to the democratic ideals and perspectives that are so critical to effective governance but have too often become overshadowed by other efforts to use business values and approaches to reinvent and otherwise *fix* government.

Subsequent editions of this book (2007, 2011) included new materials on how the principles of the New Public Service can be put into practice and factors to consider in choosing among the many approaches to citizen engagement that have been found successful.

In 2014, the original *Public Administration Review* (*PAR*) article, "The New Public Service: Serving Rather than Steering" (2000) was selected as one of the 75 most influential out of the more than 3,500 articles appearing in the journal since its inception in 1940. We were asked to revisit the key features of the New Public Service and provide an update on how and to what extent those ideas have been discussed, promoted, practiced, and applied over the last 15 years. That review became the basis for a new chapter in this edition titled, "Fifteen Years Later: Are We Rowing, Steering, or Serving?" Our review of the empirical evidence suggests that New Public Service principles and practices have become increasingly evident in scholarship and practice. Citizen engagement has proven to be both effective and widely used, the "public interest" is increasingly significant both as an ideal and as a guide to practice, and the reliance of governments on entrepreneurship and privatization has decreased.

We do not pretend that these developments are a result of this book. Rather, they are a result of the dedication of public servants to the difficult and all-important task of making democratic governance work for citizens. We have never claimed to provide the answers or to define the *correct* values of the field; rather, we want people to continue to thoughtfully examine what values ought to guide action in public service. Ultimately, our purpose is to reinforce the nobility and calling of public service and to help public servants rediscover the soul and meaning of what they do and why they do it.

Janet and Robert Denhardt

Acknowledgments

We are indebted to many people for their guidance and help during our work on this project. We especially want to acknowledge the important models of public service and civic engagement provided by forward-looking public servants and active and engaged citizens across the country and around the world. These are the people who have already established the "New Public Service." We have simply given their work a name.

We also want to thank friends and colleagues in the academic community for their assistance and support during our work on this project. Among the many practitioners and academics we might mention, we especially want to recall the intellectual contributions, support, and friendship of Marvin Andrews, Maria Aristigueta, Lynn Bailey, Eric Bergrud, Dick Bowers, Harry Briggs, Joe Cayer, Linda Chapin, Jeff Chapman, Manuella Cocci, Paul Danczyk, Tom Eichler, Eileen Eisen, Frank Fairbanks, Mark Glaser, Elizabeth Graddy, Elizabeth Granda, Joe Gray, Joe Grubbs, Jay Hakes, John Hall, Mary Hamilton, Mark Holzer, Ed Jennings, Jim Keene, Cheryl King, Jack Knott, Christiaan Lako, Lena Langlet, Juliet Lee, Roz Lasker, Brian Marson, Barbara McCabe, Cynthia McSwain, John Nalbandian, Nico Nelissen, Robert O'Neill, Phil Penland, Jan Perkins, Jeff Raffel, Randy Reid, Dan Rich, Faye Schmidt, Scott Steele, Camilla Stivers, James Svara, Larry Terry, John Thomas, Karen Thoreson, and Orion White.

We also owe a very special thanks to Gregor McGavin, Kelly Campbell, Qian Hu, and Ljubinka Adonoska, our brilliant research assistants, who have made and will continue to make great contributions to the field of public administration. We are also thankful for the assistance of our publisher at Routledge, Laura Stearns. A sincere thanks to all! And, as always, we want to express our love and admiration for our children: Michael, Ben, Cari, and Mary.

Chapter 1

Public Administration and the New Public Management

Government shouldn't be run like a business; it should be run like a democracy. Across this country and around the world, both elected and appointed public servants are acting on this principle and expressing renewed commitment to such ideals as the public interest, the governance process, and expanding democratic citizenship. As a result, they are learning new skills in policy development and implementation, recognizing and accepting the complexity of the challenges they face, and treating their fellow public servants and citizens with renewed dignity and respect. Public employees are feeling more valued and energized as this sense of service and community expands. In the process, public servants are also reconnecting with citizens. Administrators are realizing that they have much to gain by *listening* to the public rather than *telling*, and by *serving* rather than *steering*. At the invitation of public servants, even their urging, ordinary citizens are once again becoming engaged in the governance process. Citizens and public officials are working together to define and to address common problems in a cooperative and mutually beneficial way.

These developments can be understood as part of a movement that we call the "New Public Service." The New Public Service seeks to pose and inform a number of central, normative questions about the field. How can we define the essential character of what we do in the public service? What is the motivating force that propels our actions? What gives us strength and capacity when the trials and turmoil of our work get us down? How can we keep going, even as we face problems that are complex and intractable, with extremely limited resources and a public that often resents and criticizes what we do? We think the answer lies in our commitment to public service.

We find no other reasonable explanation for the extraordinary dedication and commitment of the people who work to make the world safer and cleaner, to improve our health, to teach our children, and to unravel the host of societal maladies that confront us. Where else can we find the foundations for our efforts to facilitate citizenship and public engagement as a central part of our work? What else can keep the firefighters, the police officers, the social workers, the planners and the inspectors, the receptionists and the clerks, the managers and the analysts serving their communities and their country with energy, resolve, and determination?

Research tells us that the ideals of public service are critically important in understanding how public servants can be successful in the work they do. Our objective is to present a unifying set of themes and principles that both express and reaffirm the importance of these public service values. Questions about these values have, of course, been debated throughout the history of public administration in this country, and elsewhere, but there seems to be more concern for these issues today than before. Certainly, there are some important *driving forces* that have been widely discussed in the field of public administration: the New Public Management and the Managing for Results movement, to name just two. Although these influences have been important, none has satisfied our more basic yearning to answer some core questions: Who are we? Why are we here? What does all this mean? People in public administration throughout the history of our field have been encouraged to make things work, but that's only a partial answer. We also want to do something of societal value.

Therein lies the soul of public administration. What is most significant, and most valuable, about public administration is that we serve citizens to advance the common good. Public administrators are responsible for improving the public health, for maintaining public safety, for enhancing the quality of our environment, and myriad other tasks. Ultimately, for them, for us, what really matters is not how efficiently we have done our jobs, but how we have contributed to a better life for all. In this book, we call for an affirmation of the soul of the profession through the New Public Service, a movement grounded in the public interest, in the ideals of democratic governance, and in a renewed civic engagement. This movement, we will argue, is more than ever being manifest in the way we interact with political leaders, in the way we engage with citizens, and in the way we bring about positive changes in our organizations and our communities.

We will approach the task of describing the various elements of the New Public Service by contrasting it with both traditional and more contemporary approaches to public policy and public administration. In this chapter, we will very briefly review the history and development of traditional public administration, what we must now call the Old Public Administration. Then, we will outline what has been the dominant or mainstream approach to contemporary public administration, the New Public Management. In Chapter 2, we will note some of the most important alternative views of public administration, views that have been less than "mainstream" throughout the history of the field, but are now being voiced with increasing urgency. Having examined the context and historical grounding for understanding the New Public Service, in Chapters 3 to 9, we will explore seven aspects of the New Public Service that we find most compelling. In Chapter 10, we provide some examples of how New Public Service values are being implemented in the United States and around the world. At the outset, we should note that we have not attempted to develop a complete theoretical argument for the New Public Service, nor catalog all of the many examples of its practice. Rather, our purpose is to simply lay out, in a very basic way, the normative issues and the alternative ways of thinking about public administration that may be helpful to those working to build the New Public Service.

The Old Public Administration

Although governments have used complex structures of management and organization throughout human history, public administration as a self-conscious field of study and practice is generally thought to have begun around the turn of the century. Its American version, for example, is typically dated to a well-known essay by Woodrow Wilson, then college professor, later president of the United States. Wilson acknowledged the growing and increasingly complex administrative tasks of government by commenting that, "it is getting harder to run a constitution than to frame one" (Wilson 1987/1887, 200). In order to more effectively run government, Wilson advised that we look to the field of business, as, "the field of administration is a field of business" (209). In order to follow the model of business, Wilson advised, government should establish executive authorities, controlling essentially hierarchical organizations and having as their goal achieving the most reliable and efficient operations possible.

Those residing at these centers of power, however, were not to be actively or extensively involved in the development of policy. Their tasks were, instead, the implementation of policy and the provision of services, and in those tasks they were expected to act with neutrality and professionalism to execute faithfully the directives that came their way. They were to be watched carefully and held accountable to elected political leaders, so as not to deviate from established policy. Wilson recognized a potential danger in the other direction as well; the possibility that politics, or more specifically corrupt politicians, might negatively influence administrators in their pursuit of organizational efficiency. This concern led to Wilson's well-known dictum, "Administration lies outside the proper sphere of politics. Administrative questions are not political questions. Although politics sets the tasks for administration, it should not be suffered to manipulate its offices" (Wilson 1987/1887, 210). Thus, Wilson established what was known for many years as the politics–administration (or policy–administration) dichotomy.

Two Key Themes

In Wilson's essay, we find two key themes that served as a focus for the study of public administration for the next half-century or more. First, there was the distinction between politics (or policy) and administration, with its associated ideas of accountability to elected leaders and neutral competence on the part of administrators. Second, there was concern for creating structures and strategies of administrative management that would permit public organizations and their managers to act in the most efficient way possible. Each of these ideas deserves further comment.

First, the idea of separating politics and administration received much early commentary and came to guide practice in a number of important ways. For example, the dichotomy is clearly the basis for the council–manager form of local government, which involves the council being given the responsibility of establishing policy and the city manager being charged with implementing it. Of course, in the council–manager example, as in other areas, a strict separation of politics and administration proved difficult. Members of governing bodies, whether members of city councils or state or federal legislators, always maintained an active interest in the operations of administrative agencies. Especially through the oversight function, they exercised considerable influence in the operations of agencies. Conversely, administrators came to play a more active role in the policy process, especially as they brought expert advice to bear on the legislative process. Over time, many commentators, such as Luther Gulick, first city administrator of New York and a founder of the American Society for Public Administration (ASPA), argued that policy and administration could not be separated, that every act of a public manager involves a "seamless web of discretion and action" (1933, 561). Others, such as Paul Appleby, dean of the Maxwell School at Syracuse University, were even more to the point: "public administration is policymaking" (Appleby 1949, 170).

The distinction Wilson drew between politics and administration has certainly blurred over time. Yet, in many ways, the relationship between politics and administration remains important to the field of public administration. Although a *dichotomy* between politics and administration is overdrawn, the interaction of political and administrative concerns is certainly key to understanding how government operates, even today. Perhaps more important, however, the separation of politics and administration lies at the heart of the Old Public Administration's version of accountability, one in which appointed administrators were held to be accountable to their political "masters"—and only through them to the citizenry. In this view, the requirements of democratic governance are satisfied where a neutral and competent civil service is controlled by and accountable to elected political leaders. Frederick Cleveland, an early writer, commented that democratic accountability is maintained where there is a "representative body (such as a legislature) outside of the administration with power to determine the will of the membership (the citizens) and to enforce (that) will on the administration" (Cleveland 1920, 15; parentheses added). In this view, the legislature operates somewhat like a board of directors overseeing a business operation.

Second, Wilson held, and others agreed, that public organizations should seek the greatest possible efficiency in their operations, and that such efficiency was best achieved through unified and largely hierarchical structures of administrative management. Certainly, that view was consistent with thinking among business managers of the period. Many, such as the efficiency expert Frederick W. Taylor (1923), employed a "scientific management" approach to try to learn, through detailed "time and motion" studies, exactly how the productive process could be improved. Taylor, for example, sought to determine the "one best way" to shovel dirt by designing an experiment that would calculate the ideal weight of a single shovelful of dirt—ideal in the sense of producing the most shoveled dirt per day!

Other early theorists, such as Leonard White (1926) and W.F. Willoughby (1927), focused on building organizational structures that would operate with high efficiency. Again, most found attractive the idea of a strong chief executive vested with the power and authority to carry out the work assigned to the agency. Moreover, that chief executive would be most successful if he or she operated through an organizational structure characterized by unity of command, hierarchical authority, and a strict division of labor. The job of the executive, therefore, was to determine the best division of labor, then to develop the appropriate means of coordination and control.

Or, following Gulick's classic acronym POSDCORB, the work of the executive was planning, organizing, staffing, directing, coordinating, reporting, and budgeting (1937, 13). But again, efficiency was the key value accepted by most early writers and practitioners.

Dissenting Views

That is not to say, however, that *all* accepted efficiency is the ultimate criterion by which to judge administrators. Marshall Dimock, an academic and practitioner, challenged that idea, writing that mechanical efficiency is "coldly calculating and inhuman," whereas, "successful administration is warm and vibrant. It is human" (Dimock 1936, 120). Successful administration, he continued, "is more than a lifeless pawn. It plans, it contrives, it philosophizes, it educates, it builds for the community as a whole" (133). Others suggested that administrators, as well as political leaders, were ultimately concerned with issues such as justice, liberty, freedom, and equality—issues far more formidable and difficult than efficiency alone.

Finally, many writers noted that the search for organizational efficiency might easily occur at the expense of involving citizens in the work of government. Writing somewhat later, Dwight Waldo, perhaps the best-known public administration theorist of his generation, summarized the emerging orthodoxy in the field of public administration by writing that, "The means and measurements of efficiency, it was felt and strongly stated, were the same for all administration. Democracy, if it were to survive, could not afford to ignore the lessons of centralization, hierarchy, and discipline" (Waldo 1948, 200). Moreover, he commented, "Both private and public administration were in an important . . . sense false to the ideal of democracy . . . by reason of their insistence that democracy, however good and desirable, is nevertheless something peripheral to administration" (Waldo 1952, 7).

So, in contrast to using efficiency as the sole criterion for assessing administrative performance, one might employ other criteria, such as responsiveness to the concerns of citizens. An appealing view, one might say. Yet these alternative voices were counterpoint at best, as the emerging field of public administration moved firmly through the ideas of "politics and administration," "scientific management," "administrative management," and "bureaucratic management." In each case, theory and practice confirmed the importance of tightly integrated hierarchical structures, controlled from the top by managers interested in achieving the organization's goals and objectives in the most efficient manner possible. Interestingly, even as the field moved through the next several decades and into its behavioral or "scientific" phase, these same issues continued to be highlighted. Though the justification was somewhat different, the resulting recommendations were much the same.

The Rational Model

The classic *Administrative Behavior* (1957), written by Herbert Simon, a political scientist who later won a Nobel Prize in economics, laid out the argument best. According to the positive science viewpoint Simon represented, statements may be classified according to whether they are true or false. Scientists, of course, are concerned with establishing the truth of certain propositions. In order to do so, they must strip away those pesky "values" that tend to interfere in human affairs. So, those terms that speak to individual or group preferences are not to be admitted into scientific study, in this case the study of administrative behavior. Rather, Simon argued that a single standard, the standard of efficiency, may be used to help remove values from the discussion of organized action.

The key to this argument is the concept of rationality. According to Simon, human beings are limited in the degree of rationality they can obtain in reference to the problems they face, but they can join together in groups and organizations to deal effectively with the world around them, and they can do so in a rational manner. After all, in the abstract, it's not hard to develop a rational course of action to achieve most objectives. The problem comes when we insert real live people, with all their human concerns and idiosyncrasies, into the picture. The issue then becomes one of how to match these people with the rational plan and how to assure that human behavior follows the most efficient path possible.

In contrast to a long philosophical tradition that holds human reason to be concerned with such issues as justice, equality, and freedom, Simon's more restricted view is that rationality is concerned with coordinating the proper means to accomplish the desired ends. In this view, rationality is equated with efficiency. For what Simon called "administrative man," the most rational behavior is that which moves an organization efficiently toward its objectives.

> Administrative man accepts the organizational goals as the value premises of his decisions, is particularly sensitive and reactive to the influence upon him on the other members of the organization, forms stable expectations regarding his own role ... and has high morale in regard to the organization's goals.
>
> (Simon, Smithburg, and Thompson 1950, 82)

Then, through what is called the inducements–contributions model, by controlling the inducements offered to members of the organization, its leaders could secure their contribution and compliance with the rational design of the organization, the result being a far more efficient and productive organization.

Public Choice

Some years after Simon's work, an interesting interpretation of administrative behavior, and one more closely allied with the classic "economic man" position, emerged. This new approach, called "public choice theory," actually provides an interesting bridge between the Old Public Administration and the New Public Management, for, although public choice theory was developed during the time period we generally associate with the Old Public Administration, as we will see later, public choice became much more significant as the key theoretical basis for the New Public Management. For this reason, we will only briefly outline public choice theory here, but return to it frequently throughout the material that follows.

Public choice theory is based on several key assumptions. First, and most important, public choice theory focuses on the individual, assuming that the individual decision maker, like the traditional "economic man," is rational and self-interested and seeks to maximize his or her own "utilities." According to this view, individuals "always seek the biggest possible benefits and the least costs in [any decision situation]. People are basically egoistic, self-regarding and instrumental in their behavior" (Dunleavy 1991, 3). Even if people are not that way, economists and public choice theorists argue that it enables us to better explain human behavior if we *assume* that they are. Second, public choice theory focuses on the idea of "public goods" as the output of public agencies. These can be distinguished from private goods in that a public good, such as national defense, when provided to one person will be provided to all.

A third idea associated with public choice is that different kinds of decision rule or decision situation will result in different approaches to choice making. For this reason, structuring decision rules to influence human choice, and in turn human behavior, is a key to the operations of public agencies and the governance system more generally. In this view, "public agencies are viewed as a means for allocating decision-making capabilities in order to provide public goods and services responsive to the preferences of individuals in different social contexts" (Ostrom and Ostrom 1971, 207). In other words, the public choice approach involves the application of economic models and approaches to nonmarket circumstances, especially government and political science, so as to provide structures and incentives to guide human behavior.

There are a number of questions that have been raised about public choice theory. The first and most obvious is the empirical one. Do individuals really consistently act in a self-interested way so as to maximize their utilities? Obviously, there are many situations in which they do, but also many in which they do not. This means that the public choice model must sacrifice behavioral accuracy in order to put forward a key construct upon which the rest of its theorizing is based. The result is a set of logical propositions based on assumptions that may only remotely correspond to actual human behavior. To an even greater extent than Simon's model of "administrative man," the more purely "economic man" of the public choice model is based on an assumption of complete rationality. One might ask, "Why not focus on other aspects of the human experience, such as feelings or intuition?" For the public choice theorist, the answer is that, in order to provide better explanations for human behavior, we should concentrate on the way individuals and groups attempt to maximize their own interests and on the way that market mechanisms both influence and respond to individual choices.

As Yale political scientist Robert Dahl (1947) pointed out in a critique of Simon's view, a critique also applicable to the more recent public choice model, to say that an action is rational is not to say that it serves moral or politically responsible purposes, but merely to say that it moves the organization forward more efficiently. Dahl suggested that, in contrast, efficiency is itself a value and should compete with other values, such as individual responsibility or democratic morality. In many cases, argued Dahl, efficiency would not be the primary value chosen. For example, how would we evaluate the operation of the German prison camps in World War II, camps that by all accounts were run quite efficiently? Or, more to the current point, how would we balance a concern for administrative efficiency in a public agency with the need for that agency to involve citizens in its decision processes? We think that is an important question. But Dahl's point, like similar arguments made by Waldo and others, was relegated to a position somewhat outside the mainstream in the emerging dialogue about the structure and conduct of public organizations.

Core Ideas

Obviously, many other scholars and practitioners contributed to the early development of the field of public administration. And, as we have seen, there is not a single set of ideas agreed to by all those who contributed over the decades to the Old Public Administration. However, we think that it is fair to say that the following elements generally represent the mainstream view of the Old Public Administration:

- The focus of government is on the direct delivery of services through existing or through newly authorized agencies of government.
- Public policy and administration are concerned with designing and implementing policies focused on a single, politically defined objective.
- Public administrators play a limited role in policymaking and governance; rather, they are charged with the implementation of public policies.
- The delivery of services should be carried out by administrators accountable to elected officials and given limited discretion in their work.
- Administrators are responsible to democratically elected political leaders.
- Public programs are best administered through hierarchical organizations, with managers largely exercising control from the top of the organization.
- The primary values of public organizations are efficiency and rationality.
- Public organizations operate most efficiently as closed systems; thus citizen involvement is limited.
- The role of the public administrator is largely defined as planning, organizing, staffing, directing, coordinating, reporting, and budgeting.

There's no question that the Old Public Administration should be given a considerable amount of credit. Administrators operating largely within the confines of this view made (and continue to make) dramatic and important contributions to society, in areas ranging from national defense, to social security, to transportation, to public health, and to the protection of the environment. The Old Public Administration has allowed us to deal effectively with extremely complex and difficult problems and to maintain a balance between political and administrative concerns. Given the circumstances of its time, the Old Public Administration served well, even if imperfectly. It continues to do so. Most government agencies still follow this basic model of organization and management—or at least this model seems to be the "default" position for agencies at all levels of government. But the old model has come under increasing attack, especially by proponents of what we will call the New Public Management.

The New Public Management

As it is used here, the New Public Management refers to a cluster of contemporary ideas and practices that seek, at their core, to use private-sector and business approaches in the public sector. Although, as we have seen, there have long been calls to "run government like a business," the current version of this debate involves more than just the use of business techniques. Rather, the New Public Management has become a normative model, one signaling a profound shift in how we think about the role of public administrators, the nature of the profession, and how and why we do what we do.

Over the past couple of decades, the New Public Management has literally swept the nation and the world. As a result, a number of highly positive changes have been implemented in the public sector (Barzelay 2001a; Kettl 2005; Kettl and Milward 1996; Lynn 1996; Lynn 2006; Osborne and Gaebler 1992; Osborne and Plastrik 1997; Pollitt and Bouckaert 2000; Shamsul 2007). The common theme in the myriad of applications of these ideas has been the use of market mechanisms and terminology, in which the relationships between public agencies and their customers is understood as involving transactions similar to those that occur in the marketplace. "Painted with the broadest brush, these reforms sought to replace the traditional rule-based, authority-driven processes with market-based, competition-driven tactics" (Kettl 2000a, 3).

In the New Public Management, public managers are challenged either to find new and innovative ways to achieve results or to privatize functions previously provided by government. They are urged to "steer, not row," meaning they should not assume the burden of service delivery themselves, but, wherever possible, should define programs that others would then carry out, through contracting or other such arrangements. The key is that the New Public Management relies heavily on market mechanisms to guide public programs. Harvard's Linda Kaboolian explains that these arrangements might include "competition within units of government and across government boundaries to the non-profit and for profit sectors, performance bonuses, and penalties" (Kaboolian 1998, 190). The aim is to loosen what advocates of the New Public Management see as an inefficient monopoly franchise of public agencies and public employees. Elaborating on this point, Christopher Hood, of the London School of Economics, writes that the New Public Management moves away from traditional modes of legitimizing the public bureaucracy, such as procedural safeguards on administrative discretion, in favor of "trust in the market and private business methods ... ideas ... couched in the language of economic rationalism" (1995, 94).

Following these ideas, many public managers have initiated efforts to increase productivity and to find alternative service-delivery mechanisms based on economic assumptions and perspectives. They have concentrated on accountability to customers and high performance, restructuring bureaucratic agencies, redefining organizational missions, streamlining agency processes, and decentralizing decision making. In many cases, governments and government agencies have succeeded in privatizing previously public functions, holding top executives accountable for measurable performance goals, establishing new processes for measuring productivity and effectiveness, and reengineering departmental systems to reflect a strengthened commitment to accountability (Barzelay 2001b; Boston et al. 1996; Pollitt and Bouckaert 2000).

Donald Kettl, of the Brookings Institution, sees what he calls the "global public management reform," focusing on six core issues (adapted from Kettl 2000a, 1–2):

1. How can government find ways to squeeze more services from the same or a smaller revenue base?
2. How can government use market-style incentives to root out the pathologies of bureaucracy; how can traditional bureaucratic command-and-control mechanisms be replaced with market strategies that will change the behavior of program managers?
3. How can government use market mechanisms to give citizens (now often called "customers") greater choices among services—or at least encourage greater attention to serving customers better?
4. How can government make programs more responsive? How can government decentralize responsibility to give front-line managers greater incentives to serve?
5. How can government improve its capacity to devise and track policy? How can government separate its role as a purchaser of services (a contractor) from its role in actually delivering services?
6. How can government focus on outputs and outcomes instead of processes or structures? How can it replace top-down, rule-driven systems with bottom-up, results-driven systems?

Similarly, New Zealand's Jonathon Boston had earlier characterized the central features or doctrines of the New Public Management, as follows:

> [An] emphasis on management rather than policy; a shift from the use of input controls ... to a reliance on quantifiable output measures and performance targets; the devolution of management control coupled with

the development of new reporting, monitoring, and accountability mechanisms; the disaggregation of large bureaucratic structures into quasi-autonomous agencies, in particular the separation of commercial from non-commercial functions . . . a preference for private ownership, contracting out, and contestability in public service provision; the imitation of certain private sector management practices, such as . . . the development of corporate plans (and) performance agreements, the introduction of performance-linked remuneration systems . . . and a greater concern for corporate image; a general preference for monetary incentives rather than non-monetary incentives, such as ethics, ethos, and status; and a stress on cost-cutting, efficiency, and cutback management.

(Boston 1991, 9–10)

Around the World

The effectiveness of this practical reform agenda in such countries as New Zealand, Australia, Great Britain, and later the United States put governments around the world on notice that new standards were being sought and new roles established. That is not to say that each of these countries followed exactly the same pattern in seeking management reform in the public sector. As leading European scholars Christopher Pollitt and Geert Bouckaert are careful to point out, efforts to reform are constrained by the philosophy and culture of governance within a particular country, by the nature and structure of that country's government, and by luck and coincidence. However, "Certain regimes look as though they are much more open to the 'performance-driven,' market-favouring ideas of the New Public Management than others, particularly the 'Anglo-Saxon' countries, Australia, Canada, New Zealand, the UK, and the USA" (2000, 60–61).

New Zealand's reform efforts were noteworthy, beginning in the mid 1980s as the Labor Party came to power after nine years out of office. At the time, New Zealand's economy had stagnated, and the country found it hard to sustain its traditionally generous social programs and economic support. "The New Zealand reforms began with a top-down approach that sought to privatize programs wherever possible, to substitute market incentives for command-and-control bureaucracies; and to focus single-mindedly on outputs and results instead of inputs" (Kettl 2000a, 8). The key principles underlying the model seemed to be that the government should only be involved in activities that could not be more efficiently and effectively handled elsewhere, and that government should, wherever possible, be organized along the lines of private enterprise. Additionally, there was a strong dependence on incentive systems and the use of explicit contracts between ministers and managers or between purchasers (agencies) and providers (contractors) (Boston et al. 1996, 4–6). In terms of management systems, New Zealand essentially did away with its civil service system, allowing managers to negotiate their own contracts with employees and to introduce budget systems more focused on performance and results. The result was a massive transformation of public management in New Zealand.

Similar changes in the Australian approach to public administration and management in the 1980s and beyond were also triggered by difficult economic times, but went far beyond simply enabling the government to make deep cuts in public programs. As early as 1983, the government under Prime Minister Robert Hawke had endorsed the notion of "managing for results" and had initiated a series of financial management and other reforms to achieve this objective. Again, a variety of efforts at privatization and governmental restructuring and efforts to evaluate programs in terms of specific desired results were implemented. Managers were encouraged to use corporate-style planning processes to identify priorities, goals, and objectives, to reconstitute financial management processes so as to better track expenditures in light of desired results, and to emphasize efficiency, productivity, and accountability for results.

The British reforms largely were triggered by Margaret Thatcher's neoconservative efforts to reduce the size of the state. A key early effort was to reduce costs and spin off those activities that might be better accomplished in the private sector, while subjecting those that remained to market competition wherever possible. Additionally, the Financial Management Initiative centered on identifying specific centers of responsibility, associating costs with outcomes, and holding managers contractually responsible for achieving those outcomes. A later "citizen's charter" exercise sought to hold agencies responsible for meeting specific service standards.

> The [British version of] the new public management stemmed from the basic economic argument that government suffered from the defects of monopoly, high transaction costs, and information problems that bred great inefficiencies. By substituting market competition—and marketlike incentives—the reformers believed they could shrink government's size, reduce its costs, and improve its performance.
>
> (Kettl 2000a, 14)

(For recent reviews of the New Public Management in other countries, see Dent, Chandler, and Barry 2004; Lægreid and Christensen 2007; Levy 2010; Lynn 2006; Pollitt, Van Thiel, and Homberg 2007; Ramesh, Araral, and Wu 2010.)

The American Experience

These ideas were first crystallized and popularized in the United States by David Osborne and Ted Gaebler's best-selling book, *Reinventing Government* (1992; see also Barzelay 2001a; Osborne and Plastrik 1997). Drawing on the experiences of other countries, especially New Zealand, as well as experiences at the state and local level in America, Osborne and Gaebler, a journalist and a former city manager, provided a number of now-familiar "principles" through which "public entrepreneurs" might bring about massive governmental reform, ideas that remain at the core of the New Public Management:

1. *Catalytic Government, Steering Rather than Rowing*: Public entrepreneurs move beyond existing policy options, serving instead as catalysts within their communities to generate alternative courses of action. They choose to *steer*, recognizing a wide range of possibilities and striking a balance between resources and needs, rather than rowing, concentrating on a single objective. Those who steer define their future, rather than simply relying on traditional assumptions (35).

2. *Community-Owned Government, Empowering Rather than Serving*: Public entrepreneurs have learned that past efforts to serve clients produced dependence, as opposed to economic and social independence. Rather than maintain this approach, these entrepreneurs shift ownership of public initiatives into the community. They empower citizens, neighborhood groups, and community organizations to be the sources of their own solutions (52).

3. *Competitive Government, Injecting Competition into Service Delivery*: Public entrepreneurs have recognized that attempting to provide every service not only places a drain on public resources but also causes public organizations to overextend their capabilities, thus reducing service quality and effectiveness. These entrepreneurs counter this trend by fostering competition among public, private, and nongovernmental service providers. The results are "greater efficiency, enhanced responsiveness, and an environment that rewards innovation" (80–83).

4. *Mission-Driven Government, Transforming Rule-Driven Organizations*: Public entrepreneurs have seen how excessive rule making in bureaucratic organizations stifles innovation and limits government performance. Such rule making is further supported by rigid systems of budgeting and human resources. In contrast, public entrepreneurs focus first on the mission of the group—what the organization strives

for internally and externally. Then, the budget, human resources, and other systems are designed to reflect the overall mission (110).

5. *Results-Oriented Government, Funding Outcomes, Not Inputs*: Public entrepreneurs believe that government should be dedicated to achieving substantive public goals, or outcomes, as opposed to concentrating strictly on controlling the public resources expended in doing the job. Current evaluation and reward systems focus mainly on fiscal efficiency and control, rarely asking what impacts were gained from each public initiative. Public entrepreneurs transform these systems to be more results-oriented—that is, accountability based on government performance (140–141).

6. *Customer-Driven Government, Meeting the Needs of the Customer, Not the Bureaucracy*: Public entrepreneurs have learned from their private-sector counterparts that, unless one focuses on the customer, the citizen will never be happy. As legislative bodies provide most public resources to government agencies, these agencies operate completely blind of their customer base. They function according to their own priorities, and those demanded of them by the funding source, instead of what their customers actually need. Public entrepreneurs stand this system on its head, serving the customer first (166–167).

7. *Enterprising Government, Earning Rather than Spending*: Public entrepreneurs face the same fiscal constraints as their traditional counterparts, but the difference is in the way they respond. Rather than raise taxes or slash public programs, public entrepreneurs find innovative ways to do more with less. By instituting the concept of profit motive into the public realm—for example, relying on charges and fees for public services and investments to fund future initiatives—public entrepreneurs are able to add value and ensure results, even in tight financial times (203–206).

8. *Anticipatory Government, Prevention Rather than Cure*: Public entrepreneurs have grown tired of funneling resources into programs to resolve public problems. Instead, they believe the primary concern should be prevention, stopping the problem before it ever occurs. Government in the past prided itself on service delivery—on being able to put forth initiatives aimed at curing public ills. However, as the problems in postindustrial society became more complex, government lost its capacity to respond. By returning to prevention, public organizations will be more efficient and effective for the future (219–221).

9. *Decentralized Government, from Hierarchy to Participation and Teamwork*: Public entrepreneurs appreciate the role centralized organizations served in the industrial age. These institutions represented the

first steps toward professionalization in the field of public adminis-tration. Yet, the age of the hierarchical institution has passed. Advances in information technology, improved communications systems, and increases in workforce quality have brought in a new age of more flexible, team-based organizations. Decision making has been extended throughout the organization—placed in the hands of those who can innovate and determine the high-performance course (250–252).

10. *Market-Oriented Government, Leveraging Change through the Market*: Public entrepreneurs respond to changing conditions, not with traditional approaches, such as attempting to control the entire situation, but rather with innovative strategies aimed at shaping the environment to allow market forces to act. Each jurisdiction—whether a nation, a state, or a local community—represents a market, a collection of people, interests, and social and economic forces. Public entrepreneurs realize that these markets remain beyond the control of any single political body. So, their strategy centers on structuring the environment so that the market can operate most effectively, thus ensuring quality of life and economic opportunity (280–282).

Osborne and Gaebler intended these 10 principles to serve as a new conceptual framework for public administration—an analytical checklist to transform the actions of government.

> What we are describing is nothing less than a shift in the basic model of governance used in America. This shift is underway all around us, but because we are not looking for it—because we assume that all governments have to be big, centralized, and bureaucratic—we seldom see it. We are blind to the new realities, because they do not fit our preconceptions.
>
> (321)

In the United States, the effort to "reinvent government" came later than those in other Anglo-Saxon countries, was more highly politicized, and, in part for that reason, had its effect less on the overall structure of governance in the country and more on managerial practices. Two efforts were particularly important, the National Performance Review (NPR) and the Government Performance and Results Act. The NPR was President Bill Clinton's effort, spearheaded by Vice President Al Gore, to create a government that "works better and costs less." To do so, scores of government employees were sent throughout government agencies seeking out ways in which operations could be streamlined and made less costly. Specific recommendations numbered in the hundreds and included procurement reforms, changes in personnel policy, and developments in information technology. Moreover, there was a strong emphasis on serving the "customers" of government. The NPR, however, took place against a political backdrop necessitating serious cutbacks in federal employment, because this was the one activity that could produce rapid savings. Meanwhile, the congressionally driven Government Performance and Results Act required managers to establish specific performance standards and to "manage for results." Summarizing the first five years of the NPR, Kettl writes that, despite its shortcomings, the NPR "saved a significant amount of money, brought substantial managerial reforms (especially in customer service and procurement processes), and promoted a more performance-based discussion about the functions of government" (Kettl 2000a, 29).

Intellectual Support

To this point, we have discussed the New Public Management in terms of the practical efforts undertaken in governments around the world to reform government operations. But we should also note the various intellectual justifications for the New Public Management. These justifications, as Lynn (1996) notes, largely came from the "public policy" schools that developed in the 1970s and from the "managerialist" movement around the world (Pollitt 1993).

The policy perspective that emerged in schools of public affairs and especially schools of public policy in the last few decades had its roots more clearly in economics as opposed to the more political, science-oriented programs in public administration. Many, though certainly not all, policy analysts and those engaged in policy evaluation were trained in, or at least familiar with, economics and were quite at home with terms such as "market economics," "costs and benefits," and "rational models of choice." In turn, these schools began to turn their attention to policy implementation, which they called "public management" to distinguish it from the earlier "public administration," notwithstanding the fact that both public management and public administration are concerned with implementing public policy through the conduct and operation of the various agencies of government. (The two terms can be used synonymously and often are, but, if there is a difference, it is that discussions of public management tend to show a bias toward economic interpretations of managerial behavior, as opposed to discussions of public administration, which are more likely based in political science, sociology, or organizational analysis.)

As the ultimate extension of the economic view, the New Public Management is clearly linked to the rationalist perspective and, as we noted earlier, especially public choice theory. One important variation on public choice theory that has also influenced the development of the New Public Management is what is called "agency theory" or "principal agent theory." Simply put, agency theory is concerned with the relation between principals and agents. "Agency" refers to a situation in which one individual (the agent) acts on behalf of another (the principal). For example, if I hire a lawyer, I am the principal, and the lawyer is my agent, but the lawyer has multiple incentives—win the case (my goal) and maximize billable hours (his goal). Because our objectives aren't consistent, all sorts of problems arise. In the New Public Management, agency theory can be employed either to analyze issues arising within a particular bureaucracy (e.g., what incentives might a principal provide to assume compliance on the part of an agent?) or to assess the effects of different institutional structures (e.g., how might the multiple interests influencing police officers' behavior affect a decision to privatize a police force?).

Public choice and its companion, agency theory, not only afford an elegant and, to some, compelling model of government, they have also served as a kind of intellectual road map for practical efforts to reduce government and make it less costly. For example, Boston and colleagues argue that, "one of the most distinctive and striking features of New Zealand's public management reforms was the way they were shaped by . . . public choice theory and organizational economics, especially agency theory" (1996, 16). As we have seen, in its simplest form, public choice views the government from the standpoint of markets and customers. In turn, the commitment of public choice theory to rational choice implies a selection of values, most often a commitment to efficiency and productivity. It is not surprising then, as Hood suggests, that the New Public Management has clearly placed its emphasis on values such as efficiency, eliminating waste, or matching resources to clear goals (what he calls "sigma values"). However, he also points out that achieving those values may come at the expense of honesty and fair dealing, the avoidance of bias, or the pursuit of accountability ("theta values"), or security, resilience, and the capacity to adapt ("lambda values") (Hood 1991; see also Hood and Jackson 1991, 14).

The second intellectual justification suggests that the New Public Management is deeply rooted in what has been termed "managerialism" or "neomanagerialism." In the managerialist view, business and public-sector success depends on the quality and professionalism of managers. Christopher Pollitt has described "managerialism" as the belief that the road to social progress is through greater productivity, that such productivity will be enhanced by the discipline imposed by managers oriented toward greater efficiency and productivity, and that to perform this important role, managers must be given what is variously termed the "freedom to manage" or even the "right to manage" (Pollitt 1993, 1–3; see also Lynn 2006).

Some have argued, in addition, that the rise of the New Public Management is attributable, not only to managerialism, but also to the increasing influence of "managerialists." Interestingly, in both New Zealand and Australia, a part of the transformation that occurred was very clearly linked to the emergence of a managerial class dominated by economists and those trained in economics. The Australian scholar Anna Yeatman, for example, argues that the turn toward managerialism in the Australian public service occurred when a large number of university-educated candidates, highly committed to a rationalized and task-oriented concept of public administration, were hired into high-level positions (Yeatman 1987). Michael Pusey, of the University of New South Wales, supports that view, arguing that, in Australia's central agencies, staff drawn from economics or business-related professions—a group he terms "economic rationalists"—were able to capture the line bureaucracies and, especially by threatening to withhold resources, draw them into the rationalist perspective (Pusey 1991).

We have seen that the New Public Management, as the Old Public Administration before it, is not just about the implementation of new *techniques*, but that it carries with it a different set of *values*, a set of values in this case largely drawn from market economics and business management. As already noted, there is a longstanding tradition in public administration supporting the idea that, "government should be run like a business." For the most part, this recommendation has meant that government agencies should adopt those practices, ranging from "scientific management" to "total quality management," that have been found useful in the private sector. The New Public Management takes this idea one step further, arguing that government should adopt, not only the *techniques* of business administration, but certain business *values* as well. Today, the New Public Management is presented as a normative model for public administration and public management.

Engaging the Debate

Certainly, the New Public Management has not been without its critics. Many scholars and practitioners have expressed concerns about the implications of the New Public Management and the role for public managers this model suggests. For example, in a *PAR* symposium on leadership, democracy, and public management, a number of authors thoughtfully considered the opportunities and challenges presented by the New Public Management. Those challenging the New Public Management in the symposium and elsewhere ask questions about the inherent contradictions in the movement (Fox 1996); the values it promotes (Box, Marshall, Reed, and Reed 2001; deLeon and Denhardt 2000; Frederickson 1996; Schachter 1997); the tensions between the emphasis on decentralization promoted in the market model and the need for coordination in the public sector (Bumgarner and Newswander 2009; Dent et al. 2004; Levy 2010; Meier and O'Toole 2009; Peters and Savoie 1996); and the implied roles and relationships of the executive and legislative branches (Carroll and Lynn 1996; Lynn 2006). Others have questioned the implications of the privatization movement for democratic values and the public interest (McCabe and Vinzant 1999) and how entrepreneurship and what Terry (1993, 1998) has called "neomanagerialism" threaten to undermine democratic and constitutional values such as fairness, justice, representation, and participation.

Osborne and Gaebler (1992) told us to steer, not row, the boat. Our question is this: As the field of public administration has increasingly abandoned the idea of rowing and accepted responsibility for steering, has it simply traded one "adminicentric" view for another? In other words, have we traded one model in which public managers seek to achieve greater efficiency and productivity by controlling their agencies and their clients for another model in which the same thing occurs? Osborne and Gaebler write, "those who steer the boat have far more power over its destination than those who row it" (1992, 32). If that is the case, the shift from rowing to steering may have not only left administrators in charge of the boat—choosing its goals and directions and charting a path to achieve them—but also given them more power to do so.

In our rush to steer, perhaps we are forgetting who owns the boat. In their book, *Government is Us* (1998), King and Stivers remind us that the government belongs to its citizens (see also Box 1998; Box et al. 2001; Cooper 1991; Eikenberry and Kluver 2004; Kelly 2005; King and Zanetti 2005; King, Feltey, and O'Neill 1998; Romzek and Johnston 2005; Stivers 1994a, 1994b; Thomas 1995). Accordingly, public administrators should focus on their responsibility to *serve and empower citizens* as they manage public organizations and implement public policy. In other words, with citizens at the forefront, the emphasis should not be placed on either steering or rowing the governmental boat, but rather on building public institutions marked by integrity and responsiveness.

Importantly, in making their case, proponents of New Public Management have often used the Old Public Administration as the foil against which principles of entrepreneurship can be seen as clearly superior. Note, for example, how Osborne and Gaebler contrast their principles to an alternative of rigid bureaucracies plagued with excessive rules, restricted by rule-bound budgeting and personnel systems, and preoccupied with control. These traditional bureaucracies are described as ignoring citizens, shunning innovation, and serving their own needs. According to Osborne and Gaebler, "The kind of governments that developed during the industrial era, with their sluggish, centralized bureaucracies, their preoccupation with rules and regulations, and their hierarchical chains of command, no longer work very well" (1992, 11–12). In fact, although they served their earlier purposes, "bureaucratic institutions . . . increasingly fail us" (15).

If the principles of New Public Management are compared with the Old Public Administration, the New Public Management clearly looks like a preferred alternative. However, even a cursory examination of the literature in public administration clearly demonstrates that these two approaches do not fully embrace contemporary government theory or practice (Adams and Balfour 2009; Agranoff 2007; Bevir 2009; Box 1998, 2008; Bozeman 2007; Bryer 2010; Bryson and Crosby 1992; Carnavale 1995; Catlaw 2007; Cook 1996; Cooper 1991; deLeon 1997; Denhardt 1993, 2008; Farmer 1995, 2005; Fox and Miller 1995; Frederickson 1997; Gawthrop 1998; Goldbard 2010; Goodsell 1994; Harmon 1995, 2006; Hummel 1994; Ingraham et al. 1994; Ingraham and Lynn 2004; Jun 2006; Kettl 2009; Lee 2005; Light 1997, 2008; Luke 1998; McSwite 1997; Meier and O'Toole 2006; Miller and Fox 1997; Moynihan 2008; Nabatchi and Mergel 2010; O'Leary 2006; Perry 1996; Rabin, Hildreth, and Miller 1998; Rohr 1998; Sorensen and Torfing 2008; Stivers 1993; Svara 2007; Terry 1995, 1998; Thomas 1995; Van Wart 2005; Vinzant and Crothers 1998; Wamsley et al. 1990; Wamsley and Wolf 1996). The field of public administration, of course, has not been stuck in progressive reform rhetoric for the last hundred years. Instead, there has been a rich and vibrant intellectual and practical evolution in thought and practice, with important and substantial developments that cannot be subsumed under the title "New Public Management." Thus, there are more than two choices.

We reject the notion that the reinvented, market-oriented New Public Management should be compared only with the Old Public Administration, which, despite its many important contributions, has come to be seen as synonymous with bureaucracy, hierarchy, and control. As we said, if that is the comparison, then New Public Management will always win. In contrast, we will suggest that what is missing in the debate is a set of organizing principles for a more contemporary alternative to the New Public Management. We would like to suggest that the New Public Management should be contrasted with what we will term the New Public Service, a set of ideas about the role of public administration in the governance system that places public service, democratic governance, and civic engagement at the center.

Chapter 2

The Roots of the New Public Service

In the first chapter, we traced the development of the Old Public Administration and the New Public Management. Before moving on, it will be helpful to review some of the themes that emerged in that analysis. First, for at least the first three-quarters of the twentieth century, the mainstream model of public administration was that articulated by writers such as Woodrow Wilson, Frederick Taylor, Luther Gulick, and Herbert Simon. Even though many of its advocates portrayed orthodox public administration as neutral with respect to values, it wasn't. It was a normative model for the conduct of public agencies. Among the value choices made in the construction of this model were a particular description of the public administrator's role, especially in relation to the political (or policy) process, the choice of efficiency (as opposed to responsiveness, etc.) as the primary criterion for assessing the work of administrative agencies, and an emphasis on designing public agencies as largely closed systems, featuring a single "controlling" executive having substantial authority and operating in a top-down fashion. Perhaps the most striking feature of this model, evident in its early versions but especially clear in its later versions, was the use of "rational choice" as the primary theoretical foundation of public administration.

Second, despite the dominance of this model, the prevailing assumptions of the mainstream version of the Old Public Administration were countered, frequently and eloquently, by a series of writers and practitioners who argued for greater discretion, greater responsiveness, and greater openness in the administrative process. These alternative views—which we associate with figures such as Marshall Dimock, Robert Dahl, and, most of all, Dwight Waldo—provided a counterpoint to the overall model, important to remember and often accepted in particular situations, but rarely, if ever, dominant. Indeed, it might be proper to say that these ideas were "embedded" within the prevailing model, to which they were largely subservient.

Third, the New Public Management has presented itself as an alternative to the traditional "bureaucratic" way of conducting the public's "business." The New Public Management holds that government should engage in only those activities that cannot be privatized or contracted out and that, more generally, market mechanisms should be employed wherever possible, so that citizens will be presented with choices among service-delivery options. In addition, the New Public Management suggests a special role for managers, especially entrepreneurial managers, who are given greater latitude in improving efficiency and productivity, primarily through "managing for results." Finally, the New Public Management suggests that public managers "steer rather than row," that is, that they move toward becoming monitors of policy implementation or purchasers of services, rather than being directly involved in service delivery itself. At the base of these recommendations, there are theoretical commitments to such ideas as public choice theory, agency theory, and, in general, the use of economic models in the design and implementation of public policy.

What is interesting is that, although the New Public Management has been touted as an alternative to the Old Public Administration, it actually has much in common with the mainstream model of public administration, specifically a dependence on, and commitment to, models of rational choice. For example, as we discussed earlier, principal agent theory can be applied to the relationship between public executives and those who report to them. When used in this way, a central question would be: What incentive structure is appropriate to secure the cooperation or even compliance of lower employees? Such an approach bears striking similarity to Herbert Simon's inducements–contributions model of more than a half-century ago. In that view, a chief question facing the organization's "controlling group" is how to provide sufficient and appropriate inducements so that lower participants would contribute to the work of the organization. In either case, what makes the model work is a commitment to rational choice. So, although there are clearly differences between the Old Public Administration and the New Public Management, the basic theoretical foundations of these two "mainstream" versions of public administration and public policy are in fact very much alike.

In contrast to these mainstream models of public administration or public management that are rooted in the idea of rational choice, we suggest an alternative, the New Public Service (see Table 2.1, on pages 26–27). Like the New Public Management and the Old Public Administration, the New Public Service consists of many diverse elements, and many different scholars and practitioners have contributed, often in disagreement with one another. Yet there are certain general ideas that seem to characterize this approach as a normative model and to distinguish it from others. Certainly, the New Public Service can lay claim to an impressive intellectual heritage, including the work of those we mentioned earlier who provided constructive dissent to the rationalist prescriptions of the mainstream model (e.g., Dimock, Dahl, and Waldo). However, here we will focus on more contemporary precursors of the New Public Service, including (1) theories of democratic citizenship, (2) models of community and civil society, (3) organizational humanism and the New Public Administration, and (4) postmodern public administration. We will then outline what we see as the main tenets of the New Public Service.

Democratic Citizenship

Concerns about citizenship and democracy are particularly important and visible in political and social theory, both of which call for a reinvigorated and more active and involved citizenship (Barber 1984, 1998; Dagger 1997; Gutman and Thompson 2004; Krause 2008; Mansbridge 1990, 1994; Pateman 1970; Sandel 1996; Weale 2007). However, citizenship can be viewed in different ways. A first and obvious definition focuses on the rights and obligations of citizens as defined by the legal system; that is, citizenship is seen as a legal status. An alternative, broader view considers citizenship as concerned with more general issues related to the nature of one's membership in a political community, including such issues as the rights and responsibilities of citizens, regardless of their legal status (Turner 1993, 3). In this view, citizenship is concerned with the individual's capacity to influence the political system; it implies active involvement in political life. It is this latter view we will focus on here and throughout this book.

Beyond these definitional concerns, there are different ways to understand what is involved in democratic citizenship. For example, one might argue that government exists primarily in order to advance the economic interests of the community and individuals within the community. In this case, the state and the relationship of citizens to the state should be based simply on the idea of self-interest. According to Sandel (1996), the prevailing model of the relationship between state and citizens is in fact based on the idea that

Table 2.1

Comparing Perspectives: Old Public Administration, New Public Management, and New Public Service

	Old Public Administration	New Public Management	New Public Service
Primary theoretical and epistemological foundations	Political theory, social and political commentary augmented by naive social science	Economic theory, more sophisticated dialogue based on positivist social science	Democratic theory, varied approaches to knowledge including positive, interpretive, and critical
Prevailing rationality and associated models of human behavior	Synoptic rationality, "administrative man"	Technical and economic rationality, "economic man," or the self-interested decision maker	Strategic or formal rationality, multiple tests of rationality (political, economic, and organizational)
Conception of the public interest	Public interest is politcally defined and expressed in law	Public interest represents the aggregation of individual interests	Public interest is the result of a dialogue about shared values
To whom are public servants responsive	Clients and constituents	Customers	Citizens
Role of government	Rowing (designing and implementing policies focusing on a single, politically defined objective)	Steering (acting as a catalyst to unleash market forces)	Serving (negotiating and brokering interests among citizens and community groups, creating shared values)

Mechanisms for achieving policy objectives	Administering programs through existing government agencies	Creating mechanisms and incentive structures to achieve policy objectives through private and nonprofit agencies	Building coalitions of public, nonprofit, and private agencies to meet mutually agreed upon needs
Approach to accountability	Hierarchical—Administrators are responsible to democratically elected political leaders	Market-driven—The accumulation of self-interests will result in outcomes desired by broad groups of citizens (or customers)	Multifaceted—Public servants must attend to law, community values, political norms, professional standards, and citizen interests
Administrative discretion	Limited discretion allowed administrative officials	Wide latitude to meet entrepreneurial goals	Discretion needed but constrained and accountable
Assumed organizational structure	Bureaucratic organizations marked by top-down authority within agencies and control or regulation of clients	Decentralized public organizations with primary control remaining within the agency	Collaborative structures with leadership shared internally and externally
Assumed motivational basis of public servants and administrators	Pay and benefits, civil-service protections	Entrepreneurial spirit, ideological desire to reduce size of government	Public service, desire to contribute to society

government exists to ensure that citizens can make choices consistent with their self-interest by guaranteeing certain procedures (such as voting) and individual rights. The role of government is to make sure that the interplay of individual self-interests operates freely and fairly. Obviously, this perspective is consistent with public choice economics and the New Public Management (see Kamensky 1996), and public choice theorists have largely endorsed this view. For example, James Buchanan, a leading public choice theorist, has argued that, although altruism often enters into public deliberations, political institutions should be designed so as to minimize the extent to which institutions rely on altruistic behavior (quoted in Mansbridge 1994, 153).

Others have argued that political altruism, or what Mansbridge calls "public spirit," plays an important, even an essential role in the process of democratic governance. Sandel, for example, offers an alternative view of democratic citizenship in which individuals are much more actively engaged in governance. Citizens look beyond their self-interest to the larger public interest, adopting a broader and more long-term perspective that requires a knowledge of public affairs and also a sense of belonging, a concern for the whole, and a moral bond with the community whose fate is at stake (Sandel 1996, 5–6). Mansbridge argues that this view of citizenship provides a certain "glue" that holds the political system together. In her view, public spirit (or political altruism) involves both love and duty, each playing an important role:

> If I make your good my own through empathy (love), I will be less likely to act in ways that hurt you. If I make the collective good my own (love of nation), I will forgo my individual benefit for that good. If I am committed to a principle that for one reason or another prescribes cooperation, I will forgo self-interest for reasons of duty.
>
> (Mansbridge 1994, 147)

Mansbridge is quick to point out, however, that unrestrained altruism is not necessarily good. There is the possibility that political elites might manipulate public spirit through indoctrination or charisma, through limiting the possibilities of its expression, or through structuring public debate so that challenges to their power are prohibited.

Public spirit needs to be nourished and maintained, and that can be aided by constant attention to principles of justice, public participation, and deliberation. A sense of *justice* evokes strong emotions in those who feel mistreated or exploited, and their resistance can often become quite forceful. On the other hand, a political system that seems intent on promoting justice

In evaluating four large-scale cases of deliberative citizen engagement efforts in Sacramento, California, Eugene, Oregon, and Fort Collins, Colorado, Weeks found that, "it is possible to convene a large-scale public deliberative process that enables local government to take effective action on pressing community problems," using "off-the-shelf research methods" (2000, 371). In each case, the community used a broadly inclusive and iterative process that "provides citizens with extensive information about the nature of the policy problem, engages citizens in the same problem solving context as elected officials, and uses rigorous methods including multiple data sources, multiple measures, and multiple data collection methods" (663).

is likely to engender affection and involvement. *Participation* is a second device for promoting public spirit. Those who are involved in decisions feel better about those decisions and are more likely to aid in their implementation, but participation can be structured so as to give people a false sense of involvement, and so must be balanced with conditions of open deliberation and discourse. *Deliberation* can clarify and sometimes ameliorate perceived differences; it can provide a common ground of information, so that people are at least starting "on the same page"; and it can build a sense of solidarity and commitment to solutions that may be proposed. "And good deliberation will often lead all but the most contrary-minded to change at least some of their preferences, sometimes producing agreement, sometimes clarifying conflict in ways that reveal what steps to take next" (Mansbridge 1994, 156).

Note that this alternative view of citizenship does not suggest the elimination of self-interest as an individual or social motive or its naive replacement by the notion of public spirit. To do so would neglect important and appropriate concerns—as well as longstanding debates in America and elsewhere. But this view does suggest a balancing of these "motives" and, ultimately, recognition of the primary importance of civic virtue and the public interest, such as we might expect in a democratic society. The idea of deliberation, for example, suggests an initial interchange between ideas borne out of self-interest, but it also suggests that such an interchange may open one to new ideas and even to new practices, including some that may eventually be pursued, even though they may work against narrow self-interest.

In any case, there have been increasing calls for a restoration of a citizenship based on civic interests rather than self-interest. In this view, citizens would be concerned with the broad public interest, they would be active and involved, and they would assume responsibility for others. As Evans and Boyte put it so eloquently, a reinvigorated notion of citizenship would include:

> a concern for the common good, the welfare of the community as a whole, willingness to honor the rights for others that one possesses, tolerance of diverse religious, political, and social beliefs, acceptance of the primacy of the community's decisions over one's own private inclinations, and a recognition of one's obligations to defend and serve the public.
>
> (Evans and Boyte 1986, 5)

In other words, citizens would do what citizens are supposed to do in a democracy—*they would run the government.* As they did so, they would contribute, not only to the society's betterment, but also to their own growth as active and responsible human beings.

Though we will elaborate this point later (indeed, throughout this book), these lessons concerning a more active and vital citizenship have clearly found their way into the literature and practice of public administration. An early symposium on "citizenship and public administration," published in the *PAR*, considered a variety of theoretical and practical issues connecting emerging ideas of civics and citizenship to the profession of public administration (Frederickson and Chandler 1984). Three important books, *Government is Us* (King and Stivers 1998), *Citizen Governance* (Box 1998), and *Transformational Public Service* (King and Zanetti 2005), have focused on how public administrators might contribute to the creation of a more citizen-centered government. Consistent with this perspective, King and Stivers (1998) assert that administrators should see citizens as citizens (rather than merely voters, clients, or "customers"), should share authority and reduce control, and should trust in the efficacy of collaboration. Moreover, in contrast to managerialist calls for greater efficiency, King and Stivers suggest that public managers should seek greater responsiveness and a corresponding increase in citizen trust. Box moves the argument specifically to the local government level, suggesting ways in which local governments might be restructured to allow for greater citizen involvement in the governance process. King and Zanetti explore cases of exemplary public service. As we will see, these and other adaptations of recent work in democratic theory, and especially theories of citizenship and civic engagement, have contributed to what we will term the New Public Service.

Models of Community and Civil Society

We can also locate important roots of the New Public Service in discussions about community and civil society. The widespread current interest in community is an interesting phenomenon, arising as it does in so many different arenas (Bellah et al. 1985, 1991; Etzioni 1988, 1995; Gardner 1991; Selznick 1992; Wolfe 1989) and being articulated by commentators of both the left and the right. On the one hand, those toward the left see community as an antidote to the excessive and unrestrained greed and self-interest that mark modern society, a cure for individualism run rampant. Meanwhile, those toward the right see community as an avenue to restore basic American values that were once held, but are now being challenged by forces that seem to be beyond our making or our control.

Why so many should be interested in community is an interesting question. Some suggest that Americans have become alienated by the overwhelming force of a technological society, epitomized by the assembly line or the computer, and seek a return to more "human" associations. Others blame the social and political dislocations connected with the Vietnam War and the Civil Rights movement and hope for a time and circumstance of greater gentility and perhaps remorse. Still others cite the excesses of capitalism and the moral ineptitude of those involved in questionable market practices and "insider trading" schemes as requiring a renewed sense of social responsibility. Still others become wary at the prospect of a global economy not necessarily dominated by the United States and hope for economic certainty. Finally, some point to the degradation of the environment and the possible end of human existence implied by the existence of weapons of mass destruction; they want ecological balance and security. All seem to somehow recognize that life has gotten "out of control," and that people need a way to take back their lives.

In any case, community has become a dominant theme in American life. Although different writers focus on different aspects of community, the work of John Gardner is exemplary in its clarity and persuasiveness. Gardner (1991) holds that a sense of community, which might be derived from many different levels of human association, from the neighborhood to the work group, might provide a helpful mediating structure between the individual and society. Gardner writes:

> In our system, the "common good" is first of all preservation of a system in which all kinds of people can—within the law—pursue their various visions of the common good, *and* at the same time accomplish the kinds of mutual accommodation that make a social system livable and workable.

The play of conflicting interests in a framework of shared purposes is the drama of a free society.

(1991, 15)

The shared values of a community, according to Gardner, are important, but he urges that we also recognize that wholeness must also incorporate diversity. Gardner writes:

To prevent wholeness from smothering diversity, there must be a philosophy of pluralism, an open climate for dissent, and an opportunity for sub-communities to retain their identity and share in the setting of larger group goals. To prevent diversity from destroying wholeness, there must be institutional arrangements for diminishing polarization, for teaching diverse groups to know one another, for coalition-building, dispute resolution, negotiation and mediation. Of course the existence of a healthy community is in itself an instrument of conflict resolution.

(Gardner 1991, 16)

Beyond these features, according to Gardner and others, community is based on caring, trust, and teamwork, bound together by a strong and effective system for communications and conflict resolution. The interactive nature of community mediates between and reconciles the individual and the collectivity. Rosabeth Moss Kantor, the well-known management theorist, comments on this idea in some of her early work on community. She writes:

The search for community is also a quest for direction and purpose in the collective anchoring of the individual life. Investment of self in a community, acceptance of its authority and willingness to support its life can offer identity, personal meaning, and the opportunity to grow in terms of standards and guiding principles that the member feels are expressive of his own inner being.

(Kantor 1972, 73)

In part, this effort depends on building a healthy and active set of "mediating institutions" that simultaneously serve to give focus to the desires and interests of citizens and to provide experiences that will better prepare those citizens for action in the larger political system. As Robert Putnam (2000) argues, America's democratic tradition is dependent on the existence of civically engaged citizens, active in all sorts of groups, associations, and governmental units. Families, work groups, churches, civic associations, neighborhood groups, voluntary organization clubs, and social groups—even athletic teams—help establish connections between the individual and the larger society. Collectively, these small groups constitute a "civil society" in which people need to work out their personal interests in the context of community concerns. Civil society is one place where citizens can engage one another in the kind of personal dialogue and deliberation that is the essence, not only of community building, but of democracy itself (see Walzer 1995).

A great deal of commentary on the notion of citizenship and civil society has focused on the apparently decreasing involvement of American citizens in politics and government. People seem disillusioned with government, they are withdrawing from the political process, and they are becoming more and more isolated in their private spaces. Public opinion polls, for example, have shown a sharp decrease in people's trust in government, especially at the federal level. For several decades, the University of Michigan's Survey Research Center has been gathering Americans' responses to the question, "How much of the time do you trust the government in Washington to do the right thing?" Forty-five years ago, more than three out of every four Americans said that they trusted the government "just about always" or "most of the time." Today, fewer than one out of four give this response. Trust in government seems to be at an all-time low.

Some, however, have argued for a more balanced view. David Mathews of the Kettering Foundation, for example, has suggested that, although the interest of citizens in the political process may have been sublimated over the years, it is not dead. Mathews (1994) cites a Kettering-sponsored study that discovered strong feelings of powerlessness and exclusion among citizens, but also deep concerns and an untapped sense of civic duty. Citizens felt great frustration and anger that:

> They had been pushed out of the political system by a professional political class of powerful lobbyists, incumbent politicians, campaign managers and a media elite. They saw the system as one in which votes no longer made

In Los Angeles, city officials and neighborhood councils developed and signed agreements that outlined "the processes and guidelines for more collaborative delivery of services," based on a "Learning and Design Forum" model. This process had three stages: "(1) pre-assessment and planning, (2) implementing Learning and Design Forums, and (3) agreement coordination" (Kathi and Cooper 2005, 564).

any difference because money ruled. They saw a system with its doors closed to the average citizen.

(Mathews 1994, 12–15)

As a consequence, citizens felt alienated and detached.

On the other hand, citizens still want to act. They are proud of their communities and their country and they want to help bring about positive change. In fact, many citizens are becoming engaged in political activities of a new sort, not spending their time in electoral or party politics, which they see as closed and impenetrable, but in grass-roots, citizen-based movements within neighborhoods, work groups, and associations. These activities constitute laboratories of citizenship, arenas in which people are seeking to work out new relationships with one another and the larger political order, relationships cognizant of the dilemmas of participation imposed by the modern world, but also informed by the new possibilities for activism and involvement that modern conditions offer (Boyte 2005; Boyte and Kari 1996; Fishkin and Laslett 2003; Gutman and Thompson 2004; Jacobs, Cook, and Carpini 2009; Lappé and Du Bois 1994; Meijer 2011; Nabatchi and Mergel 2010; Woolum 2010).

There also seems to be an important role for government in encouraging community building and civil society. Interestingly, many progressive and forward-looking civic and political leaders are coming to recognize the importance and the viability of such efforts—and are becoming involved themselves. Political leaders are reaching out to citizens in substantial ways, through both modern information technology and more conventional means. Similarly, public managers are redefining their role with respect to the involvement of citizens in the governmental process (Creighton 2005; Thomas 1995). Again, government can play an important and critical role in creating, facilitating, and supporting connections between citizens and their communities.

How are public administrators affected by, and how do they affect, community and civil society? Although this question will occupy us throughout the remainder of this book, there are several general comments we can make at the outset. First, where strong networks of citizen interaction and high levels of social trust and cohesion among citizens exist, public administrators can count on these existing stocks of social capital to build even stronger networks, to open new avenues for dialogue and debate, and to further educate citizens with respect to matters of democratic governance (Woolum 2000). Second, public administrators can contribute to building community and social capital. Some argue that the primary role of the public administrator is that of building community (Borins 2013; Gergen and

Kellerman 2003; Nalbandian 1999; Zeemering 2008). Others certainly argue that public administrators can play an active role in promoting social capital by encouraging citizen involvement in public decision making. Based on their experience in conducting broad-scale efforts in civic engagement, Joseph Gray and Linda Chapin comment, "citizens don't always get what they want, but including them personalizes the work we do—connects public administration to the public. And this connection leads to understanding for both citizens and administrators" (1998, 192). Such an understanding enriches both government and the community.

Organizational Humanism and the New Public Administration

A third important theoretical root of the New Public Service is organizational humanism. Over the past 30 years, public administration theorists have joined colleagues in other disciplines in suggesting that traditional hierarchical approaches to social organization are restrictive in their view of human behavior, and they have joined in a critique of bureaucracy and a search for alternative approaches to management and organization. Collectively, these approaches have sought to fashion public organizations less dominated by issues of authority and control and more attentive to the needs and concerns of internal and external constituents.

Just as writers such as Dimock, Dahl, and Waldo provided a contrast to the prevailing view of public administration theory, writers such as Chris Argyris and Robert Golembiewski provided counterpoint to the prevailing view of organizational management through the last part of the twentieth century. In an early book, *Personality and Organization*, Argyris explored the impact of traditional management practices on the psychological development of individuals within complex organizations. Argyris noted that studies of the human personality indicated that people growing from infancy to adulthood move from passivity to activity, from dependence to independence, from a limited range of behaviors to a greater range, from shallow to deeper interests, from shorter to longer time perspectives, from a subordinate position to a position of equality or superordination, and from a lack of awareness to greater awareness (1957, 50). In contrast, what Argyris saw as the standard management practices of that time (and one could argue that they have not changed all that much, even today) seemed to inhibit the development of employees rather than enhancing it. For example, in most organizations, people have relatively little control over their work. In many cases, they are expected to be submissive, dependent, and limited in what they can do. Such an arrangement ultimately backfires, Argyris argued, as it limits the contributions employees can make to the organization. In order to promote individual growth, as well as improved organizational performance, Argyris sought an approach to management in which managers would develop and employ "skill in self-awareness, in effective diagnosing, in helping individuals grow and become more creative, [and] in coping with dependent-oriented . . . employees" (Argyris 1962, 213). As Argyris's work matured, he increasingly focused on ways that organizations could move in this direction through programs of planned change known as "organization development."

We should note that Argyris's ideas stood in direct contrast to the prevailing rational model of administration, articulated most clearly, as we saw, by Herbert Simon. Indeed, in 1973, Argyris used the pages of *PAR* to explore some limitations of the rational model (Argyris 1973). Argyris began by pointing out that Simon's rational model is quite similar to traditional administrative theory, in which management defines the objectives of the organization and the tasks to be performed, as well as training, rewarding, and penalizing employees—all within the framework of formal pyramidal structures in which authority flows from the top down. What Simon adds to this model is a focus on rational behavior, that is, behavior that can be defined in terms of means and ends. (Again, in this view, "rational" is not concerned with broad philosophical concepts such as freedom or justice, but rather with how people can efficiently accomplish the work of the organization.) Given this emphasis, the rational model focuses on "the consistent, programmable, organized, thinking activities of man," it gives "primacy to behavior that is related to goals," and assumes "purpose without asking how it has developed" (Argyris 1973, 261).

Such a view fails to acknowledge the full range of human experience, the fact that people act spontaneously, that they experience chaos and unpredictability in their lives, and that they act on feelings and emotions that are far from rational. Moreover, because human growth is not a fully rational process, organizations built on this model would not support the growth, development, and "self-actualization" of the individual. Rather, the rational model would give preference to those changes that would improve the rationality (the efficiency) of the organization. Those changes would likely be highly conservative, reinforcing the status quo by focusing "more on what is than what might be" (Argyris 1973, 261). In contrast to this view, Argyris urges greater attention to "individual morality, authenticity, [and] human self-actualization," attributes associated with the "human side of enterprise" (253).

In the field of public administration, the organization development (OD) perspective has been explored most thoroughly by Robert Golembiewski. In an early work, *Men, Management, and Morality* (1967), Golembiewski developed a critique of traditional theories of organization, with their emphasis on top-down authority, hierarchical control, and standard operating procedures, arguing that such approaches reflect an insensitivity to the *moral* posture of the individual, specifically the question of individual freedom. In contrast, Golembiewski sought a way to "enlarge the area of discretion open to us in organizing and to increase individual freedom" (1967, 305). Following an OD perspective, Golembiewski urged managers to create an open, problem-solving climate throughout the organization, so that members can confront problems rather than fight about or flee from them. He encouraged them to build trust among individuals and groups throughout the organization, to supplement or even replace the authority of role or status with the authority of knowledge and competence. He suggested that decision-making and problem-solving responsibilities be located as close as possible to information sources, and to make competition, where it exists, contribute to meeting work goals, as opposed to win–lose competition. He said the idea was to maximize collaboration between individuals and units whose work is interdependent, and to develop reward systems that recognize both the achievement of the organization's mission and the growth and development of the organization's members. Managers should work, he said, to increase self-control and self-direction for people within the organization, to create conditions under which conflict is surfaced and managed appropriately and positively, and to increase awareness of group process and its consequences for performance (Denhardt 1999, 405).

Interestingly, Golembiewski, like Argyris, contrasted his more humanistic view of organization with the rational choice model, in this case through a critique of the public choice model. Golembiewski first argued that the assumption of classical rationality is a methodological construct that simply doesn't reflect reality (a point that even public choice theorists acknowledge). People don't always act rationally or even approximate rational behavior. To base a theory of choice on the assumption that they do, means that one is limited to logical propositions about how people would behave if they did act rationally. Such a view, Golembiewski argues, neglects important political or emotional considerations, which should be taken into account in developing any comprehensive theory of human behavior. Otherwise one might conclude, with Norton Long, that public choice theorists "argue with elegant and impeccable logic about unicorns" (quoted in Golembiewski 1977, 1492).

Other important contributions to constructing more humanistic organizations in the public sector were made by a group of scholars collectively known as the New Public Administration, essentially the public administration counterpart to the late 1960s/early 1970s radical movements in society generally and in other social science disciplines. Although the New Public Administration was never a very coherent movement, with its contributors often differing substantially with one another, some of the ideas associated with the New Public Administration are important to recall. Certainly, with respect to the issue of organizational humanism, several of the scholars during that period emphasized the need to explore alternatives to the traditional, top-down, hierarchical model of bureaucratic organization. Indicting the old model for its objectification and depersonalization of organizational members and calling for models built around openness, trust, and honest communications, these scholars discussed alternatives with such names as the "dialectical organization" and the "consociated model." Denhardt put it this way in his book *In the Shadow of Organization*:

> The creation of settings in which creativity and dialogue can occur, in which mutuality and respect contribute both to individual growth and development as well as to enabling groups and organizations to deal more effectively and responsibly with environmental complexity, is an effort that begins with the acts of individuals.
>
> (1981, xii)

We should note that the New Public Administration contributed other dissenting viewpoints to the mainstream discussion of public administration. Specifically, there was an argument for having administrators play a more active role in the development of public policy than had previously been the case, in part because the complexity of contemporary problems required the expertise of professionally trained administrators and their associated technical specialists, and in part simply because "somebody has to take on the challenges." There was a more explicit recognition and discussion of the role of values in public administration. For example, George Frederickson, in his *New Public Administration*, argued on behalf of social equity as a guiding concept in administrative and political decision making: "It is incumbent on the public servant to be able to develop and defend criteria and measures of equity and to understand the impact of public services on the dignity and well-being of citizens" (1980, 46). Essentially, providing equitable solutions to public problems involves offering, not just the same services to all, but greater levels of service to those in greater need. Frederickson argues that public administration is not neutral and certainly should not be judged by the criterion of efficiency alone. Rather, concepts such as equality, equity, and responsiveness should also come into play.

The Art at Work project in Portland, Maine, engaged public servants and community artists to explore issues of inclusion and diversity and to provide a new way of thinking about community problems. Police officers worked with community writers to create a "Police Poetry Calendar" to address police–community relations and low morale, and Immigration and Refugee Services staff and Public Services employees used printmaking to explore community issues.

Postmodern Public Administration

A fourth, important theoretical root of New Public Service is postmodernism. In the late 1960s and early 1970s, scholars in public administration began to explore more critically the approach to knowledge acquisition that underlay the mainstream rational model of administration. The basis for this exploration was the idea that mainstream public administration, like other social sciences, had become dependent on a particular approach to knowledge acquisition—positivism—and that this approach subtly but dramatically limited the range of thinking possible in the field. To put it simply, the positivist approach argues that social sciences can be understood using the same approaches employed in the natural sciences. In this view, the facts of social or organizational life can be separated from values; the role of science is to focus on fact rather than value. Facts can be observed and measured, just as the behavior of physical or chemical elements can be measured. In turn, concepts and theories can be built based on these observations of "manifest behavior." The positivist approach was acknowledged as the foundation of Simon's rational model of administration and clearly came to dominate other aspects of the study of public administration, especially the policy sciences.

Critics of this view pointed out that observing human behavior "from the outside" tells us far less than understanding the *meaning* of human action. For example, you might see a man running through the woods, but you would know more about what was happening if you knew he was a criminal fleeing the sheriff. Similarly, in social life, facts and values are extremely difficult to separate, and, indeed, in many cases, *values* are more important than facts in understanding human action. In any case, as human behavior differs from time to time and from culture to culture, it's impossible to formulate the same kind of enduring, lawlike statements that the hard sciences seek.

Moreover, describing human action in terms of "objective" observations and "lawlike relationships" fails to recognize the nonrational components of human experience—intuitions, emotions, and feelings. Finally, scholars pointed out that social science is not neutral (as it claims); the measurement of human behavior can affect the behavior, as in the Hawthorne experiments, when workers reacted more to the fact they were being observed than to changes the researchers made in their work environment.

On the one hand, critics pointed out that reliance on the positivist model reinforced tendencies toward objectification and depersonalization that were already part of the mainstream model of public administration. On the other hand, they also argued that relying on positivism alone simply didn't permit the fullest and most complete understanding of the meanings and values that are so much a part of human life. In a search for alternatives, scholars turned to *interpretive* approaches to knowledge acquisition, approaches that focused on understanding the meanings that people bring to their experiences, especially those experiences that they share with others (Harmon 1981). Others turned to a *value-critical* examination of the forces that underlie human experiences, especially those forces of power and domination that distort communications among human beings (Denhardt 1981). Through approaches such as these, scholars hoped to build alternative approaches to the study and practice of public administration, alternatives more sensitive to values (not just facts), to subjective human meaning (not just objective behavior), and to the full range of emotions and feelings involved in relationships between and among real people (White 2002).

These ideas have been even further extended in recent efforts to employ the perspectives of postmodern thinking, especially discourse theory, in understanding public organizations. Although there are significant differences among the various postmodern theorists, they seem to arrive at a similar conclusion—because we are dependent on one another in the postmodern world, governance must increasingly be based on sincere and open discourse among all parties, including citizens and administrators. And although postmodern public administration theorists are skeptical of traditional approaches to public participation, there seems to be considerable agreement that enhanced public dialogue is required in order to reinvigorate the public bureaucracy and restore a sense of legitimacy to the field of public administration.

Although postmodernism is extremely complex and diverse, most postmodernists would argue that a problem we face today is that we have lost the capacity to tell what is *real*. All those previously held "worldviews," as well as "scientific explanations" that seemed to work in the past, have been revealed to have fatal flaws, most of these related to the fact that these explanations were the products of particular places and particular times and could only address the world from that largely unique standpoint. If we create the world through our language and our interactions, then there will inevitably be limitations on what we can claim to be "real."

The situation is even more complicated because a vast and confusing world of symbolism has come to dominate our thinking and our feeling. For example, in television commercials, sex is used to sell cars, and frogs are used to sell beer. The communication is all one way. We, the passive viewers, don't have a chance to talk back. Ultimately, these symbols, and others like them in the worlds of art, music, architecture, and politics (to name only a few), come to replace the "reality" from which they grew and to constitute the only culture we share in common. At the cultural level, we can communicate with each other only in terms of abstractions devoid of "reality." More and more, we are forced to recognize that the only authentic communication in which we can fully engage is face-to-face interaction based on our recognition of the other as a self we share.

Public administration theorists employing the postmodern perspective are particularly critical of the field's apparent preoccupation with rationalism (especially market-based rational choice theory) and technocratic expertise (Farmer 1995, 2005; Fox 2002; Fox and Miller 1997; Harmon 2006; Jun 2006; McSwite 1997).

> In bureaucracy, the world of robust social action is displaced by the world of rationally organized action. Obedience of hierarchically commanded routines supersedes empathetic relationships with others. . . . In monologic communication there is no back-and-forth, no opportunity to engage in a verbal struggle to define a problem and decide what should be done about it.
>
> (Fox and Miller 1997, 70–71)

In contrast, postmodern public administration theorists have a central commitment to the idea of "discourse," the notion that public problems are more likely resolved through discourse than through "objective" measurements or rational analysis (McSwite 1997, 377).

The ideal of authentic discourse sees administrators and citizens as engaging fully with one another, not merely as rationally self-interested individuals being brought together to talk, but as participants in a relationship in which they engage with one another as human beings. The resulting process of negotiation and consensus building is one in which individuals engage with one another as they engage with themselves, fully embracing all aspects of the human personality, not merely rational, but experiential, intuitive, and emotional. However, that change is an immensely difficult one, requiring that we come to understand (1) how it is possible to act without relying on reason and (2) how to come to terms with the idea of otherness. O.C. McSwite offers a practical first step—to open ourselves to one another:

> The alternative is to *listen*, to become hollowed out, and to receive the other as oneself. This . . . is not so much the end of reason as its transformation. . . . By making people and their lives an object in its contemplations, reason separates us from one another when the reality of the human condition is, I am you.
>
> (1997, 276–277)

The New Public Service

Theorists of citizenship, community and civil society, organizational humanism and the new public administration, and postmodernism have helped to establish a climate in which it makes sense today to talk about a New Public Service. Though we acknowledge that differences, even substantial differences, exist in these various viewpoints, we would suggest there are also similarities that distinguish the cluster of ideas we call the New Public Service from those associated with the New Public Management and the Old Public Administration. Moreover, there are a number of practical lessons that the New Public Service suggests for those in public administration. These lessons are not mutually exclusive; rather, they are mutually reinforcing. We will outline these ideas here, and then discuss each one in more detail in the seven chapters that follow. Among these ideas, we find the following the most compelling:

1. *Serve Citizens, not Customers*: The public interest is the result of a dialogue about shared values rather than the aggregation of individual self-interests. Therefore, public servants do not merely respond to the demands of "customers," but rather focus on building relationships of trust and collaboration with and among citizens (Chapter 3).
2. *Seek the Public Interest*: Public administrators must contribute to building a collective, shared notion of the public interest. The goal is not to find quick solutions driven by individual choices. Rather, it is the creation of shared interests and shared responsibility (Chapter 4).
3. *Value Citizenship over Entrepreneurship*: The public interest is better advanced by public servants and citizens committed to making meaningful contributions to society than by entrepreneurial managers acting as if public money were their own (Chapter 5).

4. *Think Strategically, Act Democratically*: Policies and programs meeting public needs can be most effectively and responsibly achieved through collective efforts and collaborative processes (Chapter 6).
5. *Recognize that Accountability isn't Simple*: Public servants should be attentive to more than the market; they should also attend to statutory and constitutional law, community values, political norms, professional standards, and citizen interests (Chapter 7).
6. *Serve Rather than Steer*: It is increasingly important for public servants to use shared, value-based leadership in helping citizens articulate and meet their shared interests, rather than attempting to control or steer society in new directions (Chapter 8).
7. *Value People, not just Productivity*: Public organizations and the networks in which they participate are more likely to be successful in the long run if they are operated through processes of collaboration and shared leadership based on respect for all people (Chapter 9).

Chapter 3

Serve Citizens, not Customers

Serve citizens, not customers. The public interest is the result of a dialogue about shared values rather than the aggregation of individual self-interests. Therefore, public servants do not merely respond to the demands of "customers," but rather focus on building relationships of trust and collaboration with and among citizens.

The New Public Service begins, of course, with the concept of public service, but the idea of public service is intertwined with the responsibilities of democratic citizenship. In the words of Benjamin Barber:

> Service to the nation is ... the duty of free men and women whose freedom is wholly dependent on and can survive only through the assumption of political responsibilities. In this tradition service is something we owe ourselves or that part of ourselves that is embedded in the civic community.

> (Barber 1998, 195)

Public service derives, therefore, from the civic virtues of duty and responsibility.

Respect for the idea of public service has varied over time. In some periods, the commitment of citizens to public service has been far stronger than in others. Similarly, the relationship between the public servant and the public has been characterized in different ways over time. In this chapter, we will first review several important aspects of democratic citizenship and then consider these varying views of public service in relation to citizenship. We will then examine the particular interpretation of public service in the Old Public Administration, the New Public Management, and the New Public Service.

Civic Virtue and Democratic Citizenship

We noted earlier a distinction between a legal definition of citizenship and what we might call an ethical definition of citizenship—citizenship as concerned with the nature of one's membership in a political community, including such issues as the rights and responsibilities of citizens. We will focus here on ethical interpretations of citizenship; however, even here there are questions about (1) how a "theory" of citizenship might be formulated, (2) how modern society has shaped and—we would say—restricted the role of the citizen, and (3) whether there is a rationale and hope for building more active citizen involvement in the governance process. In this section, we will briefly examine each of these topics.

Theories of Citizenship

Efforts to understand the proper roles and responsibilities of the citizen trace back to ancient Greek philosophy. Political theorist J.G.A. Pocock, in fact, suggests that the history of the concept of citizenship in Western political thought can be seen as an "unfinished dialogue" between the ideal and the real, between persons and things (Pocock 1995, 42). According to Pocock, the classical account of citizenship, that which best expresses the "ideal," was first developed in Aristotle's *Politics*. In this view, the citizen engages in the work of the *polis* because it is in that work that the individual attains his or her (for Aristotle, it was only "his") fullest humanity. Because humans are active, social, and moral beings, concerned with the purpose of life, they seek to attain higher ends and must, in doing so, engage in self-determination. "Therefore, the citizen rules and is ruled; citizens join each other in making decisions where each decider respects the authority of the others, and all join in obeying the decisions ... they have made" (31). Citizens are more concerned with the "ends" to be attained in social life; they have less concern for the "means" of industry or production. Citizenship is not seen as an instrumental activity (a means to an end). To be an active citizen is an end in itself. It is valued for the freedom that is obtained by participating in the work of the polity.

There is an alternative view, one that Pocock traces to the Roman jurist Gaius, who moved from a concept of the citizen as a *political* being to the citizen as a *legal* being, existing in a world of persons, actions, and things. The concept of "things" is the one that particularly makes a difference. Aristotle's citizens were, of course, concerned with things (such as land or trade), but they did not act through the *medium* of things. Quite to the contrary, "Aristotle's citizens were persons acting on one another, so that their active life was a life immediately and heroically moral" (34).

For Gaius, people acted primarily on things, and indeed most of their actions were focused on taking or maintaining possession of things. The resulting disputes over things were what led most directly to the need for regulation. The individual as a citizen was first concerned with the possession of things and second with legal actions taken with respect to things— authorization, conveyance, litigation, and so on. In this view, the world of things became the reality, the medium through which human beings lived their lives and, indeed, defined their lives. Citizenship then became a legal status, one associated perhaps with certain "rights," especially property rights, but not a moral or political one.

> The Greek citizen . . . stepped out of a world of things into a world of purely personal interactions, a world of deeds and words, speech and war. The Roman citizen, subject to both law and prince, was constantly reminded by the Gaian formula that he lived in the world of things, as well as the world of persons and actions.
>
> (40)

Much later, Jean-Jacques Rousseau, following in the Aristotelian tradition, basically defined the citizen as one who acts with the good of the community in mind. Citizenship is a way of life that involves a commitment to the community and to its members, a significant level of involvement in public affairs, and an occasional willingness to put one's own interest below those of the broader society, what Alexis de Tocqueville later called "self-interest properly understood" (Tocqueville 1835/1969, 526–527). Others, such as John Stuart Mill, also envisioned citizen participation as a vital and necessary component of democratic government. As Mill stated, "good government . . . depends . . . [on] the qualities of the human beings composing the society over which the government is exercised" (Mill 1862, II, 2).

The legal tradition, which is often skeptical of public participation, was maintained in the writing of the U.S. Constitution. Consistently with the tradition of legalism and jurisprudence, the founding fathers created a government with careful attention to the balance, or one might say the dilution, of power, in order to protect the public from governmental tyranny. At the same time, however, the framers were extremely suspicious of rule by the masses. For this reason, suffrage was severely limited. The concept of "citizen" pertained only to white male landowners, who were believed to have enough at stake, and presumably enough knowledge, to participate through voting and public service.

James Madison was particularly concerned about the notion of citizen action. He believed that among the "heaviest misfortunes" of the new republic was the "unsteadiness and injustice [with] which a factious spirit has tainted our public administration" (Madison, Hamilton, and Jay 1787/1987, #10, 1). To Madison, factions were:

> a number of citizens, whether amounting to a majority or minority of the whole, who are united and actuated by some common impulse of passion, or of interest adverse to the rights of other citizens, or to the permanent and aggregate interests of the community.
>
> (#10, 1)

Thomas Jefferson, on the other hand, strongly defended the involvement of citizens in the conduct of government, writing in the Declaration of Independence that, "Governments are instituted among Men, deriving their just Powers from the Consent of the Governed" (Declaration of Independence 1776/1970). And so the debate continued.

Although the U.S. constitutional system does not fully support the democratic ideal, having a more legalistic focus, designed in part to protect government from excessive intrusions on the part of citizens, there has been a strong informal commitment to the democratic ideal. As an abstract value, the concept of citizen participation is unquestionably accepted as an un-mitigated good. Abraham Lincoln, in the Gettysburg Address, echoed the sentiment in the well-known phrase, "government of the people, by the people, for the people." Thus, there is a strong and explicit value placed on the role of the citizen in American democratic ideology.

Moreover, Americans have a strong tradition of *acting* in a way consistent with the ideal of democratic citizenship. Summarizing the history of civic involvement in this country, Terry Cooper writes:

> From the covenantal tradition of the early Puritan communal with their forms of participatory self-governance; the New England town meetings; the experience of forming voluntary associations, which captured the attention of Tocqueville; Anti-federalist thought; and the cooperative establishment of frontier settlements, there has emerged a set of values,

> customs, beliefs, principles, and theories which provide the substance for ethical citizenship.
>
> (1991, 10)

This strong tradition of ethical citizenship stands in contrast to the more formal legal approaches and provides the basis for an active and involved citizenry in this country.

Earlier, we noted a difference between a perspective on governance in which citizens look beyond their self-interest to the larger public interest, and one in which government exists to ensure that citizens can make choices consistent with their self-interest by guaranteeing certain procedures and individual rights. What has now become clear is that theories of citizenship diverge in a strikingly similar way. The democratic ideal of persons actively engaged in the work of the community or nation, benefiting both the society and themselves as they become more complete human beings through their involvement in the political system, is contrasted with the world of jurisprudence and legal rights, both shaped to protect our interest in things, our possessions. In this chapter, we argue that the prevailing view in both politics and administration is associated with self-interest, but that a resurgence of democratic spirit might have great benefits for society and for its members.

The Role of the Citizen

Unfortunately, in recent times, the ideals of citizenship have been largely overwhelmed by increased power, professionalism, and complexity. Robert Pranger (1968), for example, argues that much of what is termed "politics" today is actually "power politics," largely concerned with the activities of leaders, officials, and other power holders in society. Pranger contrasts this orientation to an alternative, the politics of citizenship or the "politics of participation." In the politics of participation, ordinary citizens engage in dialogue and discourse concerning the directions of society and act based on moral principles such as those associated with the term "civic virtue." A similar distinction has been made between high and low views of citizenship. High definitions of citizenship, associated with such writers as Aristotle, Rousseau, and Mill, assume a wide distribution of power and authority and view citizens as sharing equally in the exercise of authority. Low citizenship, associated with such names as Thomas Hobbes or the more contemporary democratic elitists, assumes a hierarchical distribution of authority, with the greatest power wielded by those "at the top" and little power exercised by others (Cooper 1991, 5). In either case, it appears that, in modern American society, the "politics of power" or "low citizenship" has come to dominate—perhaps not to the exclusion of the "politics of participation" or "high citizenship," but certainly to its disadvantage.

Carole Pateman argues that "low" theories of citizenship have become self-fulfilling. She is disturbed by the fact that much contemporary theory is not "centered on the participation of 'the people,' or . . . the development of politically relevant and necessary qualities in the ordinary individual." Further, she states that:

> In the contemporary theory of democracy it is the participation of the minority elite that is crucial and the non-participation of the apathetic ordinary man lacking in the feeling of political efficacy that is regarded as the main bulwark against instability.
>
> (Pateman 1970, 104)

She suggests that the present institutional setting is hostile to citizen participation and creates feelings of apathy and low political efficacy. Therefore, the development of a "democratic character" among the citizenry, which she suggests is necessary for participation, is thwarted in the current system.

Similarly, Innes and Booher accentuate that citizen bodies are often "made up of elites" and not "representative of a range of interests and voices." Public hearings, for example, are frequently attended by people who either strongly support or oppose policy initiatives. Because these participants are passionate about a particular issue, they "cannot afford polite speech, which could be misinterpreted" (Innes and Booher 2004, 423, 424). As a result, public hearings more often than not involve one-way, angry communication, where citizens express their opinion using metaphors of war and battles. Obviously, this is not an environment that promotes collaboration and the development of high citizenship and civic engagement.

In addition to questions about the quality and civility of participation, as we noted earlier, the level of political participation today is generally down, at least when measured in terms of formal involvement, such as voting or attending meetings (Callahan 2010). At the same time, trust in government has dropped precipitously, and people seem quite cynical about the means and motives of politicians. The gap between leaders and citizens seems substantially greater than before. In fact, Barber points out the irony that, although democracy needs both strong leadership and vigorous citizenship, strengthened leadership, especially when it is associated with the manifest exercise of power, may in fact undermine a more active, participatory citizenship (1998).

Active citizenship may also be discouraged by the professionalization of government and its increasing dependence on "experts." Fisher, for example, argues that experts are seen as "social trustees," but, rather than providing "neutral" expertise and information, professions have become "more the self-serving monopolies of particular services than forces for social quality and human betterment" (2009, 21). Nonetheless, as expert advice is increasingly heralded as essential to solving the problems faced by modern government, the opinions of ordinary citizens are largely devalued. Under these circumstances, officials and administrators may be inclined to disregard views they dismiss as lacking clarity and sophistication. Indeed, having to listen to such views becomes an "annoyance," interfering with the resolution of the technical problems that experts are trained to solve. Moreover, ordinary citizens may themselves become overwhelmed by the intricacies of problems and feel they have nothing to contribute—even though their "common sense" may be extremely valuable.

Finally, the sheer complexity of today's society makes civic involvement difficult. The pressures of making a living, raising children, and meeting all the other demands of modern life make many people feel they simply don't have enough energy for politics. Involvement in the public sphere takes time, and many people simply don't feel they can devote the time necessary to make democracy work.

Building Citizen Involvement

There are a number of reasons we might hope for high levels of public participation in a democratic society. The first reason is our belief that, through active participation, we can most likely achieve the best political outcomes, outcomes that reflect the broad judgments of the people as a whole or the considered judgments of specific groups *and* are consistent with the norms of democracy. Second, through participation, we might fulfill what Thompson calls the democratic objective, "attaining rules and decisions which satisfy the interests of the greatest number of citizens" (Thompson 1970, 184). Through widespread public participation in civic affairs, citizens can help assure that the individual and collective interests are being heard and responded to by governmental officials. Moreover, they can prevent rulers from violating the interests of citizens. Third, democratic participation enhances the legitimacy of government. People who are involved in decision making are more likely to support those decisions and the institutions involved in making and carrying out those decisions.

These ideas come together in what Emmett S. Redford (1969) calls "democratic morality," an expression of the democratic ideal resting on three premises. First, democratic morality assumes that the individual is the basic measure of human value. Our social and political system can only be considered successful to the extent that it promotes the realization of the fullest potential of the individual. Second, democratic morality means that all persons have full claim to the attention of the system. Although some people, for example, may have more wealth than others, that shouldn't give them undue advantage in political affairs. Third, democratic morality assumes that individual claims can best be promoted through the involvement of all persons in the decision-making process, and that participation is not only an instrumental value, but is essential to the development of democratic citizenship. The ideal of universal participation may take various forms; however, Redford indicates some basics:

> Among these are (1) access to information, based on education, open government, free communication, and open discussion; (2) access, direct or indirect, to forums of decision; (3) ability to open any issue to public discussion; (4) ability to assert one's claims without fear of coercive retaliation; and (5) consideration of all claims asserted.
>
> (1969, 8)

Through such processes, advocates of democracy believe the best government will be obtained and maintained. But what about the other side of the equation? From the standpoint of the citizen, what is there to be gained by further involvement in the body politic? Generally speaking, political theorists have come up with three answers, the ethical, the integrative, and the educative. We have already explored the ethical argument—that active involvement in political life is a part of realizing one's fullest potential. To Barber, for example, the aim of participation is to create communities of active, interested citizens "who are united less by homogeneous interests than by civic education and who are made capable of common purpose and mutual action by virtue of their civic attitudes and participatory institutions" (1984, 117). He sees citizens being transformed from having only private, selfish interests to having a regard for the public good. Similarly, Pranger writes that:

> The conduct of citizens in the culture of power is basically unvirtuous in that it has little to do with the citizen's main duty as an agent responsible for common participation based on independent points of view, eventually fostering that mutual responsibility which alone enriches the common-wealth's life.
>
> (1968, 53)

> Local governments have used a civic engagement approach in dealing with the recent fiscal crisis. In Delray Beach, Florida, for example, small groups were organized. Participants were reminded that everyone has an equal voice and they were encouraged to listen as well as talk, share their feelings, be honest, even if their opinions were unpopular, ask each other questions, and refrain from giving advice to each other. The groups discussed three questions—Why do you love living in Delray Beach? What can Delray Beach do today to be sustainable tomorrow? What do you fear most about budget changes?—and reported key points to the entire group.

Active participation and the occasional sacrifice of one's own interest that is often involved in a democracy build "character." Through discipline and self-sacrifice, citizens may become more virtuous. Involvement in the work of the polity teaches responsibility and tolerance. Active citizenship may not lead to spectacular deeds, but, according to Tocqueville:

> Every day it prompts some small ones; by itself it cannot make a man virtuous, but its discipline shapes a lot of orderly, temperate, moderate, careful, and self-controlled citizens. If it does not lead the will directly to virtue, it establishes habits which unconsciously turn it that way.
>
> (1835/1969, 526–527)

To put it simply, the person who remains actively involved in civic life will become a better person.

The integrative argument in support of more active citizenship suggests that people play many roles in society—employer, employee, teacher, student, parent, consumer, union representative, churchgoer—but that the citizenship role is one of very few roles that bring these different aspects of our lives together. (Religion might be another.) The political theorist Sheldon Wolin writes, "Citizenship provides what other roles cannot, namely an integrative experience which brings together the multiple role activities of the contemporary person and demands that the separate roles be surveyed from a more general point of view" (1960, 434). My role as a parent may sometimes conflict with my role as an employee. Where this is the case, I need a broader way of bringing together the various roles in a synoptic fashion. The citizenship role can provide such integration.

This argument is especially interesting as we consider the question of civil society, because it is those smaller groups, associations, and day-to-day patterns of interactions that provide the "social glue" that holds society together. Michael Walzer points out that citizenship is one of many roles that members play, but the state itself is unlike all the other associations:

> It both frames civil society and occupies space within it. It fixes the boundary conditions and the basic rules of all associational activity (including political activity). It compels association members to think about a common good, beyond their own conceptions of the good life.
>
> (1995, 169)

Through the citizenship role, we may integrate the interests and experiences that we have in other, less comprehensive realms. Moreover, acting as a citizen, exercising the civic virtues, brings us into a closer relationship with others. It increases the feeling that people belong to a community. So, "the activity of citizenship performs an integrative function in two respects, first, it enables the individual to integrate the various roles he or she plays; second, it integrates individuals into the community" (Dagger 1997, 101).

The educative argument in support of active and public-spirited participation is especially well developed in Carole Pateman's classic discussion of Rousseau's views on the matter. According to Rousseau, as the individual engages in the political process, he or she learns the importance of taking into account the views of others in order to gain their cooperation. "As a result of participating in decision making the individual is educated to distinguish between his own impulses and desires, he learns to be a public as well as a private citizen" (Pateman 1970, 25). As individuals engage in participation, they begin to learn and develop the skills appropriate to the process of participation, so that the process becomes self-sustaining. That is, the more the individual participates, the better he or she is able to do so. The classical or ideal theory of democratic citizenship, then, has an ambitious agenda—"the education of an entire people to the point where their intellectual, emotional, and moral capacities have reached their full potential and they are joined, freely and actively in a genuine community" (Davis, quoted in Pateman 1970, 21).

The educative argument is, of course, based on a faith in the "improvability" of the ordinary citizen. If there are problems with the involvement of citizens, if their participation doesn't bring about political improvements as well as heightened legitimacy, then the response is not to end participation, but to further educate the citizenry. Thomas Jefferson was clear on this point:

Many local governments have academies to provide information about the government and to develop leadership skills. Montgomery, Ohio, has stressed hands-on learning that acquaints the participants with the kinds of decision that city government officials make in its Montgomery Citizens Learning Academy. Through simulations, residents learn about the process and the tradeoffs involved in tax increment financing, participate in table-top street snow removal and park improvement project prioritization exercises, and examine the potential conflict between economic development and historic preservation.

I know of no safe depository of the ultimate power of the society but the people themselves, and if we think them not enlightened enough to exercise their control with a wholesome discretion, the remedy is not to take it from them, but to inform their discretion.

(Jefferson 1903, 278)

If there are problems encountered in a participatory society, the answer is not to limit participation (the Madisonian response), but rather to further educate and to inform.

Public Service as an Extension of Citizenship

Clearly, the idea of civic virtue, at least in the democratic ideal, incorporates the notion of service to the public. For this reason, discussion of democratic theory must attend to the roles and responsibilities or the duties and obligations of citizenship. A part of that discussion of particular relevance to our argument here is related to the idea of service to the community or nation. The virtuous citizen obviously is a citizen engaged in the work of the community, but the virtuous citizen also has a duty or responsibility to serve others. The idea of democratic citizenship has, since the earliest times, implied a certain duty or obligation on the part of the citizen to contribute to the betterment of the community. Many will recognize the Athenian Oath, from ancient Greece:

We will never bring disgrace on this our City by any act of dishonesty or cowardice.

We will fight for the ideals and Sacred Things of the City both alone and with many.

We will revere and obey the City's laws, and will do our best to incite a like reverence and respect in those above us who are prone to annul them or set them at naught.

We will strive increasingly to quicken the public's sense of civic duty.

Thus in all these ways we will transmit this City, not only not less, but greater and more beautiful than it was transmitted to us.

(Quoted in Bennett 1993, 217)

Similarly, Thomas Jefferson once wrote to a friend, scolding him for not being more active in national affairs, saying, "There is a debt of service due from every man to his country, proportioned to the bounties which nature and fortune have measured him" (Jefferson, quoted in Staats 1988, 605). The democratic ideal clearly posits an active and engaged citizen, one propelled at least in part by a commitment to serve others and to serve the community. As one contemporary political theorist puts it:

Civic virtue, the cultural disposition apposite to citizenship was thus two-fold, a willingness to step forward and assume the burdens of public office; and second, a willingness to subordinate private interests to the requirement of public obedience. What Aristotle called the "right temper" of a citizen was thus a disposition to put public good ahead of private interest.

(Ignatieff 1995, 56)

For some, the impulse to engage in public processes extends beyond voting, going to community meetings or public hearings, writing letters or e-mails, or engaging in focus groups and visioning projects. It leads to a full-time commitment to engage in what we typically call "public service." The call to public service that many people experience is based on the responsibility of all citizens to serve, but it goes far beyond this responsibility, to become a full-time occupation, even a preoccupation. The public servant may be someone who runs for and serves in elective public office, perhaps for a short time, perhaps throughout a career, but he or she may also be someone who works in an agency of government—in social services, public health, environmental protection, law enforcement, or any one of myriad other public and governmental agencies. Today, the public servant may even be someone who works outside government, perhaps in a nonprofit organization or in a public advocacy role. Wherever public servants are found, they are likely to be motivated by the desire to make a difference, to improve the lives of others, to do something meaningful with their own lives, to do something "significant."

What we think of as public service, therefore, is an extension of the virtues expected of all citizens in a democracy, a point most eloquently and thoroughly captured by Terry Cooper in his book *An Ethic of Citizenship for Public Administration* (1991). Cooper argues for the citizenship role as a basis for understanding the role of public servant and, more explicitly, the role of public administrator. He begins by noting that, historically, the connection between citizenship and administration was extremely close. For example, the two oldest schools of public administration, Syracuse and the University of Southern California, began as schools of citizenship. Although the field of public administration has drifted away from its roots in this regard, Cooper argues that public servants and public administrators still derive their standing and legitimacy from their role as professional citizens. In this view, the public administrator is not merely a technician, a problem solver, or an employee of government. Rather, the public servant or public administrator is best understood as someone who extends the responsibilities of citizenship into his or her life's work. Public administrators are, in the words of Michael Walzer, "citizens in lieu of the rest of us; the common good is, so to speak, their specialty" (quoted in Cooper 1991, 139).

If administrators derive their ethical identity from a base in democratic citizenship, then they assume special roles and responsibilities, including specific understandings of issues such as responsiveness and accountability, that are inherent in the idea of democratic morality. Cooper writes:

> The ethical identity of the public administrator then, should be that of the citizen who is employed *as* one of us to work *for* us; a kind of professional citizen ordained to do the work which we in a complex large-scale political community are unable to undertake ourselves. Administrators are to be those "especially responsible" citizens who are fiduciaries for the citizenry as a whole.
>
> (1991, 139)

As such, administrators will naturally be held to a set of ethical standards appropriate to the conduct of public affairs. Indeed, a substantial literature on the ethics of public service has developed. Without going into the details of that material, we should mention several important components of ethical concern in the public service. Some years ago, Paul Appleby urged that administrators attain a "special attitude of public responsibility" and that, in addition to learning the skills of management, they would be imbued with the "democratic spirit" (1945, 4).

Stephen K. Bailey interpreted Appleby's remarks to mean that administrators needed an understanding of the moral ambiguity of public policies, a recognition of the moral priorities and paradoxes of the public service, and the moral qualities of "(1) optimism, (2) courage, and (3) fairness tempered by charity" (1966, 24). Many more recent writings have followed in this tradition of elaborating the administrator's sense of democratic responsibility. For example, Patrick Dobel (1990) suggests that the administrator's integrity involves several different justifications for the exercise of discretion. These include regime accountability, personal responsibility, and prudence, justifications that in practice must be balanced and integrated:

> First, be truthfully accountable to relevant authorities and publics. Second, address the public values of the regime. Third, respect and build institutions and procedures to achieve goals. Fourth, ensure fair and adequate participation of relevant stakeholders. Fifth, seek competent performance in the execution of policy and program. Sixth, work for efficiency in the operation of government. This builds up the legitimacy of the regime, is true to the basic purposes and genealogy of public funds, and buttresses concerns with conscientiousness and competence. Seventh, connect policy and program with the self-interest of the public and participants in such a way that the basic purposes are not subverted.
>
> (Dobel 1990, 363)

If, as Cooper argues, the administrative role derives from the role of the citizen, then surely a part of the administrator's responsibility is to assist citizens in fulfilling their own civic duty to be fully engaged and involved in the work of the polity. Although administrators oriented toward efficiency and productivity may find the involvement of citizens awkward and time consuming, encouraging that involvement is nonetheless an essential element of the public servant's role. Dennis Thompson points out that the demand that citizens take a significant role in the political process means that leaders, and here we would include all public servants, such as elected public administrators, should "not only share the values and beliefs of the ordinary citizen, not only that they remain sensitive to his needs, but also that *leaders strive to activate the inactive citizen*" (1970, 26).

We argue here that public servants have an ethical obligation to extend the boundaries of public participation in the political process in whatever way they can. Often, such an effort will be uncomfortable for administrators. In many cases, "unwarranted" delays and confusion may result. Frequently, the time involved in engaging citizens will be maddening for administrators, but this will be the case only if administrators see their role as a primarily technical one focused on efficient problem solving. If they see their role as engaging citizens in the work of democracy, then such efforts will hardly be

> Plano's Workplace CARES Program (City Advocates Recruiting
> Employees into Service) began in 1998 as a way to assist employees
> to provide service in the community. The benefits of the program
> are both external, as volunteers contribute to enriching community
> life, and internal, as staff members experience higher morale,
> build leadership skills, and increase collaboration between city
> departments.

confounding. As difficult as they may be, these efforts will be a source of
exhilaration and joy.

The Old Public Administration and Client Service

Traditional public administration or the Old Public Administration was
largely concerned with either the direct delivery of services or the regulation
of individual and corporate behavior. Those on the "receiving" end were
generally referred to as "clients." The word "client," of course, means
"a party for which professional services are rendered" (*American Heritage
Dictionary* 2000). What is interesting is that the word "client" is derived
from the Latin *cliens*, which means "dependent" or "follower." In many cases,
public agencies operating under the Old Public Administration dealt with
their clients in just such a manner. Clients were seen as in need of help,
and those in government made honest efforts to provide the help that was
needed through the administration of public programs. Inevitably, those in
the agency came to be seen as being "in control" of those dependent on the
agency. For many clients, the agency's view appeared to be quite patronizing
and even dismissive. The stereotype of the thoughtless, uncaring bureaucrat
is surely overdone, but perhaps contains a modicum of truth.

The New Public Management and Customer Satisfaction

The New Public Management addresses the relationship between government
and citizens, not just as a practical concern, but from a distinct theoretical
position. Earlier in this chapter, we examined in detail the ideal concept of
citizenship as being active, involved, and public-spirited. We also pointed
out the alternative legal definition of citizenship—a view we find to be based
not only on legalism but also on self-interest. This theoretical viewpoint so

clearly underlies the way in which the New Public Management views the relationship between those in government and those served or regulated by government that it is worthwhile to elaborate the theoretical notion of citizen as *consumer*. This view is largely derived from the so-called economic theory of democracy, a theory that explains political behavior in terms of economic competition. Political parties, for example, are seen as competing for votes, just as corporations are seen as competing for profits. Citizens, in turn, are seen as consumers, for whose votes the parties compete. These citizen–consumers make decisions based on their efforts to maximize their own utilities, casting their votes for one or the other party, or simply turning away from politics and seeking great utilities by spending their time and energy elsewhere (Dagger 1997, 105).

This view of citizens as consumers is certainly consistent with the self-interested interpretation of political life we examined earlier: the view that government ultimately reflects the accumulated self-interests of largely disconnected and utility-maximizing individuals. This interpretation is also consistent with the legal definition of citizenship, as the citizen–consumer enjoys certain rights and liberties protected by the state's system of juris-prudence. Finally, this view is consistent with an economic interpretation of political life. Proponents of this view:

> conceive of citizenship in economic terms, so that citizens are transformed into autonomous consumers, looking for the party or position that most persuasively promises to strengthen their market position. They need the state, but have no moral relation to it, and they control its officials only as consumers control the producers of commodities, by buying or not buying what they make.
>
> (Walzer 1995, 160)

The New Public Management brings this idea of consumerism directly into the debate about the appropriate relationship between public adminis-trators and citizens by conceiving of the recipients of government services (or services delivered by contracted agencies) as consumers or "customers." Like other elements of the New Public Management, the customer-service orientation is clearly related to the experience of business, in this case the customer-service movement of the last several decades. In such books as *In Search of Excellence* (Peters and Waterman 1982) and *Service America* (Albretch and Zemke 1985), management consultants made the argument that, if businesses are fully attentive to customers, then everything else, including profits, will fall into place. The customer is conceived as constantly calculating satisfaction utilities: "We can think of the customer as carrying around a kind of 'report card' in his or her head, which is the basis of a grading system that leads the customers to decided whether to partake of the service again or go elsewhere" (32). The customer is clearly a construct derived from the classic model of economic man.

Osborne and Gaebler argue that customer-driven government is superior to bureaucratic government, having the advantages of greater accountability, greater innovation, the possibility of generating more service choices, and less waste (1992, 180–185). Similarly, Barzelay contends that thinking in terms of customer service helps public managers articulate their concerns about performance and come up with innovative solutions to problems that arise (Barzelay 1992, 6–7). For those agencies that interact directly with the public, the recipient of the service is the "customer." For some staff agencies (such as budgeting or purchasing), there is rather an internal customer, the agencies whose work they support.

The language of customer service has become central to the New Public Management. The NPR, for example, had a goal of "providing customer services *equal to the best in business*" (Gore 1993, 44). Noting that government's customers often face long lines, busy signals, inadequate information, and indifferent employees, the report urged "entrepreneurial" federal agencies to assess the needs of customers, to set standards for the delivery of services, and to take those steps necessary to meet those standards. Similar language was used, and similar approaches were taken, at the state and local level, as governments and their agencies sought to "reinvent" themselves as customer-driven operations. In other countries, comparable efforts were undertaken, actually in many cases predating the United States' efforts in this regard. The British "citizen's charter" movement set minimum standards of service, backed by ministerial authority, and in some cases even provided redress when those standards were not met. Similar efforts were undertaken in other countries, including Australia, New Zealand, France, and Belgium.

Although improving the quality of governmental services is an idea no one would dispute, using the rhetoric and approach of "customer service" has both practical and theoretical difficulties. In the first place, the notion of choice is essential to the economic concept of the customer. Generally, in government, there are few, if any, alternatives. There is only one fire department, for example (and the fire department cannot choose to go into another line of work). Moreover, many services provided by government are services the specific recipient may not want—receiving a speeding ticket, being held in jail, and so on. Even identifying the customers of government is problematic. Who are a local health department's customers? People who visit a clinic? Citizens who might be concerned about a particular health hazard? Doctors and nurses? Local hospitals? The general public? All of the above? Even listing all the potential customers points out another dilemma: All the customers of government seem to have different interests. For example, often there is a conflict between the interests of the immediate recipient of government services and the taxpayers who must pay the bill. And, of course, some government services—foreign policy or environmental protection, for example—do not connect with individual customers; once they are provided, they are provided for all, whether you want them or not.

Perhaps the most important objection to the customer orientation has to do with accountability. In government, citizens are not only customers; they are "owners" (Schachter 1997). As George Frederickson puts it, "Customers choose between products presented in the market; citizens decide what is so important that the government will do it at public expense" (1992, 13). Further, the interests of customers and owners do not always coincide—in business or government. Although businesses may benefit in the long term from satisfying the immediate customer, government may not. A state motor vehicle division made important efforts to improve customer satisfaction—brightening its waiting areas, cutting down on waiting time, even making the drivers' license pictures more attrractive. However, a statewide commission questioned whether these changes were made at the cost of safety on the highway. Similarly, Tom Peters supposedly tells a story of getting a building permit: "I don't want some bureaucrat at City Hall giving me a hard time. I want proper, quick, businesslike treatment. But what if my neighbor wants a permit to enlarge *his* house? Who's City Hall's customer then?" (quoted in Mintzberg 1996, 77). Government must be accountable to the larger public interest—not merely the self-interests of individual customers or consumers. In any case, the issue of accountability is critical. "The bottom line for democratic government is accountability—not profits or citizen satisfaction—and customer service does not provide a good proxy measure for accountability" (Kettl 2000a, 43). In order to properly serve the public, administrators must focus on forging relationships with citizens and identifying common understandings of shared interests and responsibilities (Bozeman 2007).

The New Public Service and Quality Service for Citizens

The New Public Service recognizes that those who interact with government are not simply customers, but rather citizens. Henry Mintzberg, the Canadian management theorist, has pointed out that there are actually several types of relationship that we have with government: "I am not a mere customer of government, thank you. I expect something more than arm's length trading and something less than the encouragement to consume" (1996, 77).

Someone engaged in a direct transaction with government—buying a lottery ticket—might indeed be considered a *customer*. However, someone receiving a professional service from government—education, for example—might more appropriately be called a *client*. Of course, we are also *subjects* of government—required to pay taxes, respect regulations, and obey the laws. Most important, we are *citizens*, and a large part of the services government provides would seem to fall under this category, "social infrastructure (such as museums), physical (such as roads and ports), economic (such as monetary policy), mediative (such as civil courts), offshore (such as embassies), and the government's own support infrastructure (such as election machinery)" (77).

There is certainly no question but that government agencies should strive to offer the highest quality service possible, within the constraints of law and accountability—and, indeed, many agencies are doing so. One of the most sophisticated efforts to improve service quality begins with a recognition of the differences between customers and citizens (Schmidt with Strickland 1998). Citizens are described as bearers of rights and duties within the context of a wider community. Customers are different in that they do not share common purposes, but rather seek to optimize their own individual benefits. The distinction, then, is made between citizens and clients, the latter either internal or external:

> The following example may serve to illustrate these definitions. A citizen may not collect employment insurance and yet has an interest in how the system functions; the actual recipient of an employment insurance payment would be an external client. A regional employment insurance office that depends on a central agency to distribute the employment insurance payments to their office would be an internal client.
>
> (3)

It is important to recognize that public servants rarely deal with a single client or citizen. The front-line employee may be assisting someone sitting across the table, but he or she is simultaneously serving the public by ensuring that the process meets legal requirements. The complexity of government's interactions with citizens and the public marks all efforts to improve service quality in government.

Despite this complexity, there have been a variety of efforts to define public-sector service quality. One especially comprehensive list developed for local government includes the following:

1. *Convenience* measures the degree to which government services are easily accessible and available to citizens.

2. *Security* measures the degree to which services are provided in a way that makes citizens feel safe and confident when using them.
3. *Reliability* assesses the degree to which government services are provided correctly and on time.
4. *Personal attention* measures the degree to which employees provide information to citizens and work with them to help meet their needs.
5. *Fairness* measures the degree to which citizens believe that government services are provided in a way that is equitable to all.
6. *Fiscal responsibility* measures the degree to which citizens believe local government is providing services in a way that uses money responsibly.
7. *Citizen influence* measures the degree to which citizens feel they can influence the quality of service they receive from the local government.
                                                        (Carlson and Schwarz 1995, 29)

What is especially interesting about this list is not only that citizens expect public services to meet such standards as timeliness and reliability, but that they should and do expect that services be delivered fairly and with attention to fiscal responsibility as well; citizens expect to have the opportunity to influence the services they receive, as well as the quality of those services.

This same point can be made more theoretically. According to Jenny Potter (1988), the theory of consumerism suggests that there is an imbalance of power between those who provide services and those who receive services. The latter carry weight only as a result of their accumulated choices. To shift greater power toward consumers, theorists have identified five key factors: access, choice, information, redress, and representation. Although these factors were originally developed in relation to private goods and services

---

In Palm Bay, Florida, the city developed a new program to better connect the public to local government. The Palm Bay Volunteer Service Corps program coordinates efforts to allow volunteer participation, input, and involvement in the daily operation of the city's departments (www.volunteermatch.org/search/org193588.jsp). In Wellington, New Zealand, the Democratic Services Department offers "Have Your Say"—an online forum set up by the city government to solicit input on specific issues. Residents do not see comments as they are received, but the city prepares a summary report of the results of the consultation process. The city also offers e-petitions and monthly surveys online.

in the marketplace, they can be adapted to the public sector, providing guidance on how the interests of citizens, both individually and collectively, might be enhanced. *Access*—deciding who will have what—is not strictly a matter of individual right; rather, it is a matter of political responsibility. However, citizens should expect to be engaged in that decision. *Choice* also is not a matter of right, but citizens should expect to be involved in shaping and extending choices available to them. They should also expect to have full *information* about goals and objectives, standards of service, their rights to service, alternatives being debated, why decisions are made, and what those decisions are. Citizens should also expect to have some means of communicating their grievances and complaints, and to receive *redress* where appropriate. *Representation* opens up wider questions of consultation and ultimately participation by citizens in making decisions.

Potter concludes that the theory of consumerism can certainly point citizens in the right direction with respect to improving service quality; however, ultimately, as an economic concept, "the theory of consumerism cannot address the political question of how power might be more extensively shared between the governors and the governed, the administrators and the administrated" (1988, 156). As already noted, the theory of consumerism starts with an imbalance of power. The key question for government is how far government is willing to go in redressing that imbalance of power between providers and users or citizens. In contrast to concentrating solely on the "charm school and better wallpaper" (Pollitt 1988, 125) approach taken by many public agencies in their efforts to improve customer service, the real issues that must be addressed as the New Public Service evolves will be those that deal with information and power. Public agencies must become better able to collaborate across jurisdictional and other boundaries and connect in substantive, meaningful ways with citizens (Feldman 2010).

The customer orientation treats the provision of information as providing better signposts or schedules. A more complete approach to the provision of information would likely include having agencies publish performance data, so that citizens can make informed decisions about choices that are available to them. It would also mean providing detailed information about standards of service and the agency's success in meeting those standards. Finally, agencies should consult and involve their users in these tasks and should provide effective remedies if things go wrong. Ultimately, those in government must recognize that public service is not an economic construct, but a political one. That means that issues of service improvement need to be attentive, not only to the demands of "customers," but also to the distribution of power in society. For too long, governments intent on measuring performance have overlooked the importance of "citizen outcomes," including social equity and capital, self-work and political participation (Wichowsky and Moynihan 2008). Ultimately, in the New Public Service, providing quality service is a first step in the direction of widening public involvement and extending democratic citizenship.

Conclusion

Despite the obvious importance of constantly improving the quality of public-sector service delivery, the New Public Service suggests that government should not first or exclusively respond to the selfish, short-term interests of "customers." The New Public Service suggests instead that people acting as citizens must demonstrate their concern for the larger community, their commitment to matters that go beyond short-term interests, and their willingness to assume personal responsibility for what happens in their neighborhoods and the community. After all, these are among the defining elements of effective and responsible citizenship. In turn, government must be responsive to the needs and interests of citizens. In any case, the New Public Service seeks to encourage more and more people to fulfill their responsibilities as citizens, and, in turn, for public administrators to be especially sensitive to their voices.

Chapter 4

Seek the Public Interest

Seek the public interest. Public administrators must contribute to building a collective, shared notion of the public interest. The goal is not to find quick solutions driven by individual choices. Rather, it is the creation of shared interests and shared responsibility.

One of the core principles of the New Public Service is a reaffirmation of the centrality of the public interest in government service. The New Public Service demands that the process of establishing a "vision" for society is not something merely to be left to elected political leaders or appointed public administrators. Instead, the activity of establishing a vision or direction, of defining shared values, is something in which widespread public dialogue and deliberation are central (Bryson and Crosby 1992; Luke 1998; Stone 1988). Even more important, the public interest isn't something that just "happens" as a result of the interaction between individual citizen choices, organizational procedures, and electoral politics. Rather, articulating and realizing the public interest is one of the primary reasons government exists.

The New Public Service sees a vital role for government in the process of bringing people together in settings that allow for unconstrained and authentic discourse concerning the directions society should take. Based on these deliberations, a broad-based vision for the community, the state, or the nation can be established and can provide a guiding set of ideas (or ideals) for the future. It is less important that this process results in a single set of goals than that it engage administrators, politicians, and citizens in a process

The Deliberative Polling® process, developed by James Fishkin at the Center for Deliberative Democracy at Stanford University, uses a multistage process to engage citizens through both surveys and facilitated deliberation. The first step is to conduct a baseline poll among a representative group of citizens. Then, a group of participants are asked to attend a session to discuss the issue and are sent balanced briefing materials to review (which are also made available to the public). During the session, small groups develop questions and then engage in partially televised dialogue with experts and political leaders. Then, the survey is readministered, with the same questions as the original. "The resulting changes in opinion represent the conclusions the public would reach, if people had opportunity to become more informed and more engaged by the issues." (http://cdd.stanford.edu/polls/docs/summary/).

of thinking about a desired future for their community and their nation. According to some, such change is inevitable, given increasing recognition of the complex nature of cross-jurisdictional, multifaceted problems with which public managers must contend (Feldman 2010).

In addition to its facilitating role, government also has a moral obligation to assure that any solutions that are generated through such processes are fully consistent with norms of justice and fairness. Government will act to facilitate the solutions to public problems, but it will also be responsible for assuring that those solutions are consistent with the public interest—both in substance and in process (Ingraham and Ban 1988; Ingraham and Rosenbloom 1989). In other words, the role of government will become one of assuring that the public interest predominates: that both the solutions themselves and the process by which solutions to public problems are developed are consistent with democratic norms and the values of justice, fairness, and equity.

In the New Public Service, government plays an important and active role in creating arenas in which citizens, through discourse, can articulate shared values and develop a collective sense of the public interest. Rather than simply responding to disparate voices by forming a compromise, public administrators will engage citizens with one another so that they come to understand each other's interests and ultimately adopt a longer range, broader sense of community and societal interests. Moreover, doing so is vitally important to the realization of democratic values in the governance process.

The issue is complex, involving not only the nature of citizen trust and governmental responsiveness but also the purposes and responsibilities of government itself (Meijer 2011). At stake is the question of whether or not citizens trust their government to act in the public interest. As Kenneth Ruscio states, "Prescriptions for establishing trust—and indeed our understanding of why it is even necessary—require staking out positions on human nature, the meaning of public interest, and the reasons for engaging in political life" (1996, 471).

This chapter will explore the concept of the public interest. We will begin with a look at the various ways the public interest has been defined, noting competing ideas about what purpose, if any, the concept serves in governance. We will then review how the notion of public interest was understood at the time the field of public administration was founded in the United States and trace some of the reasons for its decline as a central component of public administration theory and practice. We will then ask how conceptions of the public interest have changed over time, and what are the controversies and issues regarding its existence and meaning. We will also ask about the importance of the public interest from an administrative perspective. We will then discuss how the public interest has been conceived in the Old Public Administration and the New Public Management, concluding with some thoughts about how the search for the public interest shapes the New Public Service.

What is the Public Interest?

In the last 100 years, the concept of the public interest has been variously derided, applauded, dismissed, and revived—leaving little consensus on what it means or if it is even a useful concept. Walter Lippman defined the public interest as "what men would choose if they saw clearly, thought rationally, and acted disinterestedly, and benevolently" (1955, 42). Glendon Schubert, however, suggested that the concept of the public interest "makes no operational sense. . . . Political scientists might better spend their time nurturing concepts that offer greater promise of becoming useful tools in the scientific study of political responsibility" (1962, 176). Likewise, Frank Sorauf stated that the term is "too burdened with multiple meanings for valuable use" (1957, 624). Howard Smith, on the other hand, said that, although the public interest is a myth, it is a useful myth (1960). Still others have pointed out that, regardless of its ambiguity, "there has never been a society which was not, in some way, and to some extent guided by this ideal" (Bell and Kristol 1965, 5). Despite this disagreement, the concept of the public interest has remained important in public discourse and academic literature.

In one sense, attempting to define the "public interest" is a little like trying to define "love." It is clear that *love* means different things to different people under varying circumstances. It can change over time in both form and substance. It also changes us—how we think and behave. Although seeing its effects is often possible, it is difficult to observe directly. It can be simultaneously seen as both a state of being and an ongoing process. Its quality and significance are bound up in both the process of seeking it and in the realization that it must always be pursued. As a result, it defies quantification and meaningful measurement and is, therefore, difficult to use in certain kinds of analysis. Some conclude from this complexity, fluidity in meaning, and difficulty in measurement that love isn't a very useful concept. Others may question whether it even exists. Still others might readily admit that love may exist, but argue that it cannot and should not be the subject of empirical study and social science, because it cannot be appropriately operationalized. Yet, most of us would agree that any explanation of the human experience—be it personal, social scientific, or philosophical—would be sorely lacking without the use of the concept of love.

The public interest, like love, means different things to different people, changes over time, motivates behavior, frames our thinking, defies measurement, and involves both substance and process. Just as understanding the human experience virtually requires a recognition of the role of love, it is difficult, if not impossible, to understand the depth and breadth of public service without a recognition of the role of the public interest. Accordingly, the difficulties and ambiguities encountered in attempts to define and place conceptual boundaries around the public interest are more than outweighed by the richness it brings to our understanding of citizenship, governance, and public service. We acknowledge that the public interest is ambiguous and fluid, at the same time that we advocate for its centrality to democratic governance.

We should point out that exploring the idea of the public interest is not just an interesting academic pursuit. The way we think about governance and the public interest defines how we act. Depending on which view of the public interest we take, our actions will be directed in different ways. Here, we will begin the task of defining the concept of the public interest by examining four approaches to the idea. Although these categories are not entirely mutually exclusive, they give us a reasonable starting point for our discussion. In part using Clarke Cochran's (1974) schema for the different schools of thought with regard to the public interest, we will classify models of the public interest as being primarily either: (1) normative, (2) abolitionist, (3) political process-oriented, or (4) based on shared values.

Normative Models

Normative models are used by social scientists, not to describe what is, but rather what ought to be. In normative models of the public interest, the "public interest becomes an ethical standard for evaluating specific public policies and a goal which the political order should pursue" (Cochran 1974, 330). In this view, the *public interest* is a moral and ethical standard for decision making. For example, C.W. Cassinelli (1962) writes that the public interest is a standard of goodness by which political acts can be judged.

In other words, actions that can be taken in the public interest deserve approval because they meet this standard of goodness. Because Cassinelli defines the public interest as an ethical standard, he dismisses the claim that the public interest is useless as a "tool of analysis" or an "aid to scientific study" as irrelevant. He argues instead that the public interest, as an ethical concept, has functions different from those of analytic models. "Social scientists cannot ignore the fundamental issue of the final political good: this is the principal lesson to be learned from examining the concept of the public interest" (1962, 47).

To Cassinelli and other advocates of the normative model, the public interest is the "highest ethical standard applicable to political affairs" (1962, 46). In this view, when something is good for the public, that is a higher level of good than when something is good for only part of the public. Accordingly, the political system should seek a fair distribution of advantages across a community. This does not mean that all people are entitled to identical or equal benefits, but suggests that, on balance, everyone be treated fairly. According to Bozeman, public managers seeking to instill a shared notion of the public interest should avoid quick fixes to problems stemming from individual choices in favor of providing assistance in the creating of shared interests and responsibility (Bozeman 2007).

An early public administrationist, E. Pendleton Herring, for example, wrote about the public interest from a normative perspective. In his 1936 book, *Public Administration and the Public Interest*, Herring argued that laws were, by necessity, at least somewhat vague, and that the bureaucrat's job was to reconcile competing group pressures in order to interpret the statute ethically. Administrators could best meet their ethical and legal obligation to resolve these conflicts, he said, according to the ideal of the public interest. He wrote, "Under democracy the public interest is based not upon the welfare of one class but upon a compounding of many group interests. We assume the possibility of achieving a balance of forces, social and economic" (1936, vii). More succinctly, he stated, "The public interest is the standard that guides the administrator in executing the law" (23).

Similarly, Emmette Redford also defined the public interest in a normative manner: "[The public interest] may be defined as the best response to a situation in terms of all the interests and of the concepts of value which are generally accepted in our society" (1954, 1108). Likewise, Philip Monypenny's code of ethics for public administration included a section called "The Public Interest," which stated that the administrator "should follow the public interest as he understands it rather than his personal convenience or any private aim or goal" (1953, 441). This view of the public interest as a normative, ethical standard has remained important in the field of public administration to the present. In fact, ASPA, in its code of ethics for its members, states as the first principle, "Exercise discretionary authority to promote the public interest" (2013).

Abolitionist Views of the Public Interest

In contrast to the normative theorists discussed above, those who subscribe to the abolitionist view of the public interest argue that the concept of the public interest is neither meaningful nor important. These scholars tend to take one of two lines of reasoning: either (1) the public interest can't be measured or directly observed, and so isn't valid, or (2) the concept of the public interest or collective will isn't necessary, because individual choices are the best way to understand the policy process and set policy. For example, although Glendon Schubert acknowledged that people talk about the public interest, therefore making it a part of the study of political behavior, it remained an ill-defined and scientifically irrelevant idea. He claimed that, despite considerable effort:

> American writers in the field of political science have evolved neither a unified nor a consistent theory to describe how the public interest is defined in governmental decision-making; they have not constructed theoretical models with the degree of precision and specificity necessary if such models are to be used as description of, or as a guide to, the actual behavior of real people.
>
> (Schubert 1960, 220)

In order to be useful, Schubert wrote, a theory of the public interest would have to be able to describe the relationship between the public interest and behavior in a way that can be empirically validated. He concluded that, because theories regarding the public interest cannot do so, "it is difficult to comprehend the justification for teaching students of political science that subservience to the public interest is a relevant norm of official responsibility" (1960, 220).

Political Process Theories

Cochran describes process theorists as those who "define the concept by reference to the political processes through which policy is made" (1974, 331). In this view, the public interest is realized through a particular process that allows interests to be aggregated, balanced, or reconciled. For example, Howard Smith states clearly that, "The Public Interest is most properly identified with, not concrete politics as such, but rather a particular kind of a process by means of which it is decided what should be done" (1960, 159). In other words, advocates of this view suggest that it is less important what the public interest *is* than how we arrive at it. Because these theorists are concerned primarily with the process, many can be considered to be analyzing the public interest as the logical extension of a longstanding and ongoing debate among political scientists about the best way to understand the political process per se. A key point of contention in this debate is whether political parties or interest groups are considered to be the preferred mechanism for the representation of interests in a democracy.

As evidenced by James Madison's early references in *The Federalist Papers*, Number 10, factions have long been considered to be natural to the American system of government (Madison et al. 1787/1987). Although Madison and others have debated the "misfortunes" and disadvantages of politics based on interest-group activity, those views were reflected more recently in Robert Dahl's *A Preface to Democratic Theory* (1956) and in his *Who Governs?* (1961). Pluralist views of democracy are based on the idea that interest groups, rather than individual citizens or the people as a whole, are the best vehicle for representing and defending the interests of citizens in the policy process. Pluralists argue that direct participation is impractical and unworkable, and that, by forming groups, like-minded individuals can have a greater voice in policymaking than they can as individuals. Dahl suggested that interest-group pluralism was, not only the best way to describe American politics as it currently operated, but also the best way to maximize democratic principles.

The dominance of pluralism as the model for American democracy strongly influenced those who defined the public interest from the standpoint of process. Pluralists were certainly not without their critics, however, who claimed that democracy and the public interest were better served by other processes. E.E. Schattschneider, for example, was a vocal proponent of majoritarian party politics as the best way to serve the public interest. He argued that private, special, and local interests are enemies of the common interest, but political parties can synthesize and transcend special interests. Rejecting the idea that the compilation of the special interests would equal the public interest, he stated, "The public interest is not the mere sum of the special interests, and it is certainly not the sum of the organized special interests" (1952, 23).

In either case, whether advocating for interest-group politics or party politics, these scholars largely ignore the role of citizens. The assumption is that citizens will be adequately represented by either interest groups or parties, and, if we let one of these mediating institutions be the primary voice of the people in the policy process, that will approximate the public interest.

Shared Values

Cochran called models of the public interest based on shared values "consensualist." Consensualists view the public interest as a vague, but valuable, term that refers to policy debate to achieve a public value consensus. We have broadened this category to include notions of the public interest based on shared values that guide both the process for articulating these interests and the substance of the public interest itself. This shared value model was evidenced in the early writings of Paul Appleby, who stated:

> The public interest is never merely the sum of all private interests nor the sum remaining after canceling out their various pluses and minuses. It is not wholly separate from private interests, and it derives from citizens with many private interests; but it is something distinctive that arises within, among, apart from, and above private interests, focusing in government some of the most elevated aspiration and deepest devotion of which human beings are capable.
>
> (Appleby 1950, 34–35)

This idea of the public interest as referring to the broad, shared interests of society is consistent with how Deborah Stone (1988) defines the public interest in what she calls the "polis," or political community. The public interest, in Stone's view, is based on the active and conscious pursuit of collective values. She defines the polis in part by contrasting it with the market or aggregation-of-individual-interests model (described above in the section on abolitionist views). The market view, she says, is based on the idea that public policy or the public interest is the net result of all individuals pursuing their self-interest. Thus, the public interest in the market model is the by-product of individual choices.

In the polis or collective model, on the other hand, building a society in the collective interest is the aim, not the by-product. Stone suggests that:

> Public policy is about communities trying to achieve something *as communities*. This is true even though there is almost always conflict within

a community over what its goals should be and who its members are, and even though every communal goal ultimately must be achieved through the behavior of individuals. Unlike the market which starts with individuals and assumes no goals, preferences, or intentions other than those held by individuals, a model of the polis must assume both collective will and collective effort.

(Stone 1997, 18; emphasis added)

Rather than beginning with the market assumption that people are only self-interested, she suggests that values such as sharing, caring, and maintaining relationships are at least as strong in motivating behavior as competition, separation, and promotion of self-interests. Although history, loyalty, and leadership are important factors in the polis, the market does not give us any way to talk about such influences. Further, in the market model, "commons" problems are considered to be the exception. "Commons" problems refer to situations in which self-interest and the public interest are in conflict. The example often used is of a pasture that is available to all cattle owners. Self-interest dictates that each person will seek to maximize his or her individual gain by keeping as many cattle as possible on this common land. However, because each person sharing the common land makes this same decision, the commons are depleted and of no use to anyone. Thus, by pursing their individual interests, the shared interests of the cattle owners are lost.

As suggested above, commons problems are considered to be an unusual occurrence in the market. In the polis, on the other hand, commons problems are considered to be, well, common. Not only do they occur frequently, but the most significant policy problems *are* commons problems. In the polis, it is assumed that policies will rarely affect only one or two individuals. The purpose of political dialogue, then, is to encourage people to articulate shared interests and to give primacy to the broader consequences of policy

---

Ventura, California, faced the issue of handling camping by homeless persons in a dry riverbed. The city announced that, in the absence of an agreed-upon approach, it would begin enforcing an ordinance forbidding unauthorized camping. A task force of residents and homeless persons developed the idea of creating a campground for homeless persons to use legally. The River Haven campground was supported by city government.

choices. People are encouraged to do so based on influence, cooperation, loyalty, and the connections that bond people together over time.

Further, the search for the public interest in the polis is ongoing. It is, as the saying goes, more a journey than a destination. Problems in the polis are not "solved" in the way that economic needs are met in the market model. "It is not as though we can place an order for justice, and once the order is filled, the job is done" (Stone 1997, 34). Moreover, there is never full agreement on what the public interest is. Instead, the search for its meaning is the *raison d'être* of public life, much as choice based on self-interest is the cornerstone of the market. As Stone puts it:

> The concept of public interest is to the polis what self-interest is to the market. They are both abstractions whose specific contents we do not need to know in order to use them to explain and predict people's behavior. We simply assume that people behave as if they were trying to realize the public interest or maximize their self-interest.
>
> (1997, 21)

In the polis, the development of shared values and a collective sense of the public interest is the primary aim. Stone suggests that the public interest can be understood as those things desired by the "public-spirited side of citizens," such as good schools and clean air, even if it interferes with their right to have lower taxes or to burn trash. The public interest can also be expressed as those "goals on which there is a consensus" and/or "things that are good for a community as a community," such as the preservation of order, maintenance of governing processes, and defense against outsiders. There is never complete agreement on the public interest. In fact, Stone says, "Let it be an empty box, but no matter; in the polis, people expend a lot of energy trying to fill up that box" (1997, 21).

So, the public interest based on shared values suggests a process that goes beyond the interplay of special interests to include shared democratic and constitutional values. More importantly, shared-interest theorists argue that, not only are people capable of more than self-interest, but also government should work to nurture and develop that capacity. In part, that capacity depends on trust. Citizen trust and confidence are built on the belief that government is acting in response to the public interest and the shared values of the community. Trust and acting in the public interest become mutually reinforcing—as the government acts in the public interest, citizen trust is enhanced. Conversely, when citizen trust is enhanced, citizens may experience an increase in their capacity to see and act on shared interests. It may then be argued that the public allure of the basic concepts of efficiency and effectiveness espoused by the New Public Management reflected displeasure with the modern welfare state, with citizens increasingly coming to view themselves as individualized users of discrete public goods and services, and that what is required is the formation of a collaborative relationship between citizens and administrators, based on shared knowledge and decision making (Box et al. 2001).

Given this evolution in thought, what views of the public interest and what assumptions for the role of public servants are associated with the Old Public Administration, the New Public Management, and the New Public Service? As should be clear from the preceding discussion, ideas and arguments about the public interest have not unfolded in a neat, linear fashion. However, we can identify certain dominant themes associated with the Old Public Administration, the New Public Management, and the New Public Service.

The Old Public Administration and the Public Interest

In the Old Public Administration, public service was thought to be a value-neutral technical process, and the authority of the administrator was the authority of expertise. As Schubert put it:

> The public interest is found in the rationalization of the decisional process so that it will automatically result in the carrying out of the Public Will. Human discretion is minimized or eliminated by defining it out of the decisional situation; responsibility lies in autonomic behavior.
>
> (1957, 347)

This perspective was closely connected with the emphasis on neutrality and efficiency that we saw earlier associated with the progressive reform movement and the scientific management movement. In one sense, then, the Old Public Administration didn't have a theory of the administrative responsibility to defend and protect the public interest. The public interest was to be determined by elected officials. In the Old Public Administration, it was implicit, however, that focusing on neutrality, efficiency, and a strict separation between politics and administration was the best way for public servants to serve the interests of the public. Thus, there was a subordination of administrative activities and discretion to hierarchical controls, legislation, and the interplay between special interests.

When writers such as Woodrow Wilson and Frank Goodnow first attempted to define the field of public administration at the turn of the century, the concept of the public interest was important, but was considered to fall solely within the province of politics. Wilson wrote: "Policy will have no taint of officialism about it. It will not be the creation of permanent officials, but of statesmen whose responsibility to public opinion will be direct and inevitable" (quoted in Shafritz and Hyde 1997, 22). Likewise, Goodnow defined politics as the "expression of the will of the state," with administration serving a subordinate role in executing that will (quoted in Shafritz and Hyde 1997, 28).

The role of public administration in relationship to the public interest remained a passive one into the mid 1930s, when a new view was articulated in the work of E. Pendleton Herring. In this era of the New Deal, Herring found that administrators often had to interpret and define vague legislation. He wrote, "Upon the shoulders of the bureaucrat has been placed in large part the burden of reconciling group differences and making effective and workable the economic and social compromises arrived at through the legislative process" (1936, 7). Herring did not reject the notion of neutral expertise; he merely suggested that some level of discretion was needed to deal with the demands of special interests. In exercising this discretion, Herring argued that, "the public interest is the standard that guides the administrator in executing the law" (23). Again, the assumption was that the public interest could be found in the interplay of special interests. Therefore, in this model, the administrator facilitates the "reconciliation of group interests," using the public interest as a "verbal symbol designed to introduce unity, order, and objectivity" (23). Although accountability to the public interest was emphasized, Herring's model assumed that no direct citizen involvement was necessary.

Further, the role of the administrator was clearly a passive one. For example, Herring stated:

> The task of government in a democracy, we assume, is the adjustment of warring economic and social forces. The public interest is the standard that supposedly determines the degree to which the government lends its forces to one side or the other. Without this standard for judgment between contenders, the scales would simply be weighted in favor of victory for the strongest.
>
> (1936, 23)

In effect, Herring was describing the public administrator as a last resort "tie breaker" when the conflict between interests leads to an unclear outcome or seems to exclude certain important interests.

Others also suggested a relatively modest role for administrators, a role subordinate to other participants in the process. From this perspective, the public administrator becomes the voice of the underrepresented and unorganized, but that voice is subordinated to the forces of hierarchy and the political process in most cases. Monypenny, for example, advises administrators on how to serve the public interest by stating:

> The primary determination of the public interest for public servants is by the action of his political and hierarchic superiors, acting through the conventional channels, by legislation, and court decisions where applicable. However there will be areas of discretion still, and in the use of these the public servant will be exposed to a relatively small group of persons immediately affected by a proposed action. The public servant must accept their right to speak and even to be consulted, must consider the consequences, which they present. But he must remember that there are others unorganized and not directly represented, and as far as he can perceive the consequences to them, he must be their representative also in considering this discretionary action.
>
> (Monypenny 1953, 441)

In short, in the Old Public Administration, the public interest was defined by popularly elected policymakers. It was assumed that administrators could best serve the public interest by implementing laws in the most efficient, scientific, politically neutral manner possible. Although the need was for administrators to be mindful of the public interest in working through conflicts among special interests in the implementation of legislative policy, the idea was that their discretion should be limited. Public administrators would play a largely passive role in reconciling special interests, and only when necessary to allow administrative action.

The New Public Management and the Public Interest

With the ascendancy of the New Public Management in the 1980s and 1990s, the ideal of the public interest as based on shared values lost currency and relevancy. As we noted earlier, the New Public Management is predicated on the notion that government should create marketlike arenas of choice in which individuals, as customers, can make decisions based on their own self-interest. In the role of customers, individuals do not need to be concerned with the interests of their fellow customers. As we begin to think about citizens as being analogous to customers, and government as analogous to a market, the need to talk about or act upon the "public interest" largely disappears.

In this way, questions about administrative responsibility with regard to the public interest are rendered largely irrelevant in the New Public

Management. Public choice theorists, for example, would deny that the "public interest" as a concept or ideal is meaningful and would, in fact, question whether it even exists. Their reasoning is that individual choices in a marketlike arena are superior to collective action based on shared values. Because of their reliance on the market metaphor, and the assumption that self-interest is the primary and most appropriate basis of decision making, the shared public interest becomes both irrelevant and a definitional impossibility. Their perspective on the public interest would clearly be defined as abolitionist.

As Stone (1997) explains, when society is viewed as a market, it is assumed that individuals have relatively fixed, independent preferences for goods, services, and policies (9). "The market model therefore gives us no way to talk about how people fight over visions of the public interest or the nature of the community—the truly significant political questions underlying policy choices" (10). People are considered to be the best judges of their own interest. The public interest, if it exists at all, is simply the by-product of citizens (as customers) making individual choices in a marketlike arena.

In the recent past, a shared view of the public interest has been largely overshadowed by the ascendancy of the New Public Management. According to Trudi Miller (1989), the negation of the concept of the public interest, coupled with a reliance on market models of choice and the pluralist model of politics, has far-reaching and damaging effects on democratic governance and the field of public administration. In fact, she argues that, to the extent that public servants adhere to the pluralist view of politics, they actually contribute to undermining and corrupting liberal democracy. In a liberal democracy, the institutions of government respond to "shared popular views of the public interest [while respecting liberties that are beyond the reach of government] and work to "block efforts by narrow factions to coerce and tax the public for reasons not warranted by the public interest" (511). She points out that liberal democracy is based on a value system that embraces the idea of reciprocity, morality, and populism. Accordingly, one of the functions of a democracy is to correct the market imperfections of capitalism.

Miller then argues that the ascendancy of the pluralist model of politics turns liberal democracy "on its head" by rendering "shared views of the public interest meaningless and unimportant" and negating "the values that form the foundations of democracy" (1989, 511). In the pluralist model, democracy responds to the interplay of special interests, but does not respond to or recognize shared views of the public interest. In other words, government in the pluralist model, she says, "does not respond to what the citizens collectively say they want" (515). Instead, it substitutes the will of the winning coalition of special interests.

Miller cautions that, to the extent that public servants adhere to a restricted notion of politics and of social science, they in fact contribute to the demise of democracy based on a shared view of the public interest. This is so, she says, simply because our way of thinking and methods of analysis negate its possibility. When we assume that our responsibilities are defined as responding to the demands of special interests, when we act on behalf of "winning coalitions" of narrow interests, rather than trying to discover shared values, when we rely solely on quantitative analysis to determine the "right" course of action, our behavior reinforces the idea that shared public preferences either do not exist or are irrelevant.

The New Public Service and the Public Interest

In contrast, the New Public Service rejects the views of the public interest implicit in both the Old Public Administration and the New Public Management. In fact, it is the rejection of those perspectives that is a defining feature of the New Public Service. We argue that public servants have a central and important role in helping citizens to articulate the public interest, and, conversely, that shared values and collective citizen interests should guide the behavior and decision making of public administrators. This is not to say that the outcomes of the political process are wrong, or that public administrators should substitute their own judgments for policies with which they disagree. Rather, it is that public administrators must work to ensure that citizens are given a voice in every stage of governance—not just in electoral politics. Public servants have a unique and vitally important responsibility to engage with citizens and create forums for public dialogue.

Interestingly, glimpses of this viewpoint can be found in some of the early voices in the field of public administration. Although these ideas were soon overshadowed by the views of interest-group pluralists, it is interesting to note some of the early references to the public interest as based on shared values and long-term and common interests of the people. For example, although Paul Appleby would later come to see the public interest as the interplay of special interests, in 1950 he said that the job of the administrator was:

> to bring into focus—to resolve and integrate—these popularly-felt needs; to give specific form to responses of the government designed to meet the needs; to inject foresight and concern for factors not readily visible to citizens at large; to try to so organize governmental responses as to secure at least majority consensus or consent.

(155)

Here, he seems to recognize that there is a need to think, not only of special interests, but also of larger questions of the public interest and the need to build consensus.

Likewise, in 1954, Emmette Redford wrote that administrative decisions are based on "common interests and ideas," and that the administrator acting to "look for common and enduring interests is an essential safeguard for the public interest" (1107). He made a case for the administrator's attention to the underrepresented, but he talked about the importance of future and shared interests as well: "the real danger is that the interest of the unorganized and weak, the shared interests of men generally, and the interest of men for tomorrow will not have proper weight in government councils" (1109).

Despite the early voices calling for administrative attention to the public interest, the criticisms of such views were insistent and largely successful. Schubert, for example, dismissed the idea of the public interest as a guiding force in administrative decision making, deriding the idea of "benevolent bureaucrats, who are the Guardians of the democratic state" (1957, 349). He questioned, even ridiculed, the appropriateness and reasonableness of what he argued was the premise of such views, that "the public interest would be realized if bureaucrats . . . obeyed the exhortations . . . of moralists . . . [to] Be clever! Be wise! Be good!" (354).

The New Public Service regards these criticisms as simplistic and misplaced. Administrators need not simply be admonished to be clever or wise and to act as guardians in judging what is to be considered moral. Instead, the New Public Service advocates an active and positive role for administrators in facilitating citizen engagement in defining and acting on the public interest. The New Public Service also rejects the idea that the public interest can be understood as the aggregation of individual self-interests. In the New Public Service, the goal is to move beyond self-interest to discover and act upon shared interests—the public interest.

This view also affects how we look at trust in government. Ruscio, for example, argues that, in government, "the decline in trust is due to the growing perception that elected officials, administrators, and citizens seek to maximize their self interest" (1996, 464). He goes on to emphasize that, "genuine trust depends on an assumption not easily accommodated by rational choice theorists: Individuals can act on some basis other than their private interest" (464). This means that trust does not rely on self-interest. Rather, it is based on norms and values and assumes that behavior can be influenced by the shared public interest. In other words, trust will decline if people believe that the demands of self-interested citizens drive governmental responses. Citizen trust and confidence in government are built on the perception that governmental policy is focused on the public interest.

Research by Glaser, Parker, and Payton (2001) and Glaser, Denhardt, and Hamilton (2002) supports this contention: When government agencies visibly concentrate their efforts on increasing the well-being of community, it appears they can begin to close the gap between citizens and government.

The New Public Service suggests that government should encourage citizens to demonstrate their concern for the larger community, their commitment to matters that go beyond short-term interests, and their willingness to assume personal responsibility for what happens in their neighborhoods and the community. In this view, as suggested in Chapter 2, citizens adopt a broader and more long-term perspective, based both on their knowledge of public affairs and a sense of belonging, a concern for the whole, and a moral bond with the community (Sandel 1996).

This is not to suggest that determining what governmental action will best serve the public interest is a simple or straightforward proposition. As Edward Weeks points out, "any solutions to a significant public problem will likely displease some segment of the community" (2000, 362). Seeking the public interest does not mean that governmental decision makers will somehow develop policy with which all citizens will agree. Rather, the public interest is best thought of as a process of community dialogue and engagement. This process both informs policymaking and builds citizenship. "By requiring that we interact—that is engage in democratic discourse—with others, participation broadens our perspectives and helps us see beyond our own narrow interests" (deLeon and Denhardt 2000, 94). Or, as Berry, Portney, and Thomson put it, "People who participate in the life of the community share a strong appreciation of its riches" (1993, 239). It is the ability to transcend narrow interests and recognize shared community interests and "riches" that is at the core of citizenship in a democracy. Government can play a central role in facilitating such a process and elevating the discourse to focus on long-term community interests. As Weeks (2000) found, such processes may not be quick or easy, but they can be powerful instruments in engaging citizen dialogue and creating the public will to act.

What we seem to be witnessing is a renewed emphasis on the public interest and shared values as the basis for the field of public administration. In fact, several contemporary public administration scholars have used the concept of the public interest as a means to explain and legitimize the role of public administration in a democracy. John Rohr (1986), for example, asserted that the constitutional legitimacy of public administration rests upon a charge to uphold constitutional values in the public interest. In a similar vein, Charles Goodsell argued that, "public bureaucracy is . . . the leading institutional embodiment and proponent of the public interest in American life" (1994, 107).

First-person stories can be used to dramatize issues and engage the community. For example, Sojourn Theater in Portland, Oregon, created "Witness Our Schools," based on interviews with teachers, parents, students, and school officials. The resulting play toured the state in high schools, theaters, and community centers. Postperformance discussions were then used to invite others to also engage in a discussion of the future of public education.

Similarly, Gary Wamsley and his coauthors (1990) reconceptualized bureaucracy as the "Public Administration" and argued that the Public Administration is an institution of government rather than an organizational form. As such, administration should be defined in large part as competence directed toward the public interest. In this view, the role of the public administrator is about both responsiveness and responsibility (1990, 314). Wamsley and his coauthors suggested that characterizations of civil servants as seeking status and power are erroneous and harmful. Instead, we should affirm a more "transcendent" role based on a commitment to the amelioration of societal problems and improving the quality of citizens' lives. Citizens should play a crucial role in public administration and in the shift of the American political dialogue. "Administrators must seek to expand opportunities for direct citizen involvement in governance, so that citizens develop the practical wisdom that is the ultimate basis of trust in administrative good faith" (315).

The idea is not that public administrators become the guardians of democracy by substituting their superior vision of the public interest for the will of, for example, the legislative or judicial branches. For public servants to act as if their version of the public interest is somehow superior to the perspectives and values of citizens, elected officials, interest groups, and political parties is at least undemocratic, if not outright unethical. Rather, public servants play a role in facilitating dialogue about the public interest and in acting to realize those values, within the larger system of political discourse and governance. In other words, public administrators do not and cannot act as the "administrative Platonists" that Schubert feared. Acting to single-handedly define the public interest, in the style of administrative "Lone Rangers," completely ignores the active role played by elected officials, citizens, the courts, and the myriad other participants in the governance process. Rather, because so many public problems cross traditional, geographical, socioeconomic, and other boundaries, administrators must be willing to explore new options and partnerships for addressing them (Crosby 2010; Gergen and Kellerman 2003).

Conclusion

In the New Public Service, the public administrator is not the lone arbiter of the public interest. Rather, the public administrator is seen as a key actor within a larger system of governance including citizens, groups, elected representatives, as well as other institutions. As Frederickson states:

> The pursuit of self-interest through government, while commonplace, must be resisted when either citizen or public servant self-interest erodes the general interest. Rather than merely facilitating the pursuit of self-interest, the public administrator will continually strive, with elected representatives and the citizens, to find and articulate a general or common interest and to cause the government to pursue that interest.
>
> (Frederickson 1991, 415–416)

This argument, of course, has important implications for the roles and responsibilities of public administrators, emphasizing that the role of government becomes one of assuring that the public interest predominates, that both the solutions themselves and the processes by which solutions to public problems are developed are consistent with democratic norms of justice, fairness, and equity (Ingraham and Ban 1988; Ingraham and Rosenbloom 1989). One of the most important implications of viewing government as the vehicle for achieving values such as fairness and equity is that the purpose of government is fundamentally different from that of business. These differences make the exclusive use of market mechanisms and assumptions about trust as a self-interested calculation suspect, at the least. Although there are many characteristics that distinguish business from government, government's responsibility to enhance citizenship and serve the public interest is one of the most important differences—and is a cornerstone of the New Public Service.

Chapter 5

Value Citizenship over Entrepreneurship

Value citizenship over entrepreneurship. The public interest is better advanced by public servants and citizens committed to making meaningful contributions to society than by entrepreneurial managers acting as if public money were their own.

Although, in the past, government played a central role in what has been called the "steering of society" (Nelissen et al. 1999), the complexity of modern life sometimes makes such a role not only inappropriate, but impossible. Those policies and programs that give structure and direction to social and political life today are the result of the interaction of many different groups and organizations, the mixture of many different opinions and interests. In many areas, it no longer makes sense to think of public policies as the result of governmental decision-making processes. Government is indeed a player—and in most cases a very substantial player. But public policies today, the policies that guide society, are the outcome of a complex set of interactions involving multiple groups and multiple interests, ultimately combining in fascinating and unpredictable ways. Government is no longer "in charge." Rather, public servants must join with their counterparts in nonprofit and private business in order to solve problems that are simply too large in scope and cross too many boundaries to be tackled by any single organization (Marsh 2013). In this new world, the primary role of government is not to direct the actions of the public through regulation and decree (though that may sometimes be appropriate), nor is it the role of government to simply establish a set of rules and incentives (sticks or carrots) through which people will be guided in the "proper" direction. Rather, government becomes another player, albeit an important player, in the process of moving society in one direction or another. Government acts, in concert with private and nonprofit groups and organizations, to seek solutions to the problems communities face. In this process, the role of government is transformed from one of controlling to one of agenda setting, bringing the proper players "to the table" and facilitating, negotiating, or "brokering" solutions to public problems (often through coalitions of public, private, and nonprofit agencies). Whereas, traditionally, government has responded to needs by saying, "yes, we can provide that service" or "no, we can't," the New Public Service suggests that elected officials and public managers should respond to the requests of citizens, not just by saying yes or no, but by saying such things as, "Let's work together to figure out what we're going to do, then make it happen."

In a world of active citizenship, the role of the public servant changes. Public administrators will increasingly play more than a service-delivery role—they will play a conciliating, a mediating, or even an adjudicating role. And they will no longer rely on the skills of management control, but rather on the skills of facilitating, brokering, negotiating, and conflict resolution. It will be necessary to be open to learning and embracing new organizational cultures, to accepting leadership from any and all corners of an organization, and to becoming skilled negotiators, mediators, and conflict resolvers, among other duties (Davenport 2001; Schein 2008).

A Governance Perspective

One of the most important developments in political life today, and one recognized by the proponents of both the New Public Management and the New Public Service, is a dramatic change in the way that the rules and regulations, the programs and processes that guide society are being developed, or, to put it slightly differently, a change in the way public policy is being developed. As we noted earlier, in the past, government played a predominant role in the "steering of society" (Nelissen et al. 1999). That is not to say that other interests were not represented, but that government played a decisive role.

To use a sports analogy, the playing field on which the game of public policy formation occurred was one prescribed by government, and the primary players were elected public officials and policy advisors throughout government agencies. In turn, public administrators, playing on the same field, though often somewhere nearer the sidelines, were largely concerned with the implementation of public policies. They were concerned with managing their organizations so that the proper things would get done. However, times and circumstances have changed. The game of public policy formulation is no longer played primarily by those in government. You might even say that, now, the audience is no longer in the stands, but right there on the field, participating in every play. To put this more formally, there has been a reformulation of the steering mechanisms of society. Today, many groups and many interests are directly involved in the development and implementation of public policy. "This means that steering goes through channels other than the controlled hierarchical structures of central government" (Nelissen 2002, 6).

There are several reasons this has occurred. First, the more fluid character of the market, especially the expansion of international or global markets, has opened new issues to public concern. Governments are engaging more extensively with other governments and with organizations such as the World Trade Organization, to say nothing of multinational corporations and similarly large and complex nongovernmental organizations. Second, the welfare state has been reconfigured so that government itself is no longer the primary actor in the delivery of services. Especially in this country, welfare and other governmental responsibilities have been pushed down to lower levels of government and out to for-profit and nonprofit organizations.

Donald Kettl has commented on these trends in globalization and devolution as follows:

> In short, America's preeminent policy strategies have tended to grow beyond the nation-state, to linkages with international organizations, and to focus below it, to partnerships with subnational, for-profit, and nonprofit organizations. Supranational organizations have grown to new but poorly understood functions. Subnational organizations have transformed the role of state and local governments. As we have debated privatizing government, they have paradoxically also governmentalized a substantial part of the for-profit and nonprofit sectors. The federal government's institutions, political and administrative, find themselves with yet more challenges, from orchestrating these partnerships to shaping the national interest. The roles of all these players have changed dramatically. Managing these roles requires capacity that lies far beyond the standard responses, structures, and processes that have gradually accumulated in American government.
>
> (Kettl 2000b, 489–490)

Third, technology has made possible greater and greater public access to the policy process, not only in the sense that people can access information more easily and can use that information to greater impact. The transparency and public access to information are central to holding government organizations accountable in a period of rapid technological advances that have made broad dissemination of information simple (Fung 2013). Whereas, in the past, government had somewhat of a monopoly on the collection and dissemination of large amounts of data—and enjoyed a unique position because of this—today that capacity is widely distributed. As a result, government's role in the policy process has been diminished. In this sense, Harlan Cleveland was correct in predicting that the global information explosion would lead to the "twilight of hierarchy" (1985).

Similarly, H. Brinton Milward has suggested several related factors that have caused the dispersion of power and responsibility that characterizes the contemporary policy process: (1) institutional overlap, (2) overlapping authority among levels of government, (3) the fact that particular organizations have only limited responsibility for program implementation, and (4) public policy instruments that cause fragmentation (e.g., grants, contracts, and subsidies) (1991, 52). These factors have led to the development of what have been called "policy networks," networks composed of businesses, labor unions, nonprofit organizations, interest groups, governmental actors, and ordinary citizens. These policy networks now constitute the main arenas in which the game of public policy is played out.

In fact, what we are witnessing is the development of many different policy networks—each serving its own substantive interests, whether transportation, social welfare, education, or another area. Each network focuses on its own policy area and, in many ways, defines the way in which policies will be developed in that area. That is, one set of rules might define the way the "defense" game is played, and another set of rules might define how the "social welfare" game is played. In each arena, major developments in public policy, and major developments in the steering of society, are likely to occur through a difficult and convoluted process of bargaining and negotiation within that particular policy network.

Under these circumstances, the role of government is changing. As we witness a fragmentation of policy responsibility in society, we must also recognize that the traditional mechanisms of governmental control are no longer workable—or even appropriate. Traditional hierarchical government is giving way to a growing decentralization of policy interests. Control is giving way to interaction and involvement. Today, national, state, and local governments are involved in governance, *along with* thousands of citizens, other public institutions, private companies, and nonprofit organizations. For this reason, it increasingly makes sense to talk, not just about government, but about the process of governance.

We define governance as the exercise of public authority. The word "government" is usually used to refer to the structures and institutions of government and of those public organizations formally charged with setting policy and delivering services. Governance, on the other hand, is a much broader concept. *Governance* can be defined as the traditions, institutions, and processes that determine the exercise of power in society, including how decisions are made on issues of public concern and how citizens are given voice in public decisions. Governance speaks to how society actually makes choices, allocates resources, and creates shared values; it addresses societal decision making and the creation of meaning in the public sphere. As John Kirlin argues, existing conceptions of government that emphasize service delivery "undervalue the large role governments must successfully perform in providing the institutional framework for all human activity" (1996, 161). Governments exist, he says, to create value, including the value of place and the character of community.

In the overall scheme of governance, then, what role will formal government play? First, government will continue to play an overall role in establishing the *legal and political* rules through which various networks will operate. We might say that government will operate at the "meta-level," that is, government will help in ratifying, codifying, and legitimizing decisions that arise from within the various policy networks. Moreover, government will continue to establish broad principles of governance that apply to all, for example, setting the overarching rules of the game. Second,

Some cities, such as Chicago, which originated the approach in 1992 (http://imaginechicago.org/), and Memphis, have organized large-scale "Imagine" projects, with a focus on improving the quality of life and strengthening civic connections and cross-generational communication. Other cities, including Calgary (www.imagine calgary.ca/) and Durban (www.imaginedurban.org/), have focused on sustainability. An "Imagine" project uses community visioning with facilitated small-group discussions that emphasize "strength-based" communications. Participants explore questions that open up possibilities. For example, Imagine Memphis asks, "What's good in Memphis? How could what's good be better? What's your dream? How do you imagine Memphis?" (www.imaginememphis.org/# Page_1).

government will likely help in resolving resource distribution and dependency issues within various networks, but especially between and among those networks. Government will aid in protecting *economic interests* that are played out in the relationships between different sectors or policy networks; it will play a role of balancing, negotiating, and facilitating relationships across network boundaries (often through the use of incentives rather than directives), and assuring that one sector doesn't come to dominate others. Third, government will be required to monitor the interplay of networks to assure that principles of *democracy and social equity* are maintained within specific networks and in the relationships between and among the different networks. Government must make sure that democratic processes are maintained and that, ultimately, the public interest is served.

Just as the steering of society is changing, so are the roles and responsibilities of elected and appointed public officials changing—and changing in exactly parallel ways. Not surprisingly, each of the three roles we have just described—those associated with *legal or political* standards, those associated with *economic or market* considerations, and those associated with *democratic or social* criteria—is reflected in popular approaches to understanding the role of government, and especially public administration, today. As the steering of society has changed, the roles of public officials and the standards by which administrative performance will be judged have also changed.

How have these three new roles of government been translated into schools of theory and practice, and how do they affect the standards or expectations for assessing governmental performance? The first of these schools of theory and practice is the most familiar and most easily characterized. Attention to the development of legal and political standards will continue to be important in the field of public affairs. According to this school, public officials are involved in designing and implementing policies focused on limited, politically defined objectives. They are bound by the law and by political realities. They are concerned with developing programs through the traditional agencies of government. In turn, these policies are carried out by administrators in the various agencies of government. The question of accountability—the question of how administrators know that their work is consistent with the wishes of the people—is answered by the accountability of administrators to democratically elected political leaders. The school of theory and practice associated with this approach is simply traditional public policy and public administration, the Old Public Administration.

The next two approaches have emerged much more recently. The second, which has to do with *economic and market* considerations, is based on a view of political life that sees the role of government as continuing to steer, at least in the sense of acting as a catalyst to unleash the forces of the market and creating mechanisms and incentive structures to achieve policy objectives through private and nonprofit agencies. The approach to accountability reflected in this viewpoint suggests that, ultimately, the accumulation of individual self-interests will result in outcomes desired by broad groups of citizens, whom, as we saw earlier, this approach calls "customers." The school of public administration theory and practice associated with this approach is, of course, the New Public Management.

The third emerging (or perhaps reemerging) role of government focuses on *democratic and social* criteria. This view suggests that the public interest is paramount, and that the public interest is the result of a dialogue about mutual or overlapping interests. It sees the role of government as brokering interests among citizens and other groups so as to create shared values. This might mean, for example, building coalitions of public, private, and nonprofit agencies to meet mutually agreed-upon needs. Openness to such changes is vital for government and nonprofit agencies as well as private businesses, as is valuing innovation and creativity (Gilley, Dixon, and Gilley 2013), and organizations from all sectors must be willing to take their place in networks that pool resources and abilities (Feldman 2010).

John Hall states the challenge facing public administration well: "Public management that embraces the power and refines the craft of collaboration, facilitative leadership, public-private partnerships, and 'catalytic governance,' is the new formula. . . . In that spirit . . . proactive public management will need to sharpen its *capacity to listen*" (Hall 2002, 24; emphasis added). The understanding of accountability (which will be addressed more fully in Chapter 7) reflected in this approach suggests that public servants must attend to law, community values, political norms, professional standards, and citizen interests. The school of public administration theory and practice most clearly associated with this approach is, of course, the New Public Service.

The Old Public Administration and the Administrator's Role

As we saw earlier, public administration has always struggled with the question of the administrator's role in developing policy and with the relationship between administrators and other policymakers. The earliest statements on this issue suggested a separation of policy and administration. Elected political leaders were charged with making policy, and administrators were charged with carrying out policy. The administrator, though insulated from the citizenry, was accountable to elected political leaders, who were, in turn, accountable to the electorate, who could vote them out of office, thus maintaining a "chain" of democratic control by citizens over administrators.

The dichotomy of policy and administration, if it was ever fact, came quickly to be regarded as fiction. Administrators came to play an increasingly important, though often reluctant, role in the policy process. Their reluctance was understandable. If administrators came to substantially influence the policy process, one might ask whether the notion of democratic accountability envisioned under the policy–administration dichotomy would still be sufficient. Where the administrator's role only had to do with implementation, the major choices about societal direction were still being made by elected political leaders who would be held to account every two, four, or six years. But, as the administrator's influence in the policy process grew, that chain of accountability came into question. How could citizens be sure that administrators were making policy choices responsive to the public interest?

Administrators were also reluctant to engage in the policy process because they were unclear about their relationship with elected leaders. Traditional public administration, for various reasons, conceived of elected political leaders as having far greater prestige and standing than appointed officials. Administrators engaging in policymaking might be taken as an affront to the authority of elected leaders. It might be seen as taking some of the rightful power away from the people's representatives. Certainly, if power were seen as a zero-sum game, there could be no other explanation. Given that circumstance, combined with the fact that the elected leaders could still fire appointed officials, it just didn't seem like a good idea to "challenge" the elected leadership by overt involvement in the policy process.

For these reasons, when public administrators reluctantly moved into making public policy, they did so only under several "cloaks." There was, for example, the cloak of discretion. Administrators could justify their policy role by pointing out that legislation is often, even necessarily, broad and requires administrators to define more carefully what legislated policies mean. Administrators exercising discretion are, of course, making policy, but they are required to do so by the breadth of legislation. There was also the cloak of expertise. The argument was that administrators have special knowledge and expertise in the areas of their particular interest, and that their expertise needed to be brought into the policy process. Legislators, as generalists, could not be expected to know as much about any particular policy area as administrators who had spent their careers working on those specific problems. So, under the Old Public Administration, administrators were reluctant participants in the policy process, maintaining their neutrality long after it was evident that they substantially influenced public policy.

Beneath the cloaks of justification for the administrator's involvement in policymaking, there were occasional hints of something broader— a philosophy that put administrators much more at the center of the governmental process. Theorists recommended creating single centers of administrative responsibility and control through which administrators could influence the rational development of plans to meet societal goals. Specific analytic tools could be developed to calculate optimum policy choices. The result was a shift from dealing with problems through politics to dealing with problems through management. While playing this role, albeit carefully and in silence, administrators could employ their expertise and experience in order to make more rational, controlled plans and decisions for (not by) citizens. As Schneider and Ingram remark:

> Carried to its extreme, public policy becomes a scientific enterprise dominated by experts who discover the public interest, find optimal policies to achieve it, and develop decision instruments to ensure control over the implementation process. People are simply the targets of policy, available to be manipulated through inducements or penalties to achieve policy goals, rather than citizens who are integral to the democratic process and to the production of socially desirable results.
>
> (1997, 38)

The New Public Management and the Administrator's Role

The New Public Management's approach to the question of the administrator's role in policy development has two distinct faces. On one hand, the New Public Management conceives of a much more active role for the administrator in the policy process, the role of policy entrepreneur. On the other hand, the New Public Management urges managers to respond to "customer" demands and, wherever possible, to structure policies so that "customers" can choose, that is, to move as many choices as possible even further out of the political arena by converting those policy alternatives into market choices. In either case, the New Public Management even further extends the rational calculus of costs and benefits in its examination of policy alternatives.

Establishing public managers as "entrepreneurs" is an essential element of the New Public Management. Indeed, the subtitle of the "bible" of the New Public Management, the book *Reinventing Government*, is *How the Entrepreneurial Spirit is Transforming the Public Sector* (1992). Its authors, Osborne and Gaebler, describe entrepreneurship as maximizing productivity and effectiveness, but entrepreneurship embraces more than mere resourcefulness. First, there is the basic concern for "letting managers manage"— giving managers wide latitude to conduct their affairs without the constraints of typical modes of accountability, such as budget restrictions or personnel policies (Pollitt 1993). An example from Gaebler's experience as a city manager is used by Osborne and Gaebler to elaborate this point: "The idea was to get them [the city's management team] thinking like owners, 'If this were my money, would I spend it this way?'" (1992, 3).

More important, the manager is urged to take an active role in promoting policies, "arrangements," or "deals" that he or she thinks would benefit their community or agency. Moreover, the entrepreneurial public manager is encouraged to assume risks wherever necessary, in order to arrive at more creative and innovative solutions to public problems. Eugene Lewis described three entrepreneurial "giants" of public management (Hyman Rickover, Herbert Hoover, and Robert Moses) in this way: They were not "criminals in any conventional sense; rather, they were 'rule benders.' They were crafty, and they pushed the limits of what was legal and permissible time after time without getting caught or, when caught, without serious punishment" (1980, 243). In sum, as Larry Terry put it, the New Public Management supports a position in which "public managers are (and should be) self-interested, opportunistic innovators and risk-takers who exploit information and situations to produce radical change" (1998, 197).

The policy role of the public entrepreneur has been called into question by several writers. First, policy entrepreneurs may be creative and innovative, but they can also be opportunistic and uncompromising:

> As a practical matter, in real organizations, entrepreneurial managers pose a difficult and risky problem: they can be innovative and productive, but their single-mindedness, tenacity, and willingness to bend the rules make them very difficult to control. They can become loose cannons.
>
> (deLeon and Denhardt 2000, 92)

Second, there is the question of accountability. The idea of public managers independently making policy choices in the guise of "getting the best deal" and, even more important, acting as if the public's money were their own, flies in the face of a long tradition of democratic accountability and fiscal integrity in government. The public's business and the public's money, many would argue, should be treated as the *public's*.

In addition to recommending a more entrepreneurial role for public managers, the New Public Management also recommends structuring choices so that they can be made by "customers" in a market rather than by actors in the political sphere. The key, according to Osborne and Gaebler, would be to create market incentives where now there are political choices:

> In education, this might mean moving to a competitive market in which customers have choices and key stakeholders (parents and teachers) have

genuine control. In job training, it might mean injecting information about the quality of all training providers into the system, putting resources directly into customers' hands, providing them with accessible brokers, and empowering them to choose between competing providers. In unemployment insurance, it might mean creating a financial incentive for corporations to retrain employees rather than lay them off, or creating an incentive for those collecting unemployment to seek retraining.

(Osborne and Gaebler 1992, 308)

Again, recommendations such as these are consistent with the New Public Management's dependence on public choice theory and its assumption that the market is the central institution in society and can be relied on, more than other institutions (certainly more than government), to provide for free and fair choices. Through market mechanisms, individuals can pursue their own best interests with minimal constraint. Markets, it is argued, are free and without coercion, where government and public policy are coercive. In this view, the only role for government is to correct for market failures and provide goods and services that the market is not able to convey.

This argument is related to public choice theory's more general critique of the policy process. Roughly, that critique first suggests that government provides certain goods or services that could be better handled through the market, and that government is not efficiently organized to deliver many services. For example, advocates of this position argue that, if education were provided on the basis of consumer choice, say, through vouchers, the competition for students would increase the quality of the service being delivered. Schools would have to improve to attract students, their "customers." Competition would require schools to act more efficiently than if they remained under the aegis of government.

Moreover, proponents of public choice theory argue that political leaders and "bureaucrats," motivated by self-interest, seek excessive increases in programs and budgets, beyond what the public really wants. Finally, they argue that government programs breed "dependency," as recipients of services find it in their self-interest to partake of those programs rather than being self-sufficient. This argument is often made with respect to welfare, where it may appear that having a second child would increase the size of the welfare payment and, therefore, be an incentive to do so. The same argument might also be made with respect to farmers who received subsidies for growing, or even not growing, specific crops.

In contrast to centralized government programs, public choice theory recommends decentralization, privatization, and competition. Recommendations flowing from this position include privatizing government functions wherever possible, contracting with private firms (selected through a competitive bid process) in other cases, creating competitive arrangements within those government agencies that remain, and charging full market value for public goods. Specific programs might include the movement to "choice" in educational policy, contracting for social services, and the development of water policy based on market prices (Schneider and Ingram 1997, 46). Again, the effect of the New Public Management or the public choice position is to drive public policy out of the political arena and into the market, where the decisions of self-interested parties, "customers," will drive policy choices.

We should point out that the New Public Management gives the manager considerable independence with respect to policy development. On the one hand, administrators (as "entrepreneurs") are urged to act independently to move their own preferred policies or "deals" forward. At the same time, the manager must try to assess consumer preferences and then, based on that assessment, to pursue his or her own interpretation of the public's desires, largely unconstrained by external mechanisms of accountability (see Chapter 7). What is, of course, missing in all this is the involvement of citizens in the process of democratic governance. If you look, for example, at the index of *Reinventing Government*, you won't find terms such as "equity" or "justice." Nor will you find "citizens" or "citizenship." It's really quite remarkable that a reform movement as significant as the New Public Management could move forward with such sparse attention to democratic citizenship.

The New Public Service and the Administrator's Role

The New Public Service, unlike the New Public Management, is distinguished by the involvement of citizens in the administrative process. In Chapter 3, we examined various dimensions of citizenship and began to build the case for a richer and fuller engagement of citizens in the policy process. The New Public Service builds on the tradition of democratic citizenship described in that chapter, especially as it urges extensive and authentic citizen involvement in the development of public policy. Here, we review some of the reasons that governments are increasingly involving citizens in the process of making public policy, and why public administrators might find greater citizen involvement attractive. Then, we will review a number of different approaches to structuring more extensive programs for civic engagement.

Citizen involvement in government is certainly not a new concept. Indeed, some level of citizen involvement is essential to democratic governance— by definition. However, historically, our representative democracy has largely confined the role of the citizen to voting every few years and occasionally communicating with elected officials. More recently, the rise of special interest groups has restructured the relationship between citizens and their government.

At the same time, government has opened new avenues for more direct citizen involvement. Beginning with the War on Poverty in the 1960s, governments have designed opportunities for "maximum feasible participation" into their processes of policy design and implementation. Consequently, dozens of approaches to soliciting citizen input into the policy process have been tried, ranging from public hearings to citizen surveys, and from planning boards to community panels. Although many of these efforts have failed to produce what King et al. (1998) call "authentic participation," and although there is clearly a need to continue to refine the process of citizen involvement, there is no question but that public managers will need to be attentive to the question of participation. As John Clayton Thomas indicates:

> The new public involvement has transformed the work of public managers ... public participation in the managerial process has become a fact of life. In the future, this may become the case for even more managers, since the public's demand for involvement does not seem to be abating.
>
> (1995, xi)

There are a variety of both theoretical and practical reasons why public administrators should encourage great citizen involvement in the policy process. At the theoretical level, as we saw earlier, the ethical posture of the public administrator requires an attitude of caring and involvement. David K. Hart (1984) points out that the professional obligation of administrators begins with their duties as virtuous citizens, and that creates an essential link to other citizens. In exercising their public trust, not only must administrators maintain adherence to "regime values," they should also be expected to care for their fellow citizens and interact with them on the basis of trust. He suggests that administrators must learn to trust that citizens, given the opportunity, will make the right choices. Interestingly enough, given our earlier discussion of "entrepreneurial government," Hart uses the term "moral entrepreneur" to describe the administrator who is obligated to conduct public affairs on the basis of trust rather than compulsion, something that may require a certain moral "risk-taking" that is even more significant than economic risk-taking. As Louis Gawthrop states, "to commit oneself to the service of democracy requires, at least, a conscious and mature awareness of (1) the ethical impulses of democracy, (2) the transcendent values of democracy, and (3) the moral vision of democracy" (1998, 24).

Others have pointed out that the administrator bears a responsibility to help educate citizens. We noted earlier the argument that participation in the activities of citizenship can serve an educative function, helping people to entertain broader interests than their own and to understand the complexities of the governance process. Participation in democratic governance builds moral character, an empathetic understanding of the needs of others, and the skills to engage in collective action. In that process of education, some have argued, administrators are in a unique position, that of being "civic educators."

> Because they comprise that segment of the expert realm that is most insulated from the adversarial process, they are best situated to take the lead in framing questions so that public debate can be made intelligible. They have the prime responsibility for teasing out the essential social and ethical issues at stake from the welter of scientific data and legal formalisms in which those issues are enveloped.
>
> (Landy 1993, 25)

Importantly, in this context, the educative role of the administrator is not merely that of "giving advice," but rather that of creating circumstances of dialogue and engagement where mutual learning can take place.

Finally, and most basically, as Bellah et al. write, "democracy is paying attention" (1991, 254). As an active participant in democratic governance, the administrator bears a responsibility to listen to the voices of citizens and to be responsive to what is said. In the process of listening, carefully and clearly, the administrator joins self and society in a reflexive relationship. Stivers puts it this way:

> As we improve our ability to listen, we increasingly understand the extent to which we hear ourselves in others and they in us; this reciprocity is evoked in our theories and practices of justice. Instead of stripping away the qualities of unique individuals in favor of the ideal of universality, listening expands justice to include the details of the situation and the significant differences among human beings.
>
> (1994b, 366)

In addition to these theoretical considerations, there are several more practical reasons for involving citizens in the process of policy development. First, greater participation can help meet citizens' expectations that they are being heard and that their needs and interests are being pursued. Second, greater participation can improve the quality of public policy, as governments tap wider sources of information, creativity, and solutions. Third, greater

The experience of Lynchburg, Virginia, in encouraging a dialogue on race and racism illustrates how various approaches to deliberation and dialogue can be combined. The "Many Voices—One Community" initiative began with pilot study circles—small groups of diverse participants. Next, the city launched 58 communitywide study circles and added 16 youth study circles. The communitywide study circles met for two hours a week for six weeks. Following the communitywide study circles, the Lynchburg community as a whole was invited to attend a three-day action forum. The forum, held in a vacant storefront in the center of the city, incorporated some of the attributes of a charrette. Attendees were able to find out more about the study circles process, to sign up to participate in an action group, and to vote on the more than 180 ideas presented by the 500 individuals who attended this event.

participation in the policy process aids implementation, as participants have more of a stake in the outcomes. Fourth, greater participation responds to calls for greater transparency and accountability in government. Fifth, greater participation is likely to increase public trust in government. Sixth, greater participation can help meet the challenges of an emerging information society. Seventh, greater participation can create the possibility for new partnerships being developed. Eighth, greater participation can result in a better-informed public. Ninth, in a democracy, it's simply the right thing to do.

Robert Reich sums up the position of the public manager nicely when he writes:

> But sometimes, I believe, higher-level public managers have an obligation to stimulate public debate about what they do. Public deliberation can help the manager clarify ambiguous mandates. More importantly, it can help the public discover latent contradictions and commonalities in what it wants to achieve. Thus the public manager's job is not only, or simply, to make policy choices and implement them. It is also to participate in a system of democratic governance in which public values are continuously rearticulated and recreated.
>
> (Reich 1988, 123–124)

Unfortunately, in many cases, policymakers have failed to involve citizens in the policy process. Peter deLeon has examined this issue in detail and finds numerous flaws in the current approach to policy development. As opposed to Harold Lasswell's ideal of policy sciences that would "improve the practice of democracy" (quoted in deLeon 1997, 7), policy research is largely carried out by technically trained policy analysts engaged in detailed policy studies and cost–benefit analysis. In deLeon's words, these analysts are "effectively sequestered from the demands, needs and (most critically) values of the people they are reputed to be helping" (1997, 8). Without the involvement of the people in the process of policy development, the policy sciences may be in danger of becoming what Lasswell feared, the "policy sciences of tyranny." In contrast to a policy science dominated by technical expertise, engaging ordinary citizens in the process of policy development seems most consistent with the democratic dream.

Although citizens have sometimes been simply ignored in the process, in other instances they have been involved for the wrong reasons and with poor results. For example, participation has been used to put off decisions by engaging in endless discussions, or it has been undertaken with no real commitment on the part of the administrator to use the information and advice that have been developed. Even worse, as we have often seen, the decision has already been made, making the involvement of citizens a mere pretense. These "cosmetic" efforts at participation constitute failures from which we can learn, as we think about ways to more fully engage citizens in the process of governance.

There have been much more positive experiences with citizen involvement as well—in this country and around the world. These examples have been documented in numerous publications (for example, see Meijer 2011; OECD 2001; Sirianni and Friedland 2001; Thomas 1995). Based on a comprehensive worldwide survey of these activities, the Public Management Service Working Group on Government–Citizen Connections of the Organization for Economic Cooperation and Development (OECD) defines three levels of involvement: information, consultation, and active participation:

> *Information* is a *one-way relationship* in which government produces and delivers information for citizens. It covers both "passive" access to information upon demand by citizens and "active" measures by government to disseminate information. Examples include, access to public records, official gazettes, government websites.

> *Consultation* is a *two-way relationship* in which citizens provide feedback to government. Governments define the issues for consultation, set the questions and manage the process, while citizens are invited to contribute their views and opinions. Examples include, public opinion surveys, comments on draft legislation.

> *Active participation* is a *relation based on partnership* with government, in which citizens actively engage in defining the process and content of policy-making. It acknowledges equal standing for citizens in setting the agenda, proposing policy options and shaping the policy dialogue— although the responsibility for the final decision or policy formulation rests with government. Examples include, consensus conferences, citizens' juries.
>
> (OECD 2001, 23)

As important as practical designs for participation are, there are significant conceptual difficulties in structuring processes of civic engagement. Interestingly, most of these concerns center on the question of dialogue, debate, deliberation, or discourse—that is, how citizens, politicians, and administrators can engage in a full and complete discussion of the relevant issues facing the polity in a way that is representative of, or even inclusive of, the citizenry as a whole, that incorporates both technical information and political preferences, and that takes all viewpoints into account through constructive and informed debate.

Obviously, traditional avenues for participation, such as public hearings or advisory boards, involve a limited number of people and typically only those with a special interest in the topic at hand. Moreover, these approaches typically are limited in the amount of informed dialogue that can take place. For these reasons, they present policymakers with a somewhat skewed version of the public's opinion. One way to try to move beyond this limitation is to create more representative bodies and permit them to interact at length around policy issues, before arriving at a policy recommendation. James Fishkin, for example, has argued for what he calls a "deliberative opinion poll" as a way of better assessing public opinion (Fishkin 1991, 1995). The deliberative opinion poll brings together a statistically representative group of people in one place for a period of several days, immerses them in the issue through carefully balanced briefing material, and allows them to engage in a sustained process of face-to-face interaction and to ask questions of experts and political leaders, then arrive at a conclusion. Through this process of deliberation, it is hoped that the participants will learn from one another and may modify their initial positions, perhaps arriving at a consensus. In any case, a final poll of the participants may then be taken as a "proxy" for the society as a whole.

Fishkin's work is paralleled in some ways by that of Daniel Yankelovich, who begins with another concern raised above—the possibility that expert knowledge will come to dominate the policy process, allowing little room for the public. To offset this tendency, he argues for enhancing the quality of public opinion, or what he terms "public judgment," a particular form of public opinion that exhibits:

> (1) more thoughtfulness, more weighing of alternatives, more genuine engagement with the issue, more taking into account a wide variety of factors than public opinion as measured in opinion polls, and (2) more emphasis on the normative, valuing, ethical side of questions than on the factual, informational side.
>
> (1991)

To sharpen public judgment, Yankelovich recommends a structured process of deliberation, through which participants can assess options, develop information needed to make choices, engage in reasoned discussion with their peers, and arrive at a reflective judgment. In this process, participants, indeed, citizens generally, will be aided by creating circumstances for "dialogue," situations in which there is equality and the absence of coercive influences, listening with empathy, and bring assumptions into the open (1999, 41–44). Again, the key to countering technical expertise (and its potential for un-wanted control) is the process of extensive dialogue by citizens. "Information stripped of feelings is not the royal road to public judgment; dialogue, rich in feelings and values, is" (25).

Benjamin Barber takes a similar tack in his argument on behalf of "strong democracy," a form of participatory democracy involving a community of citizens "capable of common purpose and mutual action by virtue of their civic attitudes and participatory institutions" (1984, 117). In Barber's view, the masses become citizens when they deliberate. Citizen participation lacking the quality of deliberation is empty. For this reason, it is important for those involved in designing institutions that would enable great citizen involvement to understand clearly the nature of "democratic talk," which involves listening as well as speaking, feeling as well as thinking, and acting as well as reflecting (178). Again, the qualities of empathy, emotion, and activity come to the fore. Thought of in this way, democratic talk can, in Barber's view, serve many functions. Most often, we think of political talk as involving the articulation of interests, persuasion, and bargaining and exchange. Democratic talk can also assist in agenda setting, exploring mutuality, affiliation and affection, maintaining autonomy, witnessing, expressing, reformulating, and reconceptualizing. Most important, democratic talk can assist in community building, creating public interests, common goods, and active citizens (178–198).

In other words, the more citizens engage in deliberation, the better they seem to get at it. Wagenaar argues that, "ordinary citizens are able to establish

Everyday Democracy is another group that promotes the use of citizen dialogue. It focuses particularly on helping communities better understand how racism and ethnic differences may influence the problems and policy issues they face through the use of study circles. The group uses a process called Dialogue to Action, which is divided into three phases: (1) comprehensive community organizing—team development, planning, recruitment; (2) dialogue —sometimes called study circles; and (3) change—personal, collective, and policy-level change (www.everyday-democracy.org/en/Page.Organizing.aspx#).

long-term, collaborative relationships with local administrators and thereby point the way to a new democratic form of governance that carries the promise of harnessing complexity and overcoming the limits of hierarchical policy making" (2007, 21). Through the process of participation, citizens practice democratic skills such as conflict management, listening, appreciation of diversity and difference in opinions, and patience when dealing with complicated policy issues (29). Ultimately, deliberation can help citizens distinguish their private interests from the collective benefit and the common good.

A number of theorists have examined the question of deliberative democracy from a more philosophical perspective. Jurgen Habermas, for example, has argued that, although our society operates under a narrow definition of rationality, one consistent with a society dominated by technology and bureaucracy, we maintain an innate capacity to reason in a much larger sense. Moreover, it is this capacity to reason that enables us to communicate across various social and ideological boundaries. However, for reason to prevail in any given situation, (1) we must engage in a dialogue, not a monologue, and (2) the dialogue must be free of domination and distortion. Where one party to the communication has more power than another, the communication is distorted. Genuine communication in a democracy can only take place where all forms of domination, both apparent and subtle, have been eliminated. A part of our being human is a "gentle, but obstinate, a never silent although seldom redeemed claim to reason, a claim that must be recognized whenever and wherever there is to be consensual action" (quoted in Yankelovich 1991, 217).

In *Between Facts and Norms*, Habermas (1996) uses the theory of communicative action (briefly outlined above) as the basis for a form of "deliberative democracy." Although Habermas is skeptical of a whole society governing itself through deliberative processes, he feels that, within "institutionalized discursive structures," people can in fact reason together. However, remember the problem of distortion. Distortion can come about in many ways—through overt exercises of power and influence, through economic pressures and market manipulation, or through the capture of the media for political or economic purposes. Under these circumstances, creating deliberative democracy is very difficult, but at least we have some direction as to what would be required to achieve that objective.

Other efforts to elaborate theories of deliberative democracy have sought to spell out the theoretical considerations concerning the legitimacy of various forms of deliberative democracy—and the resulting debates have been intense. (See, for example, Dryzek 1999; Gutman and Thompson 1996; Macedo 1999.) Some of these have focused on the circumstances under which people would agree that outcomes of a deliberative process are valid. Benhabib, for example, has suggested three conditions required for such a process to be considered legitimate:

> (1) Participation in such deliberation is governed by the norms of equality and symmetry; all have the same chance to initiate speech acts, to question, to interrogate, and to open debate; (2) All have the right to question the assigned topics of conversation; (3) All have the right to initiate reflexive arguments about the very rules of the discourse procedure and the way in which they are applied or carried out.
>
> (1996, 70)

Postmodern theorists, including public administration theorists, have also entered into the debate. Charles Fox and Hugh Miller, for example, criticize representative democracy as neither representative nor democratic (1995). Rather, the supposedly legitimizing force of democratic deliberation has been replaced by top-down bureaucratic systems and media-infused politics. As an alternative, Fox and Miller offer a set of conditions under which legitimate and "authentic discourse" might take place. Such deliberations would have to occur in a way that would exclude insincere claims, those that are only self-serving, those from persons unwilling to attend to the discourse, and claims from "free-riders." Forums built around norms of inclusion, attentiveness, and understanding may aid in reasserting the democratic ideal. Other theorists, such as Farmer (1995) and McSwite (1997), have taken the issue a step further by arguing that our being limited to "rational" discourse may inhibit our capacity to see beyond our own experience and to engage new ideas and new relationships in a fundamentally different way. "The very

> Other methods of bringing people together to share ideas about the future of community are charrettes, which usually have a design focus, and the "world café" format for fostering small- and large-group discussions. For example, after eight months of organizing, Reading, Massachusetts, assembled more than 200 people one evening to discuss what they wanted for the future of their town. In comparison, only 50 citizens had participated in an earlier master plan update organized in a traditional way.

essence of the discourse perspective is the idea of creating a kind of relationship among people such that when they engage in dialogue, the *source of the fundamentally new* will come into play" (McSwite 2000, 60).

Conclusion

In this chapter, we have explored the new conditions under which the "steering of society" is taking place and how the Old Public Administration, the New Public Management, and the New Public Service have responded to the challenges these circumstances present for public managers engaged in the policy process. In contrast to a reliance on bureaucratic expertise or managerial entrepreneurship, the New Public Service argues for a vastly enhanced capacity for citizen involvement in all aspects of the process. We have examined a variety of approaches to engaging citizens in the governance process, as well as some of the important theoretical considerations that must go into any design choice. Although we should point out, once again, that there are differences, even dramatic differences, among these viewpoints, they all share the same concern for democratic governance and civic engagement that is central to the New Public Service, yet missing in the Old Public Administration and the New Public Management. In all cases, these theorists are concerned with improving dialogue, deliberation, or discourse to better meet the tenets of democratic governance.

The first section of this chapter was adapted from a previously published paper: Robert Denhardt and Janet Denhardt, 2001, "The New Public Service, Putting Democracy First," *National Civic Review* 90(4): 391–400. The paper was originally prepared for the Arizona Town Hall.

Chapter 6

Think Strategically, Act Democratically

Think strategically, act democratically. Policies and programs meeting public needs can be most effectively and responsibly achieved through collective efforts and collaborative processes.

In Chapter 4, we argued that the public interest is based upon widespread public dialogue and deliberation about shared values and interests. In the New Public Service, the idea is not merely to establish the vision and then leave the implementation to those in government; rather, it is to join together all parties in the process of both designing and carrying out programs that will move in the desired direction. Through involvement in programs of civic education and by helping to develop a broad range of civic leaders, government can stimulate a renewed sense of civic pride and civic responsibility. We would expect that such a sense of pride and responsibility would evolve into a greater willingness to be involved at many levels, as all parties work together to create opportunities for participation, collaboration, and community. Again, this participation should not be limited to framing the issues; it should also extend to policy implementation.

How might this be done? To begin with, there is an obvious and important role for political leadership—to articulate and encourage a strengthening of citizen responsibility and, in turn, to support groups and individuals involved in building the bonds of community. Government can't create community, but government, and, more specifically, political leadership can lay the groundwork for effective and responsible citizen action. People must come to recognize that government is open and accessible—and that won't happen

In Phoenix, Arizona, the Blight Busters program links neighborhood volunteers with training and tools to eliminate graffiti, conduct cleanup projects, and report code violations. Blight Busters volunteers help to connect other residents of the neighborhood to each other and to the city's Neighborhood Services Department to extend the reach of code inspectors, police officers, and other law enforcement officials.

unless government *is* open and accessible, both in the process of policy formulation and in program implementation. People must come to recognize that government is responsive—and that won't happen unless government *is* responsive, in both framing programs and delivering services. People must come to recognize that government exists to meet their needs—and that won't happen unless it does. The best way to do so is to create opportunities for participation and collaboration in achieving public purposes. The aim, then, is to make sure that government is open and accessible, that it is responsive, and that it operates to serve citizens and create opportunities for citizenship in all phases of the policy process.

Accordingly, assumptions regarding the role of public administrators and citizens in the implementation of public policy are key to understanding the nature of citizenship and the relationship of public administration to the larger system of democratic governance. Early writers suggested that the role of public administration consisted of the efficient implementation of politically determined goals, with little or no direct citizen involvement. Later works portrayed the implementation process as much more complex and multi-faceted, but still largely ignored the role of citizens.

In order to understand the underlying principles of implementation in the context of the New Public Service values, this chapter will first briefly consider the evolution of implementation theory from a historical perspective. We then examine contemporary models of implementation and relate them to the assumptions and values of the New Public Management. We follow that with an explanation of the theoretical foundations that support a more democratic and participative approach to implementation.

Implementation in Historical Perspective

Interestingly, the study of "implementation" did not exist per se in the early stages of the development of public administration. This is not because public agencies were not involved in implementation. Rather, in a sense, implementation was invisible as a separate concept or function, because it constituted the whole of the field of public administration. Virtually the sole purpose of public agencies was to implement politically determined policies and programs. Because the goal of public administration was to maintain neutrality and to use administrative expertise to achieve efficiency, there was no need to have a concept of implementation; the assumption was that the policy would remain largely unchanged as public agencies acted upon it. After all, as Wilson, Goodnow, and other founding scholars in the field asserted, the political sphere made the decisions, and the administrative apparatus simply and mechanically put them into action. In short, the process of policy implementation didn't call for study or theory because it wasn't considered important relative to the decisions already made by the politicians.

Accordingly, theory and practice focused on achieving politically determined ends. This led to a concentration on the structures and functions of organizations that long characterized the field. Even in the 1940s and 1950s, with growing recognition that politics and administration were not entirely separate, the focus remained on the management of organizations to achieve efficiency and cost-effectiveness.

It was not until the emergence of policy studies in the 1970s that the idea of the activities of public organizations as the implementers of policy (as opposed to the managers of organizations) took hold. The first significant work dealing with implementation as a distinct issue was Jeffrey Pressman and Aaron Wildavsky's 1973 book, *Implementation: How Great Expectations in Washington are Dashed in Oakland*. These authors chronicled a series of failures and problems in the implementation of a Federal Economic Development Administration project in Oakland, California, finding that, although the program began with good intentions and a strong commitment, the actual implementation of this large-scale federal project was very difficult and largely unsuccessful. Their conclusion was that policy is not automatically translated into action, and that the dynamics of the implementation process must be understood as a major determinant of policy outcomes. Pressman and Wildavsky's work was the launching point for numerous subsequent works that sought to understand and explain the implementation process. In fact, six years later, Wildavsky, in the preface to the second edition of their book, commented that implementation had become a growth industry (1979).

Although considerable attention has been paid to policy implementation over the past several decades, mapping the boundaries of implementation theory remains difficult. This confusion is, in part, due to the fact that implementation research has continued to overlap with and draw heavily from work in organizational theory, decision making, organizational change, and intergovernmental relations. Admitting its rather fuzzy boundaries, implementation research has become an important and relatively prominent area of inquiry. In *Implementation Theory and Practice: Toward a Third Generation* (1990), Goggin and colleagues divide the development of implementation into first-, second-, and third-generation research. They discuss first-generation research as the work immediately following Pressman and Wildavsky's book, work that succeeded in shifting the focus from how a bill becomes a law to how a law becomes a program, and demonstrated the complexity, difficulty, and frequent failures that occur in the implementation process. Second-generation research is described as focusing on predictors of implementation success or failure, such as policy form, organizational variables, and the behavior of individual actors. Third-generation research, which the authors claim has not been achieved, will be more scientific in that it will clarify key concepts and specify causal paths and frequency distributions of behavior variations, and modeling of the process. This typology of three generations of research provides a useful basis for reviewing the historical evolution of implementation theory.

First Generation

First-generation research on implementation, including the work of Wildavsky and Pressman, assumed a top-down, linear policy process that was driven by the language of the statute and the intent of elected officials. Top-down models began with the decisions of policymakers, typically expressed in statutory language, and worked "down" the policy process. This model assumed that implementation *ought* to be a linear process wherein policy directives are translated into program activities with as little deviation as possible. It suggests that policymakers are the only important actors, and that organization-level actors serve only to thwart the "correct" implementation process. First-generation research was largely based on single-site case studies, and it concentrated on two sources of implementation failure: the content of the policy and the inability of people and organizations to implement it precisely. Although early first-generation research on implementation laid out the basics of the study, it was considered methodologically weak, as it was generally atheoretical and case-specific.

Within this framework, interest in implementation studies began to build in the early 1980s. For example, two articles published in *PAR* reported the results of specific implementation cases. First, Weimer, in his 1980 analysis of the implementation of an automated case management system, found that three kinds of problem were encountered in such projects: design and cognition problems, organizational cooperation problems, and poor data quality. He concluded that technical assistance might help overcome design and cognition problems.

Second, Menzel studied the implementation of the Federal Surface Mining Control and Reclamation Act, concentrating on the role of administrative rule making, and found that statutory deadlines, complex intergovernmental relationships, and lack of supportive clientele exacerbate implementation problems (1981). In both of these instances, the research was completely program-specific; as a result, few general propositions could be produced.

The issue of implementation was also being discussed in the literature on program evaluation during this time period. Three articles appeared in *Evaluation and Program Planning* in 1982 that underscored the importance of considering what are termed "type III" errors in evaluation. Type III errors are those errors that occur because of the failure to expose the experimental group to the independent variable—in other words, when outcomes are mistakenly attributed to program activities that were never actually implemented. Rezmovic, for example, examined the results obtained for an experiment conducted in criminal justice and found that the original, positive results could not be replicated when experimental and control groups were subdivided between those that actually received treatment and those that did not (1982). Similarly, Cook and Dobson concluded that program implementation data should be included in the analysis of program outcomes (1982). Tornatzky and Johnson explored the specific issue of how evaluation can be used to guide implementation efforts and found that evaluation should specify crucial program elements related to implementation and could be used as a means to ensure that planned activities actually take place (1982).

In all these cases, the explicit focus was on the idea that implementation often goes awry and confounds the intentions of the policymakers. However, implicit in these findings is an assumption that implementation ought to be a top-down, linear process wherein policy directives are translated into program activities with as little deviation as possible.

Second Generation

In second-generation implementation research, the top-down assumption was turned on its head. In other words, dissatisfaction with the top-down perspective led theorists to develop a number of models that viewed implementation from the bottom up. Linder and Peters (1986), for example, suggested that, for successful implementation, program design must consider the needs and values of the implementers. Bottom-up models assume the existence of a network of actors whose goals, strategies, and actions must be considered in understanding implementation. In this model, implementing agencies play a positive, necessary, and appropriate role in redefining and refocusing legislation in light of organizational-level realities. The question then becomes, of course, how do you determine success? In top-down models, success occurs when implementers do not deviate from politically determined policy. In bottom-up models, the presumption is that implementers are supposed to exercise discretion and redefine programs and policies as appropriate.

Next, implementation researchers sought to meld or integrate these top-down and bottom-up models. In the integrated model, implementation is seen as occurring in an interactive, circular policy process. For example, Nakamura argued that, instead of a linear process, implementation activities were a part of a seamless, interacting whole (1987). Adaptation and discretion in the implementation process, therefore, was seen as necessary and desirable. However, legislative leadership was also seen as critical. Likewise, Burke argued that, depending on institutional factors and the degree of internal or external control that could be exercised in the process, public policies should be designed to intentionally allow a range of bureaucratic discretion within legislatively established parameters (1987). This model explicitly acknowledges that both policymakers and administrators are actively involved in the implementation process.

In short, various perspectives on policy implementation emerged. The top-down model assumes implementation to be a linear process, controlled by policymakers. The bottom-up perspective views control and the exercise of discretion at the bottom of the bureaucracy to be an appropriate part of implementation. An integrated view incorporates both the top-down and bottom-up perspectives by acknowledging the importance of both leadership from the top and discretion at the bottom.

In addition to debates about the best vantage point from which to view the implementation process, a significant amount of work focused on establishing the predictors of implementation success. For example, Van Meter and Van Horn (1975) argued that, in addition to the characteristics of the implementing organization and the political, social, and economic environment, the success of policy implementation is influenced by resource availability, interorganizational communication, as well as the attitude of implementers. O'Toole and Montjoy (1984) found that, in cases in which the cooperation of two or more agencies was required for implementation, the type of interdependence between those agencies was a factor in predicting the likelihood of implementation.

Third Generation

In the third generation of research, questions increasingly focused on policy design and policy networks and their implications for how implementation "success" is most appropriately evaluated. In other words, there was an increasing recognition that the manner in which programs and policies are designed determines how, and how successfully, they will be implemented within a particular policy network.

Unfortunately, implementation is not often considered in policy design. Scholars increasingly argue that implementation is not a failure if the policy is poorly designed or not feasible in the first place; in other words, success must be measured in light of design considerations (Linder and Peters 1987). Dennis Palumbo (1987) claims the problem is that existing research does not differentiate between implementation failure and problems that result from poor policy design. He also criticizes the top-down bias that assumes that the goals and objectives of the policymakers are superior to those of the street-level implementers, as well as the failure to see adaptation in implementation as necessary and desirable. Moreover, according to Palumbo, the field of implementation research has an ideological bias that leads investigators to assume that government can't do anything right. As a result, he says, implementation research remains a highly fractured, disjointed body of knowledge.

On the positive side, however, Palumbo argues that inquiry has given us a number of important insights that should change how implementation is understood. Among the most important of these insights is that the tools of implementation, rather than management techniques, are critical. This becomes particularly important in complex policy networks. Cline (2000) suggests that the implementation process has been defined in two ways: as a problem of organizational management based on administrative process, or as a problem of how to elicit cooperation from participants in the imple-mentation process. He concludes, "Problems of generating cooperation in situations of conflict of interest are likely to stymie implementation before issues of organizational management become an obstacle" (2000, 552). In a similar vein, O'Toole urges scholars to look at the multiple institutional actors in the implementation process "whose cooperation and perhaps coordina-tion are needed for implementation success" (2000, 266). In fact, Hall and O'Toole showed that, "the great majority of legislation requires multifactor structures spanning governments, sectors, and/or agencies" (2000, 667).

One way to view implementation networks is from an intergovernmental communication perspective. Goggin and colleagues, for example, look at implementation from an intergovernmental policymaking framework based on "messages, messengers, channels, and targets operating within a broader communications system" (Goggin, Bowman, and O'Toole 1990, 33). This communication system provides political messages with regard to inducements, constraints, expectations, and exhortations within the intergovernmental framework.

Lynn, Heinrich, and Hill also look at implementation in networked settings: "public, nonprofit, and proprietary sectors through webs of states, regions, special districts, service-delivery areas, local offices, independent organizations, collaborative associations, partnerships, or other administrative entities" (2000, 551). Unlike Goggin, these researchers examine implementation from a political economy perspective, emphasizing the "logic of governance." The logic of governance, based on the concepts of political economy, deals with rational choice and consequences of the mechanisms used by alternative institutional forms to constrain and control behavior. They argue that the logic of political economy has great utility for understanding how agencies, programs, and activities can best be organized to achieve successful outcomes, efficiency, and effectiveness. Again, the focus is on "better system performance" (551).

Because top-down models have continued to be prevalent, criticisms of that model of implementation have also continued. Fox (1987) points out that top-down analysis assumes policymakers' directives must be literally and completely followed without deviation, that all program expectations will be met, and that only intended benefits are valid. As a result, implementation research tends to arrive at negative findings and concludes that government can't do anything right. Similarly, Nakamura (1987) also attacks what he calls the textbook policy process, which views policy as a linear series of functionally discrete steps (such as policy formation, implementation, and evaluation) with a feedback loop at the end. He argues that this is unrealistic, and that these activities are a part of a seamless, interacting whole. He concludes by urging researchers to develop an alternative, more realistic model of the process. Love and Sederberg (1987) offer one such possibility. They suggest that policy can be seen as a theory, and implementation as the attempt to translate theory into action. A number of factors influence how well this translation works: the theory's internal consistency, consistency with conventional wisdom, administrative capacity, and resources and the political support or momentum available.

Although much of the most contemporary literature analyzes implementation from a policy design perspective, Linder and Peters (1986) caution that a design perspective taken to its logical extreme would lead to the view that good policy is that which is most feasible or that which can be most easily implemented. That is, they say, a misdirection of the policy sciences.

What would be more fruitful, in their view, is to focus on policy imperatives first, and then consider alternative instruments for their accomplishment. Like Burke, they urge attention to the normative issues that underlie implementation, and that researchers concentrate on the design of effective and desirable policy.

In short, moving through various generations of research on implementation, two trends seem evident. First, there has been a shift away from the view of policy implementation as a unidirectional, linear process in which the intent of the elected officials is either followed (successful implementation) or not (failed implementation). Instead, implementation is increasingly seen as an interactive, circular process. Second, numerous variables have been shown to influence the implementation process, including individual actors, human behavioral considerations, organizational factors, institutional and interinstitutional factors, and policy design. As such, implementation studies no longer focus exclusively on a single agency as the unit of analysis. Rather, they look at implementation in the context of policy networks.

Nonetheless, most implementation research has ignored or neglected the role of direct citizen involvement in implementation. Using the concepts and questions raised in this review of implementation research, we will now explore the dominant views of implementation evidenced in the Old Public Administration and the New Public Management. We will then discuss how the New Public Service differs from these perspectives, particularly in its recognition of, and emphasis on, the importance of citizen involvement in program implementation.

The Old Public Administration and Implementation

As noted at the beginning of this chapter, in public administration orthodoxy, there was little differentiation between the administrative process and the implementation process. Implementation was what public administration was responsible for. Consequently, although what later came to be termed "implementation" models did not exist per se, there were a number of implicit assumptions about the nature of implementation (which was largely equivalent to efficient and neutral administration) and the best way to achieve it.

The first assumption was, of course, that the process of policy implementation was top-down, hierarchical, and unidirectional. It was assumed that policy arrived fully formed at the doorstep of administrative agencies. These agencies would then put that policy or program in place, with little need to exercise judgment or discretion. In fact, discretion was not acknowledged as a necessary part of a public administrator's job. Instead, agencies and their managers were to apply administrative expertise to control the process, so that policies would be put into place precisely as policymakers had intended. The job of administrative agencies was to neutrally execute laws passed by legislative authorities.

Second, because of the influence of scientific management and the emphasis on formal organizations, the focus was on controlling behavior to conform to these scientifically derived principles. The task was, then, to discover the most predictable, regularized, and "correct" procedures and rules to implement a program, and then to use management techniques and controls to ensure that people within the organization did what they were supposed to do. The sole focus was on the management of the organization and the people who were responsible for providing services and functions in support of enacted policy. The preeminent value was efficiency: Deliver services at the lowest cost consistent with the law.

The third assumption was that implementation was not part of the policy process. Administrative processes and policymaking (as prescribed by the politics–administration dichotomy) were entirely separate. Accordingly, there was no question about whether a policy was good or bad, "implementable" or not; it simply was the guiding force behind what administrators were obligated to do in the most efficient manner possible. Because of these assumptions, thinking strategically—much less implementing programs democratically—would have seemed both inappropriate and unnecessary.

The New Public Management and Implementation

It is somewhat difficult to tease out the assumptions regarding the implementation process that are embedded in the New Public Management. This is owing in part to the fact that the New Public Management doesn't deal with "implementation" directly. Rather, public choice theory and the New Public Management suggest that, in essence, government "get out of the way" as much as possible, to allow market forces and incentives to accomplish public purposes. As we will explore more fully in this section, advocates of the New Public Management talk about some of the same mechanisms and approaches to implementation and citizen involvement found in the literature on the New Public Service; however, these approaches are based on different fundamental assumptions and are justified for different reasons. As a result, although the approaches sound the same in some respects, and even use the same terminology, implementation in the New Public Management is different from that in both the Old Public Administration and the New Public Service.

Two of the primary approaches to implementation applauded by the New Public Management theorists are privatization and coproduction—in other words, get implementation out of the hands of bureaucrats and into a marketlike arena. As noted previously, privatization is a hallmark of the New Public Management movement. Although Osborne and Gaebler did not advocate the wholesale privatization of government, they did state that, "It makes sense to put the delivery of many public services in private hands . . . if by doing so a government can get more effectiveness, efficiency, equity or accountability" (1992, 47). In a sense then, the view of implementation advocated by the New Public Management theorists involves removing the implementation function from bureaucracies as much as possible, and instead introducing businesslike incentives to ensure that programs are implemented correctly and efficiently.

Although the Old Public Administration sought efficient implementation from the top down, the New Public Management seeks efficient implementation from the side—from the private sector into the public domain—and from the bottom—from its customers. Coproduction is the involvement of citizens in producing and delivering public services. Public choice theorists Vincent and Elinor Ostrom were among the first to use the term "coproduction" in their discussion of public goods in relation to institutional arrangements for service delivery (Ostrom and Ostrom 1971). Ironically, some of the other early proponents of coproduction (discussed in the section that follows) advocated the use of citizen involvement to empower communities, but this idea was quickly overshadowed by the idea of using coproduction to reduce costs.

This emphasis on cost reduction and de-emphasis on empowerment was expressed by John Alford, who suggested that problems with coproduction arise when it is too dependent on volunteerism and altruism: "In a climate where market incentives are the dominant currency, [it] seems far too unreliable a motivation on which to base important public functions." The answer is not to rely on the voluntary efforts of citizens, but to base coproduction on clients who are analogous to buyers. "While some of the early theoretical literature mentioned clients or 'consumer producers' . . . it usually collapsed them into 'citizens' or slid into the notion of volunteers" (2000, 129). He goes on to say that, "although no one is seriously suggesting a return to an emphasis on direct government production," a more "hardheaded" approach to coproduction by clients is needed (129).

Alford's more hardheaded approach is based on the ideals and norms of the market. He suggests that organizations can provide incentives to clients to behave in ways that can lower organizational costs. For example, if customers write postcards in a particular way, it can make mail sorting easier and reduce costs. If customers can be induced to carry their garbage to the street, it reduces the costs of garbage collection. One way to accomplish this is simply to require certain actions by the consumer as a condition of receiving the service.

Derived as it is from the customer in the private-sector market, that model assumes an exchange, in which the organization provides goods or services and the customer provides money to the amount of the purchase price. Aside from the fact that many public-sector clients are beneficiaries who do not pay for the services they receive, client coproduction means that the provision of the service is not simply done by the organization in a one-way transfer, but rather is partly done by the client (Alford 2000, 132).

Brudney and England (1983), on the other hand, argued that coproduction works best to reduce costs and improve performance if it is based on voluntary cooperation on the part of citizens, and on active rather than passive behaviors. However, the focus remains on coproduction as a cost-saving measure in response to fiscal constraints: "By supplementing—or perhaps supplanting—the labors of paid public officials with the service-directed activities of urban dwellers, coproduction has the potential to raise both the quality and the efficiency of municipal services" (1983, 959). In other words, in the New Public Management, citizen involvement concerns "*productive* behaviors that can enhance the level and quality of services provided" (Percy 1984, 432; emphasis added).

The New Public Service and Implementation

As described in Chapter 11, many local governments that experimented with privatization in the early 1990s subsequently took back responsibility for provision of those same services (Hefetz and Warner 2004). This phenomenon of "contracting back in" was largely attributable to poor service quality and problems with contract specifications and monitoring. This suggests that the market is an insufficient mechanism for ensuring that community needs and preferences are met. In the New Public Service, a primary focus of implementation is citizen engagement and community building. Citizens are not treated as potentially interfering with "correct" implementation, nor are they used primarily as vehicles for cost reduction. Instead, citizen engagement is seen as an appropriate and necessary part of policy implementation in a democracy. Because discretion is and must be exercised in policy implementation, that discretion should be informed by citizen participation. Peter deLeon (1999) argues convincingly, for example, that, by

placing greater emphasis on democratic, participative forms of implementation, combined with a more postpositivist methodology, we will gain
a much better understanding of how implementation can be successful.

In a similar vein, Terry Cooper makes the point that:

> The public administrator should be held ethically responsible for
> encouraging participation of the citizenry in the process of planning and
> *providing* public goods and services. Participation may or may not be useful
> or satisfying to the administrator, but it is essential to the creation and
> maintenance of a self-governing political community.
>
> (Cooper 1991, 143; emphasis added)

In the New Public Service, citizen involvement is not limited to setting
priorities. In fact, we should manage public organizations so as to enhance
and encourage the engagement of citizens in all facets and phases of the
policymaking and implementation process. Through this process, citizens
"come to see themselves as citizens . . . rather than as consumers, clients, and
beneficiaries of the administrative state" (Stivers 1990, 96). Citizens become
involved in governance instead of only making demands on government to
satisfy their short-term needs. At the same time, the organization becomes
"a public space in which human beings [citizens and administrators] with
different perspectives . . . act together for the public good" (96). It is the
interaction and engagement with citizens that give purpose and meaning to
public service. As Frederickson (1997) puts it, it "ennobles" our work.

From the perspective of the New Public Service, mechanisms such as
coproduction are derived from the concept of community, not from the
concept of the market. Communities are characterized by social interaction,

The city of Morgan Hill, California, was having little success getting
residents to buy into the reduction of greenhouse gas emissions. The
22-Million-Pound Carbon Diet Club was created to encourage
residents to change their behaviors regarding carbon emissions. In
the program, small groups of five to eight households formed teams
that aimed to reduce their emissions by 5,000 pounds in 30 days.
Neighbors helped each other and engaged in friendly competition to
see who could make the biggest cuts. By 2009, 80 households were
participating in Carbon Diet Clubs and had reduced greenhouse gas
emissions by half a million pounds.

a sense of shared place, and common bonds. As explained by Richard Sundeen (1985), there are three attributes of community—social interaction, shared territory, and common bonds. "These characteristics contribute to the cohesiveness and solidarity of the community with social relations among its members marked by mutual aid, cooperation, and holistic ties—in contrast to segmented, impersonal ties" (388). In this kind of community, citizens and public servants have mutual responsibility for identifying problems and implementing solutions. The absence of these community attributes contributes to self-interested and impersonal relationships between people. In this environment, the only way to implement a policy is to offer incentives or disincentives to modify the choices of self-interested individuals.

Worse, we suggest that this view is self-perpetuating. As people are treated as self-interested, utility maximizers, they come to see themselves as consumers of government services, not as members of a community. In the New Public Management, citizens generate demands, and government is then responsible for producing services to satisfy these demands. The goal is to meet the demands of citizens so that they will favorably judge the performance of government. This model leads to an emphasis on performance measures and productivity indicators to show the citizens that government is doing its job. The consuming public makes demands on government, and government sets out to show that it has responded. Accordingly, the role of the citizen/customer is limited to demanding, consuming, and evaluating services (Sharpe 1980).

Advocates of the New Public Service argue that too little attention is paid to citizens participating in government decision making and the actual delivery of services. We suggest that coproduction in a community rests on mutual trust, cooperation, and shared responsibility. In the New Public Service, citizens and administrators share responsibility and work together to implement programs. In the process, citizens learn more about government, and government learns more about citizens. Charles Levine (1984), for example, speaks directly to this issue, arguing that debates about involving citizens in the delivery of public services too often focus on narrow economic and political criteria. Rather than asking how much money will be saved, or how a particular approach will help deal with a contentious political environment, he suggests that we evaluate alternatives according to their potential contribution to enhancing citizenship, including: "(1) citizen trust in government; (2) citizen efficacy; and (3) a shared conception of the 'common good'" (1984, 284).

With regard to privatization, Levine argues that efficiencies will often result because of the advantages of choosing between competitive bidders.

> In Derby, Kansas, city officials opened the discussion to citizens to find out what they really cared about, before performance measures were developed. The results of the citizen survey gave managers unexpected information about how citizens perceived the quality of their work. Managers were then able to take steps to improve the quality of public services in areas important to citizens. Denver used randomly selected focus groups of citizens to discuss community-wide issues and public performance. City officials also involved the inter-neighborhood committee, which was developing its own "Neighborhood Vital Signs." Vancouver, Washington, used interactive polling, focus groups, and assistance from the local community college to engage citizens in a dialogue about performance. The city also used a virtual advisory group of citizens who volunteered to help with selecting performance measures aligned to the goals in the new strategic plan.

However, in the privatization model, the ideal becomes one of government existing to provide a competitive environment where firms provide services to consumers, with or without a government contract. Such arrangements do nothing to build citizenship or citizen trust. Rather, citizens are viewed and treated as mere consumers of privatized services, behaving just as they would buying a service from a business. As a result:

> The high citizenship of Pericles, Aristotle, and Rousseau that requires citizens to be active members of a self-governing community is excused by the advocates of privatization as irrelevant in an age of rational, self-centered private interests. . . . Public-spirited action has no place in this scheme.

(1984, 285)

In short, privatization cannot lead to better citizens, only to the possibility of smarter consumers. In contrast, coproduction, as Levine understands it, "lays the foundation for a positive relationship between government and citizens by making citizens an integral part of the service delivery process" (288).

Conclusion

We can conclude by noting that the difference between the New Public Management approach to coproduction and that of the New Public Service is not just a matter of semantics. For example, one of the most widely used applications of coproduction techniques is in the area of policing. Think for a minute what a policing program might look like if it were focused only on cost savings and efficiency—the hallmarks of the New Public Management. If a police department sought to enhance efficiency and reduce costs, citizens might, for example, be recruited through a series of incentives or disincentives to report more crime and/or create neighborhood watch activities to prevent criminal activities. These alternatives and others would be evaluated based on the degree to which they reduced the cost of policing services by involving a set of consumers and engaging their assistance to meet police objectives. It might be concluded, in some cases and for some functions, that privatization was the preferable alternative, because of the potential cost savings that could accrue from private firms' hiring less-well-trained and lower-paid security officers. This would also have the advantage of creating competition among security firms to find new and better ways to deliver police services at a lower cost. The role of the police department would become one of creating a competitive environment. The role of the police officer in relation to coproduction activities would be to ensure that citizens and neighborhood groups understood their objectives clearly and absorbed as many policing functions as were practical and cost efficient, to reduce and prevent crime. There would be little need for an ongoing relationship between officers and citizens. In fact, such efforts would most likely be costly, as they would divert police personnel from their traditional duties of responding to individual crime calls.

On the other hand, coproduction as derived from the ideals of community and citizenship, as in the New Public Service, would look very different. Community policing, as it is commonly known, generally involves working with members of the community to develop creative solutions to neighborhood problems. Community policing is based on "the concept that police officers and private citizens working together in creative ways can help solve contemporary community problems" (Trajanowicz et al. 1998, 3). This requires a change in the relationship between police officers and citizens, empowering them to set police priorities and involving them in efforts to improve the quality of life in their neighborhoods.

Although some of the mechanisms employed in these efforts might appear similar to those used in cost-cutting and market-driven strategies, in practice they are different. Neighborhood watches, for example, would be approached as vehicles for building community ties and the relationship between public employees and citizens to address neighborhood problems. The goal would not be, for example, to reduce the marginal cost of a police officer's responding to a call. Rather, the goal would be to build a stronger community, with citizens who are involved and empowered to prevent and reduce crime, and who share with public servants the responsibility for making their communities better. The role of the public servant becomes one of facilitating and encouraging such involvement and helping to build the capacity of citizens.

Chapter 7

Recognize that Accountability isn't Simple

Recognize that accountability isn't simple. Public servants should be attentive to more than the market; they should also attend to statutory and constitutional law, community values, political norms, professional standards, and citizen interests.

The matter of accountability and responsibility in the public service is extremely complex. Public administrators are and should be held accountable to a constellation of institutions and standards, including the public interest, statutory and constitutional law, other agencies, other levels of government, the media, professional standards, community values and standards, situational factors, democratic norms, and of course citizens. Indeed, they are called upon to be responsive to all the competing norms, values, and preferences of our complex governance system. These variables represent overlapping, sometimes contradictory, and ever-evolving points of account-ability. As a result, there are significant challenges involved in "establishing expectations, verifying performance, maintaining responsiveness of agents, assessing blame, sorting out responsibilities, determining who the masters are, and managing under conditions of multiple accountability systems" (Romzek and Ingraham 2000, 241–242).

The New Public Service recognizes both the centrality of accountability in democratic governance and the reality of administrative responsibilities. We reject the idea that simple measures of efficiency or market-based standards can adequately measure or encourage responsible behavior, as have others (Eikenberry and Kluver 2004; van der Wal and Huberts 2008). Instead, we argue that accountability in the public sector should be based on the idea that public administrators can and should serve citizens in the public interest, even in situations involving complicated value judgments and overlapping norms. To do so, public administrators must not make these judgments by themselves. Rather, these issues must be resolved, based not only on dialogue within organizations, but also on citizen empowerment and broad-based civic engagement. Although public servants remain responsible for assuring that solutions to public problems are consistent with laws, democratic norms, and other constraints, it is not a matter of their simply judging the appropriateness of community-generated ideas and proposals after the fact. Rather, it is the role of public administrators to make these conflicts and parameters known to citizens, so that these realities become a part of the process of discourse. Doing so not only makes for realistic solutions, it also builds citizenship and accountability.

Although accountability in the public service is unavoidably complex, both the Old Public Administration and the New Public Management tend to oversimplify the issue. As will be explored more fully in this chapter, in the classic version of the Old Public Administration, public administrators were simply and directly responsible to political officials. At the other end of the spectrum, in the vernacular of the New Public Management, the focus is on giving administrators great latitude to act as entrepreneurs. In their entrepreneurial role, public managers are called to account primarily in terms of efficiency, cost-effectiveness, and responsiveness to market forces.

This chapter considers how our ideas about accountability and responsibility in public administration have evolved and changed over time. First, to define some of the key parameters of the issue, we summarize the classic debate between Carl Friedrich (1940), who argued that professionalism was the best way to ensure accountability, and Herman Finer (1941), who said accountability must be based on external controls. Then, we look at the notion of responsibility and the evolution of thought regarding answers to the three big questions of responsibility and accountability: (1) *What* are public administrators responsible for? (2) To *whom* are they accountable? (3) By what *means* should accountability and responsibility be achieved? Finally, we compare and highlight the implicit and explicit views on accountability and the approaches they suggest, in the Old Public Administration, the New Public Management, and the New Public Service.

The Classic Debate

In a sense, the field of public administration was founded on a claim made by Wilson and others that the question of administrative accountability could be answered by defining the work of public administrators as objective and businesslike—and completely separate from politics. The trouble with accountability, at least intellectually speaking, began anew when the credibility of the politics–administrative dichotomy began to crumble under the pressures of increasingly complex governmental functions. If we cannot explain administrative functions as being largely mechanical and entirely separate from politics, and administrators aren't elected, how then do we hold them responsible? If administrative functions involve discretion, how do we make sure that discretion is exercised in a responsible manner, consistent with democratic ideals? What, for that matter, is "responsible" administrative behavior? Finding answers to these questions is as difficult as it is important. As Frederick Mosher said, "Responsibility may well be the most important word in all the vocabulary of administration, public and private" (1968, 7).

Questions about how best to secure accountable and responsible administration encompass some of the most important issues in democratic governance. In fact, one of the defining principles of democracy is the notion of controlled, accountable government. As Dwivedi states:

> Accountability is the foundation of any governing process. The effectiveness of that process depends upon how those in authority account for the manner in which they have fulfilled their responsibilities, both constitutional and legal. . . . Consequently, at the very root of democracy lies the requirement for public responsibility and accountability.
>
> (1985, 63–64)

Decatur, Georgia, offers an example of how Open City Hall can work. Located on Decatur's website (at www.decaturga.com), the Open City Hall program provides background information on pending issues. It asks residents whether they support or reject such proposals as annexing more neighborhoods into the city, creating more green space, and balancing the pedestrian–vehicle experience in the downtown area. It also gives citizens a chance to explain their views, and the responses are open to all. Posted views can become an evolving conversation about the issue. City officials read the comments and consider them in the decision process during their public meetings.

The fundamental parameters of the debate about responsibility and accountability in the field of public administration were set forth in a well-known exchange between Carl Friedrich and Herbert Finer. In 1940, as America prepared for war, Friedrich wrote in the journal *Public Policy* that the key to bureaucratic responsibility was professionalism. Administrative responsibility involved much more than simply executing pre-established policy. Policy formulation and execution were, in fact, becoming largely inseparable. Further, administrators were professionals and possessed specialized knowledge and technical expertise that the general citizenry did not have. Because their responsibilities were based on professional knowledge and norms of conduct, administrators should be accountable to their fellow professionals to meet commonly agreed-to standards.

It is not, Friedrich said, that being responsive to public sentiment isn't important. Rather, the changing nature of administrative responsibility requires that, among technical experts, professionalism, or "craftsmanship," be a central component of accountability (1940, 191). In making this argument, he suggested that there are two aspects of this responsibility: personal and functional. Personal responsibility refers to the administrator's being able to justify his or her actions according to orders, recommendations, and so forth. Functional responsibility involves the administrator's looking to his or her function and professional standards for guidance. There was the potential, he warned, for personal and functional responsibility to conflict. In these cases, both technical knowledge and hierarchy have to be considered.

Friedrich suggested that there are a number of ways to measure and enforce accountability, and "only a combination of all of them offers the prospect of securing the desired results" (1940, 201). But, he said:

> Officials working in all the more esoteric fields of government service, the ever more numerous scientific activities, both national and international, are more sensitive to and more concerned with the criticism made of their activities by their professional peers than by any superiors in the organization they serve.
>
> (201)

Ultimately, as government problems had grown increasingly complex and the need for discretion had expanded, professionalism had become the cornerstone of administrative responsibility.

Herman Finer (1941), from the University of London, disagreed. Writing in response to Friedrich, he said that external controls were the best and only means of ensuring administrative accountability in a democracy. He argued that administrators should be subordinate to elected officials, because elected officials were directly responsible to the people. These officials, based on their interpretation of the public's wants, should tell the administrator what to do. Then, the administrator was responsible for carrying out those duties according to those directions. In making this argument, Finer defined responsibility in two ways. The first definition is that "X is accountable for Y to Z." The second (and, according to Finer, the wrong-headed) definition involves "a personal sense of moral obligation." He stated:

> The second definition puts emphasis on the conscience of the agent, and it follows from the definition that if he commits an error it is an error only when recognized by his own conscience, and that punishment of the agent will be merely the twinges thereof. The one implies public execution; the other hara-kiri.
>
> (1941, 336)

Finer argued instead that technical feasibility and knowledge must always be secondary to democratic controls, controls based on three doctrines or ideas. First, he referred to the "mastership of the public," suggesting that public servants don't work for the good of the public based on their sense of what the public *needs*, but rather what the public *says it wants* (1941, 337). The second idea is that institutions must be in place, most particularly an elected body, to express and exert the public authority. Most important, however, is the third idea: that these elected institutions not only express and channel public wants, but also have the authority to decide and enforce how these wants are to be satisfied.

In this process, if external controls are lacking, abuses of power are inevitable. Finer dismissed Friedrich's argument that administrators' responsibility was more of a moral than a political issue, and that adherence to the standards of their profession was the answer. He further stated that Friedrich "gives the impression of stepping over the dead body of political responsibility to grasp the promissory incandescence of the moral variety" of responsibility (1941, 339). Finer concluded that:

> Moral responsibility is likely to operate in direct proportion to the strictness and efficiency of political responsibility, and to fall away into all sorts of perversions when the latter is weakly enforced. While professional standards, duty to the public, and pursuit of technological efficiency are factors in sound administrative operations, they are but ingredients, and not continuously motivating factors, of sound policy, and they require public and political control and direction.
>
> (Finer 1941, 350)

Over the years, Friedrich reaffirmed his position, calling Finer a "pious myth-maker" whose views were unrealistic and outdated (1960). He argued that Finer's views on accountability would not work unless there were clear agreement as to what needed to be done and little or no need for administrative discretion. "When one considers the complexity of modern governmental activities, it is at once evident that such agreement can only be partial and incomplete, no matter who is involved" (3–4). He pointed out that administrative responsibility is more than trying to "keep the government from doing wrong" (4). Rather, the main concern ought to be to ensure effective administrative action. To do this, he said, the interdependencies between the realms of policymaking and policy execution had to be considered. "In so far as particular individuals or groups are gaining or losing power or control in a given area, there is politics; in so far as officials act or propose action in the name of public interest, there is administration" (6).

Friedrich once again criticized Finer's contention that external controls must be the basis for ensuring accountability. Although political controls are important:

> There is arising a type of responsibility on the part of the permanent administrator, the man who is called upon to seek and find the creative solutions for our crying technical needs, which cannot be effectively enforced except by fellow-technicians who are capable of judging his policy in terms of the scientific knowledge bearing upon it.
>
> (1960, 14)

Besides, external mechanisms of control and measures of accountability "represent approximations, and not very near approximations at that" (14). In other words, unless there is a set of standards based on professional and technical knowledge that administrators internalize and hold each other accountable to, responsibility cannot be achieved. Friedrich concluded that:

> Responsible conduct of administrative functions is not so much enforced as it is elicited. But it has been the contention all along that responsible conduct is never strictly enforceable, that even under the most tyrannical despot administrative officials will escape effective control—in short, that the problem of how to bring about responsible conduct of the administrative staff of a large organization is, particularly in a democratic society, very largely a question of sound work rules and effective morale.
>
> (Friedrich 1960, 19)

In simplest form, Friedrich claims that administrators have to use their technical and professional knowledge in order to be responsible. Therefore, for a public administrator, being accountable means not only following the law and doing what you are told to do by elected officials, but also using the expertise of your profession.

The debate between Friedrich and Finer raised several key questions that remain at the center of contemporary issues regarding democratic accountability. As Dunn and Legge state, "The concepts and methods that define accountability and responsibility constitute fundamental issues in democratic theory because they determine how public policy and administration remain responsive to public preferences" (2000, 74). It is apparent that Friedrich and Finer held very different views of the way in which the policy process ought to work. Friedrich accepted the need for administrative discretion. Finer, on the other hand, wanted to limit it as much as possible. Perhaps most fundamentally, their positions are staked on the rather unsteady foundation of the politics–administrative dichotomy: In what manner are the forces of democracy to be balanced with the structure of bureaucracy and professional expertise? What institution or institutions are best suited to articulate public needs and wants? Can the work of administrators be made predictable and objective, and therefore controllable by means of preset measures? Or is it inherently subjective and too complex to reduce to a set of preconceived standards? Is it both? These are questions that have continued to plague efforts to encourage and enforce accountability in the public service and are not likely to be definitively resolved anytime soon.

Administrative Responsibility: To Whom, for What?

The exchange between Friedrich and Finer crystallized some of the key issues with regard to administrative accountability in the democratic process. Not too surprisingly, since that time, most administrators and writers in the field have located themselves somewhere in the middle of the controversy, saying that administrative accountability requires both external controls and professionalism. As Marshall Dimock and Gladys Dimock expressed it, accountability is a legal and moral issue that is enforced both internally and externally:

> To be accountable means to act responsibly, that is, in accordance with predetermined standards of propriety. For the public administrator, however, accountability is more than a matter of manners and custom; it is a matter of law. To be accountable also describes a person on whom one can count. For the administrator, this means knowing his duty and doing it—being honest and acting with probity. Thus the combined modern meaning of accountability is duty, both legal and moral.
>
> (Dimock and Dimock 1969, 123)

Accountability in public administration is achieved by both internal and external means. Internal controls are those that are established and enforced within an agency when "the administrator himself or someone alongside or above him in the hierarchy sees that he does his duty" (123). External controls may involve legislative supervision; budget and audit activities; the use of an office such as an ombudsman; criticism from the press; and oversight by consumer groups, interest groups, and other concerned individuals.

Unfortunately, despite the appeal of this more balanced view, it does not "solve" the issue of accountability, nor does it tell us exactly what to do about it. As a result, questions about accountability have continued to revolve around a set of tensions in the field of public administration that can be expressed in three deceptively simple questions: (1) *What* are we responsible for? (2) To *whom* are we responsible? And (3) *how* is that responsibility best ensured? Depending on how these questions are answered, and in what order of importance, different perspectives on the most appropriate systems of administrative accountability are suggested. Most problematic is usually the last question: We can set forth propositions about what we are responsible for and to whom, but figuring out how to ensure accountability is not an easy proposition.

For example, Maass and Radaway (1959) clearly state their positions (which they called "working biases") on the first two questions. In fact, they largely dismiss the first question (responsible for what?) in one sentence, stating that administrative agencies should be responsible for formulating as well as executing policy. With regard to the second question (to whom are administrators responsible?), their answers are somewhat more qualified. They begin by saying that administrators should not be held directly responsible to the public at large or to political parties. However, administrative agencies should be responsible to pressure groups in order to allow them sufficient access and information to safeguard their interests. The primary responsibility of administrators is "to the legislature, but only through the chief executive, and primarily for broad issues of public policy and general administrative performance" (1959, 169), leading back to the question of what they are responsible for. Maass and Radaway suggest that administrators are responsible for conforming to the general program of the chief executive and coordinating activities with other executive branch agencies to carry out that program. Further, they should be "responsible for maintaining, developing, and applying such professional standards as may be relevant to its activities" (176).

With these answers in hand, Maass and Radaway turn to the question of how accountability is to be achieved under these circumstances. Because the basic principles of administrative responsibility are often equivocal and mutually incompatible, the question of how to ensure accountability cannot be answered generically. They suggest, therefore, that it is necessary to use the more practical and modest language of "criteria" of responsibility. Some of these criteria may conflict with others, "but all of which must be weighted and applied together in any attempt to gauge the responsibility of a specific administrative agency" (1959, 163). There is no one-size-fits-all solution. As we said at the beginning of this chapter, accountability is complex. In the words of Maass and Radaway:

> Administrative responsibility ... has been termed the sum total of the constitutional, statutory, administrative, judicial, and professional practices by which public officers are restrained and controlled in their official actions. But it is not possible to identify the *criteria* for gauging administrative responsibility by relying on such general language. It becomes necessary, therefore, to relate the general concept of responsibility to the specific functions of power (i.e., responsibility to whom?) and purpose (i.e., responsibility for what?).
>
> (Maass and Radaway 1959, 164)

One answer, then, would be to make sure that accountability and responsibility (or authority) were always in balance in a given circumstance. In other words, an administrator would only be held responsible for those things for which he or she had authority and responsibility. But there are potential problems with this as well. Herbert Spiro, in *Responsibility in Government* (1969), points out that such a proposition is not very practical and raises questions that inevitably lead to confusion. Even the word "responsibility" itself has multiple definitions and uses, and it is used more often than it is defined. This lack of definitional clarity, he says, contributes to the controversy and confusion.

His argument is that there are three different connotations used when addressing responsibility: accountability, cause, and obligation. Like several other authors, but using different terms, Spiro argues that accountability can be either explicit or implicit. Explicit accountability refers to having to answer and account for how an administrator carries out his or her official tasks. But, he says, "All of us are implicitly accountable to the extent that we may be unexpectedly affected by the consequences of decisions made by other human beings" (1969, 15). In other words, people can be held implicitly responsible for outcomes that they did not directly cause. Explicit causal responsibility, on the other hand, "consists of four elements, present in varying degrees under different circumstances: resources, knowledge, choice, and purpose" (16). Implicit causal responsibility occurs when one or more of these elements is lacking.

Discussions about responsibility that confuse accountability with causal responsibility, or that assume that responsibility and accountability are in balance are bound to be unrealistic. "As a matter of *fact*, this is simply not so. As a matter of *value*, however, advocacy of a fair balance between causal responsibility and accountability is quite possible" (17). But a reasonable imbalance is not necessarily a bad thing, according to Spiro. If the function of responsibility is to preserve social conscience, then it might be appropriate that someone is held accountable for an event that he or she did not directly, or solely, cause. On the other hand, Spiro writes:

> From the viewpoint of constitutional democracy, however, we would have to advocate a fair balance between these two faces of responsibility, between accountability and causal responsibility. We would not want to hold a person accountable for an event to which he made no causal contribution. ... We would want him to be in a sound *situation of responsibility*, in which causal responsibility stands in fair balance with accountability.
>
> (Spiro 1969, 18)

Under these circumstances, figuring out how to ensure responsibility is difficult. The issue is not whether we want public administrators to be responsible—we do. The more important issue is *how* to ensure accountability, an issue that goes directly back to the Friedrich–Finer debate. If accountability mechanisms focus on the constitutional and legal framework alone, and do not take into account other sources of knowledge and resources, the purpose becomes one of negatively restraining bureaucrats. If we take a broader approach, accountability can have the more positive purpose of enhancing responsibility across the public sphere. Spiro states:

> We must give up excessive preoccupation with the bureaucrat's situation in favor of the individual citizen's. This is true especially because bureaucrat and citizen are no longer opposites who face each other in attitudes of constant hostility. Moreover, the bureaucrat is also a citizen. By virtue of assuming his delegated, specific, additional responsibility and accountability *qua* bureaucrat, he does not surrender his original, general responsibility *qua* citizen. His situation as a citizen, and that of his fellow citizens, must be the main center of our attention.
>
> (Spiro 1969, 101)

From this perspective, then, the focus should be on the character and ethics of the individual administrator. Some have suggested, in fact, that, at its core, accountability is a question of ethics, and that the role of administrator should be reconceived as an ethical actor. As Dwivedi states, "Unethical administration is the antithesis of accountable administration" (1985, 65). The work of Terry Cooper exemplifies the thinking of those who would focus on ethics as the basis for accountable and responsible administrative action. In *The Responsible Administrator* (1998), Cooper examines the ethical decision-making process and proposes a model for addressing ethical problems. Like several other writers, Cooper discusses the objective (external) and subjective (internal) natures of responsibility. He argues that the problems that arise when there is conflict between these two forms of responsibility are fundamentally ethical in nature. Ethical conduct, Cooper suggests, is enhanced by both internal and external controls. This is so, he says, because there are four components of responsible conduct: individual attributes, organizational culture, organizational structure, and societal expectations. Individual ethical behavior, he argues, requires individual ethical autonomy and self-awareness, as well as limits to the reach and power of organizations.

What can we conclude from all this? We can suggest that several generations of scholars have determined that administrative accountability is difficult to define and even more difficult to enforce. This is in part a function of the complexity of the administrative process as a component of the larger system of governance. The result is the complex web of accountability mechanisms and systems that characterize the current American governmental system. Romzek and Ingraham (2000) provide a useful framework for understanding these multiple perspectives on accountability. They suggest that there are four primary types of accountability, based on whether they are internal or external, and whether they assume high or low levels of individual autonomy. The first type is hierarchical accountability, which is "based on close supervision of individuals who have low work autonomy." Second, legal accountability involves "detailed external oversight of performance for compliance with established mandates . . . such as legislative and constitutional structures." This would include fiscal audits and oversight hearings, for example. Third, professional accountability is based on "arrangements that afford high degrees of autonomy to individuals who based their decision making on internalized norms of appropriate practice." Finally, political accountability requires responsiveness to "key external stakeholders, such as elected officials, clientele groups, the general public, and so on" (2000, 242).

Romzek and Ingraham point out that, although all of these types of accountability relationship are present, some forms may become more dominant, while others may become largely dormant, in a given circumstance. In times of reform, they say, "there is often a shift in emphasis and priority among the different types of accountability" (242). In the sections that follow, we will discuss the assumptions about, and forms of, accountability that can be seen as dominant in the Old Public Administration, the New Public Management, and the New Public Service.

The Old Public Administration and Accountability

A formal, hierarchical, and legal view of accountability characterizes the Old Public Administration and remains, in some ways, the most familiar model for viewing administrative responsibility and accountability today. This view of accountability relies on the assumption that administrators do not and should not exercise significant amounts of discretion. Rather, they simply implement the laws, rules, and standards set forth for them by hierarchical superiors, elected officials, and the courts. Accountability, according to adherents of the Old Public Administration, focuses on ensuring that administrators adhere to standards and conform to rules and procedures established for them in carrying out their functions. It is not a matter of using discretion appropriately and responsibly; it is a matter of avoiding the use of discretion by closely adhering to the law, regulation, organizational procedures, and directives of the supervisor.

In this view, direct responsiveness or accountability to the public is, implicitly at least, seen as unnecessary and inappropriate. Elected officials are seen as solely responsible and accountable for translating the public will into policy. As Goodnow presented it, "Politics has to do with the guiding or influencing of governmental policy, while administration has to do with the execution of that policy" (1987, 28). The public has little or no direct role in the administrative or policy-execution process. Wilson, in fact, seemed to want to buffer the governing process from popular interests, thus preventing the people from becoming "meddlesome" by direct involvement. In the Old Public Administration, responsible administrators were those who possessed and relied on their expertise and "neutral competence." Accordingly, responsible administrative action was based on scientific, value-neutral principles.

It is not difficult to see the continued influence of this perspective in present-day, institutionalized accountability systems. A quick review of the topics included in Rosen's (1989) edition of *Holding Government Bureaucracies Accountable*, for example, presents a broad array of processes, institutions, and mechanisms for ensuring formal accountability. Within the executive branch, hierarchical supervision, the budget and audit process, performance evaluations systems, and oversight by staff agencies such as personnel and purchasing departments are used to hold the actions of administrators in check and to ensure compliance with laws, procedures, and regulations. The legislative branch also uses a range of accountability mechanisms, including the appropriations process, committee oversight, hearings and investigations, reporting requirements, and legislative audit. The courts also employ a number of administrative controls, through judicial review and case law, as well as their oversight and interpretation of the Administrative Procedure Act of 1946 (which governs the procedures and process that executive agencies must use in establishing and applying governmental regulations). Most of these approaches rely, to a greater or lesser degree, on formal, external notions of accountability—that is, that administrators are responsible for adhering to objective external controls and answering for their actions in relation to established standards and the preferences of key stakeholders.

The New Public Management and Accountability

In a sense, the views of accountability advocated by the adherents of the New Public Management echo those of the Old Public Administration, in that there is a continued reliance on objective measurement and external controls. There are important differences, however. First, in the New Public Management, the assumption is that traditional bureaucracy is ineffective because it measures and controls inputs rather than results. As Osborne and Gaebler state, "Because they don't measure results, bureaucratic governments rarely achieve them" (1992, 139). Controlling inputs, such as money and personnel, rather than results, such as the cleanliness of streets or the knowledge gained by children, leads to government failure. Osborne and Gaebler argue that the answer is to look to the business model: "Private organizations focus on results because they will go out of business if the key numbers go negative" (139).

Again, as with the New Public Management generally, the assumption is that business and the market model are superior and ought to be emulated in the public sector. As government agencies cannot go out of business when they do not produce results, performance measurement must be used as a surrogate measure for what in business is the bottom line—profit. The focus of accountability is, then, on meeting performance standards to produce results.

Second, the public is reconceptualized as a market made up of individual customers who each act in a manner to serve their self-interest. In this way, public agencies are not primarily accountable, either directly or indirectly, to citizens or to the public or common good. Rather, they are accountable to their "customers." The responsibility of government, then, is to offer choices to its customers and to respond to their expressed individual preferences in terms of the services and functions provided. Accountability is a matter of satisfying the preferences of the direct customers of governmental services.

The third difference in the dominant view on administrative accountability suggested in the New Public Management perspective is the reliance on privatization. There is a strong emphasis in the New Public Management on privatizing previously public functions whenever possible. Again, this shifts accountability from a public to a private perspective, focusing once more on the bottom line. As such, accountability systems in privatized government emphasize the provision of services and functions that produce desired results in the most cost-effective manner possible, while satisfying their customers.

The New Public Service and Accountability

Perspectives on accountability in the New Public Service stand in contrast to both the Old Public Administration and the New Public Management. Measures of efficiency and results are important, but they cannot address or encompass the other expectations we hold for public administrators to act responsibly, ethically, and in accordance with democratic principles and the public interest. In the New Public Service, the ideals of citizenship and the public interest are at center stage.

Accountability in the New Public Service is multifaceted and demanding in recognition of the complex roles played by public administrators in contemporary governance (Callahan 2010; Feldman 2010; Perry and Buckwalter 2010; Warner and Hefetz 2008). The New Public Management artificially oversimplifies the issue of accountability in several ways. Kettl expresses it even more strongly: that the pursuit of businesslike practices and market-driven reforms constitutes an "aggressive attack on the tradition of democratic accountability" (1998, v). First, privatization and attempts to mimic the private sector narrow the scope of accountability and place the focus on meeting standards and satisfying customers. Such approaches do not reflect the multiple, overlapping channels of accountability in the public sector because the standards in the private sector are simply less stringent (Mulgan 2000). A private company being responsible to its shareholders is not analogous to a government agency being responsive to its citizens. Although private companies are invariably and primarily accountable for producing a profit, the public sector must pay more attention to process and policy. In government, "The emphasis is on the accountability of public power, on how to make governments, their agencies and officials, more accountable to their ultimate owners, the citizens" (Mulgan 2000, 87).

Glen Cope (1997) also makes important observations in this regard. She suggests there are a number of reasons that responsiveness to citizens is different than responsiveness to customers. In order to be responsive to customers, private enterprise attempts to provide a product or service that is desirable and of acceptable quality, as inexpensively as possible. Customers don't have to like the product or buy it unless they choose to do so. The serving of customers is driven by the profit motive: Enough customers have to be satisfied so they will buy the product or service at the designated price. Response to citizens is distinctly different. Government should provide a service or product that the majority of citizens want. As buying the product or service is not voluntary, in that it is often paid for by tax revenues, "This creates a special responsibility for government not only to satisfy its immediate customers and operate in a cost-efficient manner, but also to deliver services that its citizens have requested" (1997, 464).

Second, the New Public Management does not place an appropriate degree of emphasis on public law and democratic norms. Public accountability is lessened when governmental services are performed by nonprofit or private organizations that are not bound by public law principles (Leazes 1997). As Gilmore and Jensen suggest, "Because private actors are not subject to the same constitutional, statutory, and oversight restrictions as governmental actors, delegation of public functions outside the bounds of government profoundly challenges traditional notions of accountability, making it all the more difficult" (1998, 248).

In the New Public Service, if private administrators are to function as public ones, they should become subject to public standards of accountability. Based on his examination of a state's child welfare program, Leazes concludes that:

> Efficiency and effectiveness alone are not the only public administration standards available to measure the success of privatization. The

---

Governments collaborate with citizens through social media to share views about addressing neighborhood concerns. Westminster City Council in London has augmented a crime watch approach in which neighbors look out for each other and notify the police of suspicious activity. The program uses online tools to engage a broad, diverse set of residents, giving them a say in developing and selecting the policing priorities and strategies for their neighborhood.

> accountability inherent in public law that relates to the safeguarding of democratic, constitutional administration should have an equal place at the privatization policy-implementation table.
>
> (1997, 10)

Typically, however, they cannot and do not.

The focus on results or outcomes popularized by advocates of the New Public Management does not satisfy the need for accountability to democratic norms and values either (Innes and Booher 2004; Terry 2005; Wichowsky and Moynihan 2008). As Myers and Lacey state, "The performance of civil servants should be judged . . . according to the extent to which they uphold such values, just as much, if not more than, on their success at meeting output targets" (1996, 343). That is not to say that attention to results and output measures isn't important. By focusing on results, public organizations can make important improvements, to the benefit of the people they serve. But it does suggest that results-oriented performance measures ought to be developed based on an open public process; they should not be developed and imposed by those in government simply to mimic measures of profit.

Third, in the New Public Management, the public administrator is conceived of as an entrepreneur, seeking opportunities to create private partnerships and serve customers. This perspective on the role of the public administrator is narrow and is poorly suited to achieving democratic principles such as fairness, justice, participation, and the articulation of shared interests. The very qualities that make an administrator a good entrepreneur may in fact make him or her an ineffective public servant. Cooper states, "The attributes associated with effective administration and management in the business world, such as competitiveness and profit orientation, may be unsuited to, or less appropriate to, the interests of democratic political society" (1998, 149). In fact, he points out, if concern for efficiency is given more than secondary importance, the openness to popular sovereignty may well be compromised.

The New Public Service rejects all three of these assumptions about accountability advanced by the New Public Management. The complexity of public accountability faced by public servants is recognized as a challenge, an opportunity, and a calling. It requires expertise, a commitment to democratic ideals, knowledge of public law, and judgment informed by experience, community norms, and ethical conduct. Accountability in the New Public Service suggests a reconceptualization of the role of the public servant as leader, steward, and emissary of the public interest, not as an entrepreneur. As Kevin Kearns states:

> [Despite] the fact that accountability is an untidy construct . . . debates on accountability should be informed by its poor structure, not deterred by it. To this end, any truly meaningful dialogue should be guided by an analytical framework that embraces the many dimensions of accountability and allows contextual factors and subjective judgments to surface for informed dialogue on assumptions.
>
> (1994, 187)

Legal, constitutional, and democratic principles are an incontrovertible centerpiece of responsible administrative action. The New Public Service differs from both the Old Public Administration and the New Public Management in its emphasis on elevating the importance and centrality of citizenship and the public as the basis for accountable and responsible public action. Put simply, the source of public administrators' authority is the citizenry. "Public Administrators are employed to exercise that authority on their behalf. They do so as one of citizenry; they can never divest themselves of their own status as members of the political community with obligations for its well being" (Cooper 1991, 145). Accountability requires that public servants interact with and listen to citizens in a manner that empowers and reinforces their role in democratic governance (Durant and Ali 2013; Yang and Callahan 2007). As N. Joseph Cayer states, "The purpose of citizen participation is generally to make administration more responsive to the public and to enhance the legitimacy of governmental programs and agencies" (1986, 171). Responsible behavior requires that public administrators interact with their fellow citizens, not as customers but as members of a democratic community.

In *Bureaucratic Responsibility* (1986), John Burke says that, in light of the problems with accountability, and of inherent tensions between the values of bureaucracy and democracy, our attention should focus on "how bureaucratic officials conceive of their roles, duties, and obligations and especially what principles might guide them in a more responsible, accountable direction" (1986, 5). He suggests that a "democratically grounded conception of responsibility [is] derived not just from formal rules, regulations, and laws but from a broader understanding of the bureaucrat's place within a more encompassing set of political institutions and processes" (39).

There are two major components of this model of democratic responsibility. The first is a public servant's responsibility to take political authority seriously. The second involves a set of responsibilities that hinges on obligations with respect to the duties of others, as well as the role of the responsible public servants in policy formulation and implementation. This democratic model, Burke argues, "attempts to reconcile the potentially conflicting allegiances owed politics and the profession by demarcating a domain within which expertise is granted license and autonomy" (1986, 149).

Importantly, Burke argues that the multiple views of moral obligation, responsibility, and their political relevance cannot be resolved based on an administrator's own sense of what is right. Rather, such judgments must be made as part of a participatory process. Burke states:

> Not only do the specific obligations posited by a democratic conception of responsibility enhance participatory processes and outcomes, but the general sense of responsibility it fosters—especially its democratic source and character—facilitates the goals of participation. It embodies an implicit ethos of taking democracy seriously, whether its structure is formal or informal, centralized or decentralized.
>
> (Burke 1986, 214)

This viewpoint is also exemplified by Edward Weber's (1999) discussion of the grass-roots ecosystem management (GREM) model, which looks at administrative accountability "in a world of decentralized governance, shared power, collaborative decision processes, results-oriented management, and broad civic participation" (1999, 451). The GREM model looks at political responsiveness, administrative performance, and a normative dimension when assessing accountability. Although Weber is speaking directly to the issue of accountability and responsiveness, his arguments also apply to the question of how we view and evaluate the administrative discretion exercised in policy implementation. He challenges the view that responsiveness is "a one way street" emanating from elected officials, suggesting instead that responsiveness and accountability are "a matter of both top-down policy commands from political and administrative superiors and bottom-up input from community-based stakeholders as well as others" (454–455).

Although the model gives weight to bottom-up participation, legal and hierarchical accountability are also important. He is suggesting, in essence, a holistic policy focus that provides for adaptive management and citizen involvement. In the New Public Service, accountability is broadly defined to encompass a range of professional, legal, political, and democratic responsibilities. But, "The ultimate aim of accountability and responsibility mechanisms in democratic policies is to assure responsiveness by government to citizens' preferences and needs" (Dunn and Legge 2000, 75). The accountability and responsibility are best achieved by a public service that acknowledges and responds to the multiple and conflicting norms and factors that can and should influence an administrator's actions (Perry and

Buckwalter 2010; Zeemering 2008). The key to balancing these factors in a responsible and democratically accountable fashion rests with citizen engagement, empowerment, and dialogue. Public administrators are neither neutral experts nor business entrepreneurs. They are called upon to be responsible actors in a complex governance system, in which they may play the roles of facilitators; reformers; interest brokers; public relations experts; crisis managers; brokers; analysts; advocates; and, most importantly, moral leaders and stewards of the public interest (Vinzant and Crothers 1998; Terry 1995).

If public functions are privatized, or "reinvented" so as to mirror private-sector corporations, democratic values become less important. Instead, the focus is placed on market efficiency and the achievement of the governmental "bottom line." Particularly when privatization involves functions that are vital to the public interest (such as medical care, welfare, or education), the relationship between government and citizen becomes more complex than merely the provision of a service to a customer. Accordingly, more than market-driven measures of efficiency are required to hold the government accountable (Gilmore and Jensen 1998). In the private sector, financial incentives and shareholder preferences guide an administrator's behavior. When public functions are either given over to the private sector or reconfigured to mimic the private model, public accountability for equity, citizen access, and the constitutional and statutory rights of citizens are almost by definition compromised, if not lost. As Shamsul Haque states:

> The hallmark of public bureaucracy is its accountability to the public for its policies and actions. Without the realization of such accountability, public bureaucracy loses its identity of publicness, surrenders its public legitimacy, and may relegate itself to the fetish of self-seeking private interests.

(1994, 265)

Truckee Meadows Tomorrow is a broad-based group of individuals and associations who care about the quality of life in Washoe County, Nevada. One of the initiatives the group supports is the Adopt-an-Indicator Program, where individuals, organizations, schools, and businesses are encouraged to develop action plans to improve the indicator they adopt. For example, people can develop strategies to improve voter registration efforts or clean public parks or improve youth outreach efforts.

As Michael Harmon (1995) puts it, responsibility remains a paradox. The paradox is that the nature of responsibility upholds two contrasting ideas: moral accountability versus answerability to an organization. He argues that conceptions of responsibility that rely on the concepts of agency (acting on behalf of), accountability, and obligation do not take into account the element of morality. Because of this lack of emphasis on morality, three paradoxes arise: the paradox of obligation, the paradox of blame, and the paradox of accountability. The paradox of obligation suggests that:

> [If] public servants are free to choose but at the same time are obliged to act only as others authoritatively choose for them, then they are not, for all practical purposes, free. If, on the other hand, public servants do choose freely, their actions may violate authoritative obligations, in which case, their exercise of free choice is irresponsible.
>
> (1995, 102)

The paradox of agency occurs when taking personal responsibility for acting as a moral agent conflicts with answerability to others. Conversely, "the claim of moral innocence implied in the assertion of ultimate answerability to others can only be achieved by the individual's denial of agency" (128). The paradox of accountability, Harmon says, is that:

> [When] public servants are accountable solely for the effective achievement of purposes mandated by political authority, then as mere instruments of that authority they bear no personal responsibility as moral agents for the products of their actions. If, on the other hand, public servants actively participate in determining public purposes, their accountability is compromised and political authority is undermined.
>
> (Harmon 1995, 164)

Harmon concludes, "the rational reform of government institutions is no substitute for, and in fact may well prevent, strengthening the communal bonds that form the substance of the institutions themselves" (1995, 207). In other words, public servants are rightly called upon to be accountable, answerable, responsible, and moral; to choose any one of these qualities to the exclusion of the others places democratic government at risk. Despite the inherent tensions and difficulty, if not impossibility, of perfectly and fully satisfying each facet of accountability in every circumstance, that is what we, as a society, demand of our public servants. Fortunately, with courage and professionalism, they are doing so every day, in communities across America. It is our responsibility as a field to acknowledge the difficulty of their jobs, prepare them, applaud their successes, and advance the democratic values that surround what they do.

Conclusion

The question of accountability in the public service is a complex one, involving balancing competing norms and responsibilities within a complicated web of external controls; professional standards; citizen preferences; moral issues; public law; and, ultimately, the public interest. Or, as Robert Behn puts it, "To whom must public managers be accountable? The answer is 'everyone'" (2001, 120). In other words, public administrators are called upon to be responsive to all the competing norms, values, and preferences of our complex governance system. Accountability is not, and cannot be made, simple. The tensions and paradoxes that Harmon and others identify are irreducible and unavoidable in our democratic system of governance. It is a mistake, in our estimation, to oversimplify the nature of democratic accountability by focusing only on a narrow set of performance measures or by attempting to mimic market forces—or, worse, by simply hiding behind notions of neutral expertise. To do so calls into question the nature of democracy, and the role of citizenship and a public service dedicated to serving citizens in the public interest. The New Public Service recognizes that being a public servant is a demanding, challenging, sometimes heroic endeavor involving accountability to others, adherence to the law, morality, judgment, and responsibility.

Chapter 8

Serve Rather than Steer

Serve rather than steer. It is increasingly important for public servants to use shared, value-based leadership in helping citizens articulate and meet their shared interests rather than attempting to control or steer society in new directions.

We noted in Chapter 5 that public policy is increasingly being made through the interaction of many different groups and organizations, overlapping and often competing in their interests and jurisdictions and engaged in efforts to meet both individual and collective goals through an open-ended, fluid, and often chaotic process. We also noted some of the ways in which citizens' views can be brought to bear on that process of building public policy in a democratic fashion. Here, we will focus more on the way in which various groups and interests can be brought together in a collaborative manner to achieve mutually satisfactory ends. More particularly, we will ask how leadership can be brought to bear where "no one is in charge." Under those circumstances, in which there is little evidence of formal or traditional leadership, there may seem to be a vacuum of leadership—at least if we think of leadership primarily as the exercise of power over others. Leadership is still needed; in fact, leadership is needed more than ever. What is needed, however, is leadership of a new kind.

Changing Perspectives on Leadership

Certainly there is agreement that the traditional top-down models of leadership we associate with such groups as the military are outdated and unworkable in modern society. This is an idea, in fact, that is even accepted in the military. As we have seen, today's society can be described as (1) highly turbulent, subject to sudden and dramatic shifts; (2) highly inter-dependent, requiring cooperation across many sectors; and (3) greatly in need of creative and imaginative solutions to the problems facing us. Under these conditions, public (and private) organizations need to be considerably more adaptable and flexible than in the past. Yet the traditional command and control form of leadership doesn't encourage risk and innovation. Quite to the contrary, it encourages uniformity and convention. For this reason, many people now argue that a new approach to leadership is desirable (Gilley et al. 2013; Marsh 2013; Nye 2013; Perry and Buckwalter 2010).

Leadership is changing in many ways, and we should be attentive to those changes. First, in today's world and certainly in tomorrow's, more and more people are going to want to participate in the decisions that affect them. In the traditional top-down model of organizational leadership, the leader was the one who established the vision of the group, designed ways of achieving that vision, and inspired or coerced others into helping to realize that vision. Increasingly, however, those in organizations want to be involved; they want a piece of the action. Moreover, clients or citizens also want to participate, as they should. As Warren Bennis correctly predicted a few years ago, "leadership . . . will become an increasingly intricate process of multilateral brokerage. . . . More and more decisions will be public decisions, that is, the people they affect will insist on being heard" (1992, 311).

Second, leadership is increasingly being thought of, not as a position in a hierarchy, but as a process that occurs throughout organizations (and beyond). In the past, a leader was considered the person who held a formal position of power in an organization or a society. Increasingly, however, we are coming to think of leadership as a process occurring throughout organizations and societies. Leadership is not just something reserved for the presidents, governors, mayors, or department heads; rather, it is something that everyone throughout our organizations and our society will become involved in from time to time (Borins 2013). Indeed, there are many who argue that such a shift in the distribution of leadership will be necessary for our survival. John Gardner, the former cabinet secretary and founder of the public interest group Common Cause, states:

> In this country leadership is dispersed among all elements of society and down through all levels, and the system simply won't work as it should unless large numbers of people throughout society are prepared to take leader-like action to make things work at their level.
>
> (1987, 1)

It's safe to predict that, over the coming years, we will see more and more instances of what we will term "shared leadership" in public organizations, both within public organizations and as administrators relate to their many external constituencies. In our view, the notion of shared leadership is especially important in the public sector, as administrators work with citizens and citizen groups of all kinds. As was suggested in Chapter 5, public administrators will need to develop and employ new leadership skills that include important elements of empathy, consideration, facilitation, negotiation, and brokering (Crevani, Lindgren, and Packendorff 2007; Nye 2013; Schein 2008).

Third, we should understand that leadership is not just about doing things right, it's about doing the right things. In other words, leadership is inevitably associated with important human values, including the most fundamental public values, values such as freedom, equality, and justice. Through the process of leadership, people work together to make choices about the directions that they want to take; they make fundamental decisions about their futures. Such choices cannot be made simply on the basis of a rational calculation of costs and benefits. They require a careful balancing of human values, especially as citizens and governmental officials work together in the development of public policies. Leadership, as we will see, can play a "transformational" role in this process, helping people to confront important values and to grow and develop individually and collectively. Accordingly, a number of contemporary writers on leadership have urged that we examine the "servant" role of leadership (Bolman and Deal 2008; Cronin and Genovese 2012; Northouse 2013) and that we be attentive to "leading with soul."

We will suggest in this chapter that the public administrator of today, and especially tomorrow, will have to develop quite a different understanding of leadership than that associated with the Old Public Administration or the New Public Management. Leadership will need to be dramatically reconceptualized (Crosby 2010; Feldman 2010; Marsh 2013). At a minimum, the role of public leaders will be (1) to help the community and its citizens to understand their needs and their potential, (2) to integrate and articulate the community's vision and that of the various organizations active in any particular area, and (3) to act as a trigger or stimulus for action. This reconceptualization of public leadership is variously described as shared leadership, values-based leadership, and street-level leadership. Before we examine these alternatives, which we associate most clearly with the New Public Service, we should briefly review the approaches to leadership taken by the Old Public Administration and the New Public Management.

The Old Public Administration and Executive Management

As we saw earlier, the prevailing view of leadership in the Old Public Administration was based on a model of executive management. Recall that Woodrow Wilson first argued for creating single centers of power and responsibility, an admonition upon which a number of early writers elaborated. W.F. Willoughby, for example, argued that administrative authority should first be vested in a chief executive, who should have the power and authority necessary to create a "single, integrated piece of administrative machinery" (1927, 37). The next step is to group similar activities together in units reflecting a division of labor. In turn, a management hierarchy could be created through which the executive could essentially control the behavior of those lower in the organization. The key principles underlying this interpretation of executive leadership were exactly those found in business organizations of the time—unity of command, hierarchical/ top-down authority, and the division of labor.

This preoccupation with organizational design, that is, designing organizations through which control might be effectively exercised, was certainly a topic of great interest to business leaders of the time. For example, two former General Motors executives, James Mooney and Alan C. Reiley (1939) identified four "principles" around which organizations might be built. The first was coordination through unity of command, the idea that strong executive leadership should be exercised through a hierarchical chain of authority. In such a structure, each person would have only one boss, and each boss would supervise a limited number of subordinates, leaving no question about whose orders were to be obeyed. Second, Mooney and Reiley described the "scalar" principle, the vertical division of labor among various levels of the organization. For example, in the military, the difference between a general and a private would be a "scalar" difference. A third principle, the "functional" principle, described the horizontal division of labor, as in the distinction between infantry and artillery. Fourth, there was the distinction between line and staff, with line offices reflecting directly the chain of command through which authority flows, and staff offices providing advice to those in line offices. Not surprisingly, these concerns for administrative structure were frequently illustrated by examples from the military, seen as the epitome of rationalized authority.

The top-down nature of internal organizational management in the Old Public Administration was, for the most part, paralleled by a similar approach to relations between government agencies and the citizenry or their "clients." As we noted earlier, administrators came to play a more and more influential role in the process of policy development, though always with an eye toward maintaining the primacy of the elected official. In this process, the role of the citizenry was seen as limited—largely one of periodically electing officials, then standing on the "sidelines" to watch them perform. At least until the mid 1960s, citizen involvement in agency operations was extremely limited. True enough, some writers questioned that omission. Leonard White, for example, argued against excessive centralization of power, in part because citizens need to gain experience in assuming their civic responsibility. "If administration is to be the work of a highly centralized bureaucracy, it is impossible to expect a sense of personal responsibility (on the part of citizens) for good government" (1926, 96; parentheses added). Luther Gulick, on the other hand, pursued a much more active and independent role for the administrator, one in which citizen involvement was at best a device for securing compliance, at worst an unnecessary inconvenience. According to Gulick, "the success of the operation of democracy must not be made to depend upon extended or continuous political activity by citizens nor upon unusual knowledge of intelligence to deal with complicated questions" (1933, 558). Policy determination, in other words, should be left to the "experts."

For the most part, agencies and their leaders were either concerned with the regulation of behavior or with direct service delivery. In either case, detailed policies and procedures were devised, mostly to protect the rights and responsibilities of both agency personnel and their clients. Despite their noble purposes, these policies and procedures often became so cumbersome that they restricted the capacity of the agency to meet clients' needs. Thus, government agencies and their managers came to be viewed as inefficient and rule-bound, hopelessly wrapped in "red tape."

The New Public Management and Entrepreneurship

In the New Public Management, the need for leadership is at least partially eclipsed by decision rules and incentives. In such cases, leadership does not reside in a person; rather, the aggregation of individual choices replaces the need for some leadership functions. For example, Don Kettl says that a key issue in market-based reform is, "How can government use market-style incentives to root out the pathologies of bureaucracy?" (2000a, 1). In some cases, governments have completely set adrift certain public functions, such as those performed by telephone companies, airlines, and power companies, so that they might simply compete in the market. In many other cases, governments have contracted out the delivery of services, ranging from trash collection to prisons. Still others have tried to create mechanisms for consumer choice, through alternative systems of service delivery or through such efforts as providing "vouchers" for needed services. In any case, the New Public Management aims to replace traditional, rule-based service delivery with market-based, competition-driven tactics. Citizens are "led" by their preferences to one choice or another.

Osborne and Gaebler (1992) explicitly describe a reduced service-delivery role for government as a better way of "leading" society. They recommend that government should move increasingly away from a service-delivery role (which they call "rowing") and instead attend to policy development (which they call "steering"). Steering organizations set policy, provide funding to operational agencies (whether governmental or nongovernmental), and evaluate performance. They establish a structure of "incentives" for which agencies can compete or which citizens can choose. But they are not actually involved in delivering services. What are the benefits of such an approach? Osborne and Gaebler write:

> Freeing policy managers to shop around for the most effective and efficient service providers helps them squeeze more bang out of every buck. It allows them to use *competition* between service providers. It preserves maximum *flexibility* to respond to changing circumstances. And it helps them insist on *accountability* for quality performance; contractors know they can be let go if their quality sags; civil servants know they cannot.
>
> (Osborne and Gaebler 1992, 35; italics in original)

Another element of New Public Management's approach to public leadership is its insistence on injecting competition into areas that previously were governmental "monopolies." By establishing competitive bidding processes for such services as trash collection, many cities have substantially reduced their costs, but even more dramatic departures from tradition have been urged. For example, many jurisdictions are experimenting with school choice as a device for creating competition within the educational system. The idea is simply that schools should be given enough autonomy to manage their own resources, and then the market would determine which school is most effective as students "vote with their feet." The incentive mechanism works in several directions. Schools have an incentive—high enrollments— to demonstrate high quality. Students and their families have an incentive to seek out the best school system.

What is important for our discussion here is that market incentives are employed by the New Public Management *as a substitute for public leadership*. Osborne and Gaebler, for example, enthusiastically endorse a statement from John Chubb, coauthor of an important book on school choice:

> You can get effective schools through other means—such as the force of powerful leadership. But if we have to rely on the development of truly unusual leaders in order to save our schools, our prospects simply aren't going to be very good. The current system is simply not set up to encourage that kind of leadership. A system of competition and choice, on the other hand, automatically provides the incentives for schools to do what is right.
>
> (Quoted in Osborne and Gaebler 1992, 95)

The New Public Service and Leadership

The New Public Service sees leadership in terms of neither the manipulation of individuals nor the manipulation of incentives. Instead, leadership is seen as a natural part of the human experience, subject to both rational and intuitive forces, and concerned with focusing human energy on projects that benefit humanity. Leadership is no longer seen as a prerogative of those in high public offices, but as a function that extends throughout groups, organizations, and societies. What is needed, in this view, is principled leadership by people throughout public organizations and throughout society. Here, we will examine several prominent and representative interpretations of this new approach to leadership.

Values-Based Leadership

Perhaps the most powerful formulation of leadership, whether applied to politics, business, or management, is the idea of "transformational leadership." Transformational leadership is the key concept in a classic, indeed, a Pulitzer Prize-winning study, written by Harvard political scientist James MacGregor Burns and titled simply *Leadership* (1978). In this monumental work, Burns goes far beyond trying to understand the dynamics of leadership in terms of rational efficiency, getting things done, or meeting organizational objectives. Rather, he seeks to develop a theory of leadership that would extend across cultures and time and apply to groups, organizations, and societies. Specifically, Burns seeks to understand leadership, not as something leaders do to followers, but as a relationship between leaders and followers, a mutual interaction that ultimately changes both:

> The process of leadership must be seen as part of the dynamics of conflict and power . . . leadership is nothing if not linked to collective purpose . . . the effectiveness of leaders must be judged not by their press clippings but by actual social change . . . political leadership depends on a long chain of biological and social processes, of interaction with structures of political opportunity and closures, of interplay between the calls of moral principles and the recognized necessities of power . . . in placing these concepts of political leadership centrally into a theory . . . we will reaffirm the possibilities of human volition and of common standards of justice in the conduct of peoples' affairs.
>
> (Burns 1978, 4)

Burns starts by noting that, although historically we have been preoccupied with the relationship between power and leadership, there is an important difference between the two. Typically, power is thought of as carrying out one's own will, despite resistance. Such a conception of power neglects the important fact that power involves a relationship between leaders and followers, and that a central value in that relationship is *purpose*—what is being sought and what is intended, both by the one who is exercising power and the one who is on the receiving end. In most, though perhaps not all, situations, the recipient has some flexibility in his or her response to an attempted exercise of power, so that the power one can exercise is dependent on the way both parties view the situation. Power wielders draw on their own resources and their own motives, but these must be relevant to the resources and motivations of the recipient of power.

Leadership, according to Burns, is an aspect of power, but it is also a separate process. Power is exercised when potential power wielders, acting to achieve goals of their own, gather resources that enable them to influence others. Power is exercised to realize the purposes of the power wielders, whether or not those purposes are also the purposes of the respondents (1978, 18). Leadership, on the other hand, is exercised, "when persons with certain motives and purposes mobilize, in competition or conflict with others, institutional, political, psychological, and other resources so as to arouse, engage, and satisfy the motives of the followers" (18). The difference between power and leadership is that power serves the interests of the power wielder, whereas leadership serves both the leader's interests *and* those of the followers. The values, motivations, wants, needs, interests, and expectations of both leaders and followers must be represented in order for leadership to occur.

There are actually two kinds of leadership, Burns argues. The first is "transactional" leadership, which involves an exchange of valued things (whether economic, political, or psychological) between initiator and respondent. For example, a political leader might agree to support a particular policy in exchange for votes in the next election. Or a student might write a superb paper in exchange for an "A" grade. In the case of transactional leadership, the two parties come together in a relationship that advances the interests of both, but there is no deep or enduring link between them. "Transformational" leadership, on the other hand, occurs when leaders and followers engage with one another in such a way that they raise one another to higher levels of morality and motivation. Although the leaders and the led may initially come together, either out of pursuit of their own interests or because the leader recognized some special potential in the followers, as the relationship evolves, their interests become fused into mutual support for common purposes. The relationship between leaders and followers becomes one in which the purposes of both are elevated through the relationship; both parties become mobilized, inspired, uplifted. In some cases, transformational leadership even evolves into *moral* leadership, as leadership raises the level of moral aspiration and moral conduct of both leaders and followers. Moral leadership results in actions that are consistent with the needs, interests, and aspirations of the followers, but these are also actions that fundamentally change moral understandings and social conditions. In the end, leadership, especially transformational or moral leadership, has the capacity to move groups, organizations, even societies toward the pursuit of higher purposes.

A similar, though somewhat more contemporary, interpretation of leadership is provided by Ronald Heifetz in his book, *Leadership Without Easy Answers* (1994). Heifetz argues, as we did at the beginning of this chapter, that leadership is no longer just about establishing a vision and then getting people to move in that direction. More bluntly, leadership is no longer about "telling people what to do." Instead, leadership, whether it comes from someone in a position of formal authority or someone with little or no formal authority, is concerned with aiding a group, an organization, or a community in recognizing its own vision and then learning how to move in a new direction. As an illustration of the difference between these two views of leadership, think about the following two definitions of leadership: "leadership means influencing the community to follow the leader's vision" versus "leadership means influencing the community to face its problems" (Heifetz 1994, 14). Heifetz argues that the latter view is better suited to contemporary life, where the tasks of leadership are not merely getting a job done, but rather "adapting" to new and unusual circumstances. The work of leadership, then, is "adaptive work"—work that may either involve reconciling conflicting values that people hold or finding ways to reduce the discrepancy between the values people hold and the realities they face. Leadership is all about values and learning, specifically helping people learn to identify and actualize their values. In this way, leadership is basically an educative function.

From this theoretical standpoint, Heifetz identifies several practical lessons for leaders—again, even leaders with no formal authority:

1. *Identify the Adaptive Challenge*: Diagnose the situation in light of the values at stake, and unbundle the issues that come with it.
2. *Keep the Level of Distress Within a Tolerable Range for Doing Adaptive Work*: To use the pressure cooker analogy, keep the heat up without blowing up the vessel.
3. *Focus Attention on Ripening Issues and Not on Stress-Reducing Distractions*: Identify which issues can currently engage attention; and while directing attention to them, counteract work avoidance mechanisms like denial, scapegoating, externalizing the enemy, pretending the problem is technical, or attacking individuals rather than issues.
4. *Give the Work Back to People, But at a Rate They Can Stand*: Place and develop responsibility by putting the pressure on the people with the problem.
5. *Protect Voices of Leadership Without Authority*: Give cover to those who raise hard questions and generate distress—people who point to the internal contradictions of the society. These individuals often will have latitude to provoke rethinking that authorities do not have.

(Heifetz 1994, 128)

Shared Leadership

John Bryson and Barbara Crosby (1992) set the stage for their discussion of shared leadership by contrasting the traditional model of bureaucratic

> Portsmouth, New Hampshire, has built on its study circle tradition to examine sustainability. An outgrowth of the sustainability study circles was a new regionwide organization, the Piscataqua Sustainability Initiative, which has continued to use study circles on a larger geographical scale. Similarly, Morgan Hill, California, has recruited small groups of neighbors to work together to meet a goal for reducing greenhouse gas emissions.

leadership with more contemporary leadership—where no one is in charge. On the one hand, there is the traditional, hierarchical bureaucracy, which has the capacity to "get its hands around problems" and to engage in rational and expert problem-solving and planning processes to arrive at solutions that it can then implement "on its own." On the other hand, as we saw in our discussion of the new processes of governance, today's problems increasingly require the involvement of networks of many different organizations, with different styles, agendas, and concerns. Those groups that are concerned may have serious differences—in direction, motivation, timing, assets, and so on—and these differences may be severe. In these more fluid and chaotic circumstances, the rational model of formal leadership no longer works. Instead, someone, often someone who is not in a formal position of authority, must assume leadership, bringing together all those concerned with the problem and helping to resolve or mediate their differences, while never controlling, but rather leading by example, persuasion, encouragement, and empowerment.

This alternative model of leadership, which Bryson and Einsweiler describe as "shared transformative capacity" (1991, 3), is sometimes slow and often tedious, but for good reason. Leaders in a world of shared power and shared capabilities have needs that require special time and attention:

> the need to be sure the move is politically acceptable, technically workable, and legally and ethically defensible; the need to have the move endorsed by a coalition large enough to support and protect it; and the desire to keep as many options as possible open as long as possible.
>
> (Bryson and Crosby 1992, 9)

Although shared leadership takes time, because more people and groups are involved, ironically, it is often far more successful for exactly the same reason—because more people and more groups are involved!

However, success requires an understanding of the various places in which policy decisions take place and the various steps that individuals and groups must work through to be successful. Bryson and Crosby (1992) suggest three settings that are becoming more frequently employed in bringing people together and negotiating or brokering their different points of view. *Forums* are spaces in which people can engage in discussion, debate, and deliberation. They may include discussion groups, formal debates, public hearings, task forces, conferences, newspapers, radio, television, and the Internet. *Arenas*, on the other hand, are more formal and have a more delimited domain. Examples might be executive committees, city councils, faculty senates, boards of directors, and legislatures. Finally, *courts* are settings that focus on dispute resolution according to established societal norms. Here, examples might be the Supreme Court, traffic courts, professional licensing bodies, and ethics enforcement bodies.

Bryson and Crosby then lay out several key steps in effectively solving public problems:

1. *Forging an Initial Agreement to Act*: An initial group of leaders, key decision makers, and ordinary citizens come together and agree on the need to respond to a particular problem. As more people become involved, and as each phase informs the next, this step is likely to recur in a continuous loop (as are the next two). Leaders must secure the involvement and participation of all affected groups (and perhaps some that are not).

2. *Developing an Effective Problem Definition to Guide Action*: The way in which problems are framed will dramatically affect the way different parties respond to and engage in the process and the way in which eventual solutions are structured. People must rethink problems before moving to their solution. Here, public leadership is perhaps most intense, because leaders can "help people see new problems or see old problems in new ways."

3. *Searching for Solutions in Forums*: In this phase, a search for solutions to the problems previously identified takes place. Especially in this phase, leaders facilitate the construction of alternative scenarios for moving from a problem-filled past to a problem-free future. A key here is to be sure that proposed solutions meet the problem as defined earlier and don't just capture the interests of particular groups. Leadership is required to transcend the private interests that may come forward during this phase.

4. *Developing a Proposal that Can Win in Arenas*: Here the focus shifts to the development of policies that can be put on the agendas of formal decision-making bodies. The key is that action in forums and less formal groups must produce proposals that will likely be adopted, proposals that are both technically sound and politically acceptable.

5. *Adopting Public Policy Solutions*: In this phase, those advocating change seek the adoption of their proposals by those with formal decision-making authority and the resources and support necessary for successful implementation.

6. *Implementing New Policies and Plans*: Policies don't implement themselves, and so extending the newly adopted policy throughout the system involves a multitude of details and arrangements associated with

the implementation process. Until these concerns are attended to, the change cannot be considered complete.

7. *Reassessing Policies and Programs*: Even following implementation, there is a need to reevaluate the situation. Things change, people change, resource commitments change—and any of these can lead to a new round of policy change (adapted from Bryson and Crosby 1992, 119–338).

A similar argument is developed by Jeffrey Luke in *Catalytic Leadership* (1998). Consistent with our earlier discussion of network-based governance, Luke points out that public organizations are increasingly limited in what they can do on their own. Many other groups and organizations must be involved in addressing issues such as teenage pregnancy, traffic congestion, and environmental pollution. In addition, traditional leadership, the type Luke associates with business corporations and bureaucratic government agencies, is largely based on hierarchical authority and cannot be easily transferred to situations that are dispersed, chaotic, and complex. In contrast, in these circumstances, which increasingly characterize the public policy process, leadership must "focus attention and mobilize sustained action by multiple and diverse stakeholders" (1998, 5).

The problem, on one hand, is that government is no longer "in charge" of the policy process:

> Governance in the United States is characterized by a dynamic interplay among government agencies, nonprofit service providers, business

In Redwood City, California, the council faced heated opposition to a plan to reduce water consumption by using recycled water for irrigation because of health concerns, and the city council was stymied about what to do. Ed Everett (2009, 11), as city manager, recommended creating a task force with 10 citizens who favored using recycled water and 10 who were opposed. The task force was instructed to come up with a plan to save a target amount of water within a fixed maximum cost. If the task force developed a consensus recommendation that met these criteria, it would be considered. Otherwise, the council would move ahead with the recycled water plan. In the end, the task force developed a recommendation that was better than those that staff or consultants had devised.

enterprises, multinational corporations, neighborhood groups, special-interest and advocacy groups, labor unions, academia, the media, and many other formal and informal associations that attempt to influence the public agenda.

(Luke 1998, 4)

Moreover, the most substantial problems we face today cross organizational, jurisdictional, and sector boundaries. What happens in one place or what one organization does is likely to affect the problem only in a marginal way; all the other groups and organizations interested in the same issue are also affecting the issue. In other words, there is an underlying web of interdependence and interconnectedness that ties many different groups together. Without the involvement of all these interconnected groups and organizations, little can be done to effectively address complex public problems. Moreover, given the passionate commitment and highly focused interest of most of these parties, it's often difficult to exclude anyone.

According to Luke, effective public leadership in an interconnected world, what he calls "catalytic" leadership, involves four specific tasks:

1. *Focus attention* by elevating the issue to the public and policy agendas. Moving a particular problem onto the public agenda involves identifying the problem, creating a sense of urgency about its solution, and triggering broad public interest.
2. *Engage people in the effort* by convening the diverse set of people, agencies, and interests needed to address the issue. Engaging people involves identifying all the stakeholders and those with understanding of the problems, enlisting core group members, and convening the initial meetings.
3. *Stimulate multiple strategies and options for action.* This step requires building and nurturing an effective working group, with a unifying purpose and a credible process for discussion and group learning. Strategic development involves identifying desired outcomes, exploring multiple options, and promoting commitment to the strategies that are developed.
4. *Sustain action and maintain momentum* by managing the interconnections through appropriate institutionalization and rapid information sharing and feedback. In this stage, it is necessary to build support among "champions," power holders, advocacy groups, and those holding important resources. The leader must then turn to institutionalizing cooperative behavior and becoming a network facilitator (adapted from Luke 1998, 37–148).

As we have noted before, the New Public Service requires developing skills quite different from those associated with controlling public agencies or those involved in strict economic analysis—though particular skills from those areas may be appropriate from time to time. Instead, those interested in a New Public Service will need to develop skills in other areas. Luke specifically addresses this concern by describing three specific skill sets required for catalytic leadership (1998, 149–240). The first is thinking and acting strategically—framing and reframing issues, identifying desired outcomes and connecting those with specific actions or strategies that might be undertaken, identifying stakeholders and others whose involvement is essential to success, and drawing out the interconnections so essential to effective leadership in the complex public policy universe. The second is facilitating productive work groups—engaging in skillful interventions that move a group forward, helping the group cope with conflict, and forging multiple agreements, hopefully through consensus building. The third is leading from personal passion and inner values:

> Catalytic leaders lead from strength of character, not strength of personality. Successful catalysts exhibit a strength of character that establishes their credibility to convene diverse groups. They have the personal confidence to facilitate and mediate sometimes difficult agreements, and they possess a long-term perspective that helps focus and refocus groups members' attention in the face of small defeats.
>
> (Luke 1998, 219)

This perspective is echoed in recent work that explores the emotional basis of leadership. In *Primal Leadership* (2002), Daniel Goleman, Richard Boyatis, and Anne McKee argue that emotional intelligence, the capacity to understand and respond to significant emotional cues, is a key element of leadership. Similarly, Robert Denhardt and Janet Denhardt, in *The Dance of Leadership* (2006), write that a key leadership skill is the capacity to engage with others in a way that energizes them and causes them to act. Doing so, they argue, is much more of an art than a science.

Once again, as in our discussion of the dignity and worth of public service, we argue that passion, commitment, and perseverance in the face of difficult problems are often required to "make a difference."

Servants, Not Owners

In the New Public Service, there is an explicit recognition that public administrators are not the business owners of their agencies and programs.

Accordingly, the mindset of public administrators is that public programs and resources do not belong to them. Rather, public administrators have accepted a responsibility to serve citizens by being stewards of public resources (Kass 1990), conservators of public organizations (Terry 1995), facilitators of citizenship and democratic dialogue (Box 1998; Chapin and Denhardt 1995; King and Stivers 1998), and catalysts for community engagement (Denhardt and Gray 1998; Lappé and Du Bois 1994). This is a very different perspective from that of a business owner focused on profit and efficiency. The New Public Service suggests that public administrators not only must share power, work through people, and broker solutions, but also must reconceptualize their role in the governance process as responsible participant, not entrepreneur (Innes and Booher 2004; Perry and Buckwalter 2010).

When public administrators take risks, they are not entrepreneurs of their own businesses who can make such decisions knowing that the consequences of failure will fall largely on their own shoulders. Risk in the public sector is different (Denhardt and Denhardt 1999). In the New Public Service, risks and opportunities reside within the larger framework of democratic citizenship and shared responsibility. Because the consequences of either success or failure are not limited to a private business concern, public administrators do not single-handedly decide what is best for a community. This need not mean that all short-term opportunities are lost. If dialogue and citizen engagement are ongoing, opportunities and potential risks can be explored in a timely manner. The important factor to consider is whether the benefits of a public administrator's immediate and risky action in response to an opportunity outweighs the costs to trust, collaboration, and the sense of shared responsibility.

Finally, in the New Public Service, shared and value-based leadership is seen as a function and responsibility at all levels of the organization, from

The Boston Foundation, Greater Boston's community foundation, coordinates the Boston Indicators Project in partnership with the City of Boston and the Metropolitan Area Planning Council. The project draws data from the wealth of information and research generated by the region's public agencies, civic institutions, think tanks, and community-based organizations. The project relies on the expertise of hundreds of stakeholders who engage in frequent and meaningful dialogue to assess the data and frame their recommendations.

the executive suite to the street level. Vinzant and Crothers (1998), for example, describe how public servants on the front lines are called upon to exercise discretion, involve others, and make decisions that respect and reflect a variety of factors and values. They must be responsive to agency rules, the community they serve, their supervisors, and their coworkers, as well as to situational and ethical variables. Vinzant and Crothers argue that, in many of these cases, front-line public servants are called upon to behave as value-based leaders:

> They make choices and take action to elevate the goals, attitudes, and values of the participants in a given situation in ways that may be counter to their immediate interests and desires, but that can be legitimated through reference to the broader complex of ideals and values involved in the case.
>
> (1998, 112)

Conclusion

In the New Public Service, leadership is based on values and is shared throughout the organization and with the community. This change in the conceptualization of the public administrator's role has profound implications for the types of leadership challenge and responsibility faced by public servants. First, public administrators must know and manage more than just the requirements and resources of their programs. The narrow view is not very helpful to a citizen whose world is not conveniently divided up by programmatic departments and offices. The problems citizens face are often, if not usually, multifaceted, fluid, and dynamic—and they do not easily fall within the confines of a particular office or the narrow job description of an individual. To serve citizens, then, public administrators must not only know and manage their own resources, they must also be aware of and connected to other sources of support and assistance, engaging citizens and the community in the process. They do not seek to control, nor do they assume that self-interested choice serves as a surrogate for dialogue and shared values. In short, they must share power and lead with passion, commitment, and integrity in a manner that respects and empowers citizenship.

    The first section of this chapter was adapted from a previously published paper: Robert Denhardt and Janet Denhardt, 2001, "The New Public Service, Putting Democracy First," *National Civic Review* 90(4): 391–400. The paper was originally prepared for the Arizona Town Hall.

Chapter 9

Value People, not just
Productivity

Value people, not just productivity. Public organizations and the networks in which they participate are more likely to be successful in the long run if they are operated through processes of collaboration and shared leadership based on respect for all people.

In its approach to management and organization, the New Public Service emphasizes the importance of managing through people. Systems of productivity improvement, process reengineering, and performance measurement are seen as important tools in designing management systems. However, the New Public Service suggests that such rational attempts to control human behavior are likely to fail in the long term if, at the same time, insufficient attention is paid to the values and interests of individual members of an organization. Moreover, although these approaches may get results, they do not build responsible, engaged, and civic-minded employees or citizens.

The evolution of thought with regard to how to best manage people involves a number of related topics and ideas, including motivation, "supervision" and leadership, organizational culture, organizational structure, and organizational power. It involves questions about the nature of authority, definitions of performance and responsibility, and the establishment of trust. Most fundamentally, however, it is grounded in our most basic assumptions about the nature of people and behavior. In this chapter, we explore the very different assumptions and conceptual foundations for the views about managing people exemplified in the Old Public Administration, the New

Public Management, and the New Public Service. We begin by looking at the major concepts and ideas related to motivation and management from a historical perspective. We then compare the assumptions and models that underlie the management of people from the perspective of the Old Public Administration, the New Public Management, and the New Public Service.

Human Behavior in Organizations: Key Concepts

Our beliefs about what motivates human behavior in large measure determine how we interpret, respond to, and try to influence the behavior of others. When theorists initially began to study human behavior in organizations, the assumptions they made about the nature of people were relatively simplistic and generally negative. One of the first and most central ideas in the study of organizational management was that, in order for organizations to function, workers had to be induced or forced to produce certain behaviors and perform particular tasks. These tasks were to be accomplished by people within an organization that was understood principally as a "structure" for regularizing interactions and processes. The goal of this structure was to obtain efficient and consistent performance of tasks.

Whereas we now talk of the structure of the organization as being one factor among several in influencing worker behavior, initially, it was *the* focus of management. Ott states, "The structure—an organization's shape, size, procedures, production technology, position descriptions, reporting arrangements, and coordinating relationships—affects the feelings and emotions, and therefore the behavior of the people and groups inside them" (1996, 304). These feelings and emotions were largely ignored in the study of organizations and management for many decades. Rather, it was assumed that, if the work was designed well and authority relationships were appropriately structured and regularized, optimum efficiency could be realized.

Hierarchy and Scientific Management

The German sociologist Max Weber is perhaps most closely associated with the structural approach to managing and controlling human behavior in organizations. Weber described bureaucratic organizational structure as characterized by a hierarchy of authority, regularized rules and procedures, and formalized positions with fixed duties, and said that such a structure would lead to predictable and efficient performance. "Precision, speed, unambiguity, knowledge of the files, continuity, discretion, unity, strict subordination, reduction of friction and of material and personal costs—these are raised to the optimum point in the strictly bureaucratic administration"

(Weber, quoted in Gerth and Mills 1946, 214). In part because bureaucracy was the best way to attain efficiency, Weber said, bureaucracy is the "most rational known means of carrying out imperative control over human beings" (337). This is accomplished, in part, by making the administrative processes as objective, rational, and depersonalized as possible. "The objective discharge of business primarily means a discharge of business according to calculable rules and 'without regard to persons'" (215). Weber went on to say that this dehumanization of work, "is the specific nature of bureaucracy and it is appraised as its special virtue" (216).

However, Weber himself was concerned about the consequences of bureaucracy for both democratic values and the individual human spirit. He said, "'democracy' as such is opposed to the 'rule' of bureaucracy" (Weber, quoted in Gerth and Mills 1946, 231). Even so, Weber thought that, ultimately, bureaucratic power would exceed that of the political sphere: "Under normal conditions, the power position of a fully developed bureaucracy is always overpowering" (232).

Not only was Weber concerned about the implications of bureaucracy for democratic governance, he was also worried about its consequences for people. "The individual bureaucrat cannot squirm out of the apparatus in which he is harnessed" (Weber, quoted in Gerth and Mills 1946, 228). He referred to bureaucratization as creating an "iron cage" in which "all forms of value-oriented social conduct would be suffocated by the almighty bureaucratic structures and by the tightly-knit networks of formal–rational laws and regulations, against which the individual would no longer stand any chance at all" (Mommsen 1974, 57).

Despite these concerns, the values of bureaucracy and efficiency found particularly fertile ground with early management theorists, who sought to find the best means to control workers and achieve efficiency. These early management theorists viewed workers primarily as extensions of their tools and machines. It was thought that the fear of physical or economic punishment was needed to get people to work. Only those "motivated" by money or fear would complete their assigned tasks.

For example, as we saw earlier, Frederick Taylor argued that workers would do what they were told if they were given specific instructions and then paid a piece rate to follow them. He urged managers to study the tasks to be performed, establish the best way to perform them, and then scientifically select and train workers to do the job. The workers could then be induced to perform by being paid a set amount of money for each task performed or product produced. Although Taylor saw this as a mutually beneficial approach for workers and managers, it was clear that he assumed workers to be naturally lazy and stupid. For example, in his comments about inducing men to haul big iron, he said, it is "possible to train an intelligent gorilla" to do their job (1923, 40). He also expected employees to obey their superiors without question.

The Human Factor

These ideas about obedience to authority and hierarchy were the dominant management doctrine in the early 1900s and still exert considerable influence today. Although there were a few early humanistic writings on management and workers (e.g., Follett 1926; Munsterberg 1913), it was not until the publication of the Hawthorne studies in the 1930s that there was any significant recognition of the importance of social (as opposed to economic or technical) factors in work motivation. Even the Hawthorne experiments themselves began as a study of "the relation between conditions of work and the incidence of fatigue and monotony among employees" (Roethlisberger and Dickson 1939, 3). However, the study did not go as planned, and the researchers ultimately found that human relationships (including the workers' relationship with the researchers) influenced worker behavior. Consequently, new models were needed to explain worker behavior. The researchers found that behavior and motivation are complex, influenced by attitudes, feelings, and the meanings that people assign to their work and their relationships at work. As Roethlisberger and Dickson stated, "It is [our] simple thesis that a human problem requires a human solution" (1939, 35).

Research that immediately followed the Hawthorne studies resulted in the beginnings of a more sophisticated understanding of the relationship between people, work, and organizations. Ideas such as the importance of human cooperation (Barnard 1948) and the influence of groups (Knickerbocker and McGregor 1942) were studied by researchers to determine how these factors might influence work performance. By the 1950s, there was growing agreement among management theorists that motivation was a psychological concept rather than a purely economic one.

This recognition was exemplified in McGregor's (1957) work in which he distinguished between what he called Theory X and Theory Y assumptions about workers. He argued that traditional command and control approaches (Theory X), based on the assumption that people are lazy, uninvolved, and motivated solely by money, actually cause people to behave in a manner consistent with that expectation. Theory Y, on the other hand, is based on a much more optimistic and humanistic view of people and emphasizes the inherent dignity and worth of individuals in organizations. Holding these assumptions, and acting on them, would allow these more positive qualities of workers to manifest themselves in organizations.

Other theorists looked at different aspects of worker motivation and conducted research on the behavior of individuals under differing circumstances. In simple terms, contemporary motivation theory seeks to explain voluntary, goal-directed behavior (Coursey, Yang, and Pandey 2012; Ott, Parks, and Simpson 2007). There are a variety of models that emphasize different aspects of motivation: human needs (e.g., Herzberg 1968; Maslow 1943; McClelland 1985); an individual's expectations, skills, and desires (Vroom 1964); goal setting (Locke 1978); perceptions of equity and fairness (Adams 1963); opportunities for participation (Lawler 1990); and motivation based on public service values and norms (Perry and Wise 1990).

As assumptions about workers and their motivations changed, so did the dominant framework for an understanding of the role of management and leadership. Management's role was originally conceived of as documenting tasks and procedures, and then supervising and controlling workers accordingly. With the recognition of the psychological components of human motivation came the need to broaden the definition of management to include "human relations," in order to keep workers satisfied and productive. Importantly, however, although the parameters of management changed, the goals typically remained the same—to improve and maintain productivity. In many cases, the idea was to treat people better and more humanely in order to get better performance from them. It wasn't until the last several decades that the argument that treating people with respect and dignity is important in its own right, not simply as a means to improve production, gained currency in the management literature (Bolman and Deal 2008; Crevani et al. 2007; Schein 2008).

Groups, Culture, and Democratic Administration

A number of other perspectives on managing worker behavior have also emerged and gained recognition. It has been argued, for example, that group norms and behaviors influence individual behavior (e.g., Asch 1951; Homans 1954; Lewin 1951; Sherif 1936; Whyte 1943). These theorists suggest that human beings are social and readily form groups both inside and outside of organizations. These groups create norms, roles, and expectations for members that meet individuals' needs for affiliation and belongingness, but also require a level of conformity in order for membership to be maintained. Accordingly, work groups, both formal and informal, create a normative context for our behavior in organizations. Mary Parker Follett, for example, argued that group dynamics and the motivations of the individual should form the basis of administration. Rather than simply responding to orders, managers and workers should define administrative problems jointly and respond accordingly—taking their "orders" from the circumstances. She wrote in 1926, "One *person* should not give orders to another *person*, but both should agree to take their orders from the situation" (quoted in Shafritz and Hyde 1997, 56). Still other theorists looked at how individual character-istics influence organizational behavior, such as those who emphasize the life stage of workers (Schott 1986) or personality characteristics (e.g., Myers Briggs or similar inventories). Power and politics, once the province of political scientists and philosophers, have also been used as a lens for understanding human behavior in organizations (French and Raven 1959; Kotter 1977; Pfeffer 1981).

Critiques of bureaucracy and hierarchy have also been launched from the standpoint of the inconsistency between bureaucracy and democratic governance. Waldo, in his book *The Administrative State* (1948), for example, argued not only that administrative questions were inherently value-laden, but that administration itself must be made more consistent with democratic principles. "*The Administrative State* contains a strong message: that an uncritical acceptance of an administrative outlook constitutes a rejection of democratic theory and that this is a societal problem, not simply a problem of administrative management" (Denhardt 2000, 66–67). In other words, Waldo's argument is that the extension of the hierarchical and "neutral" bureaucracy would ultimately undermine democracy.

Only by making the administrative machinery adhere to democratic norms and principles could this threat be addressed. This requires, not merely expanding the role of citizens in policy administration, but also reforming the administrative process itself. As suggested by Levitan, "a democratic state must not only be based on democratic principles but also democratically administered, the democratic philosophy permeating its administrative machinery" (1943, 359). Waldo was even more direct in his criticism of hierarchy and bureaucratic control and his hope for reform, saying that what was needed was:

> Substantial abandonment of the authority–submission, superordinate–subordinate thought patterns which tend to dominate our administrative theory. . . . In rare moments of optimism, one permits himself the luxury of a dream of society of the future in which education and general culture are consonant with a working world in which all participate both as "leaders" and "followers" according to "rules of the game" known to all. Such a society would be postbureaucratic.
>
> (Waldo 1948, 103)

This critique of bureaucracy and the call to make administration more democratic dovetailed neatly with developments in motivation theory. For instance, making administration more democratic and less hierarchical would allow individuals to express their natural tendencies to work and be responsible, as suggested by McGregor, to meet social/esteem/self-actualization needs as suggested by Maslow, and to take orders from the situation as advocated by Follett.

Another important idea with regard to managing the behavior of people in organizations is the concept of organizational culture. Rather than seeing an organization as a static "structure," the organizational culture perspective draws from the field of anthropology to understand how norms, beliefs, and values are shared by members of an organization and, in turn, define its boundaries. These shared norms and values are manifest in organizational members' language and behaviors, rituals, and symbols, and in the artifacts they produce. Culture expresses the ideas and overall values that define an organization and has a significant and long-lasting influence on its members. Schein (1987) suggested that there are three levels of organizational culture: (1) the observable social and physical environment, such as physical layout, technological preferences, language patterns, or the day-to-day operating routines that guide people's behavior; (2) the values and ideas about the way the organization "should" be; and (3) the often hidden and largely unquestioned assumptions and beliefs held by members of the organization that guide their behavior. Schein suggests that the last category constitutes the core definition of culture: "a pattern of basic assumptions . . . that has worked well enough to be considered valid and, therefore, to be taught to new members as the correct way to perceive, think, and feel in relation to those problems" (1987, 9). Or, as Ott states, "It functions as an organizational control mechanism, informally approving or prohibiting behaviors" (1989, 50).

Despite this evolution of thought, there remains a lack of consensus about what motivates people and how best to influence behavior in organizations. As will be explored later in this chapter, public choice theorists argue strenuously for a model of human behavior and motivation based solely on self-interested, individual decision making, to the exclusion of other explanations of human behavior. For others, there has been a growing recognition that, in addition to self-interest, human motivation involves both social and psychological factors. This leads to a much more complex view of the relationship between organizations and human behavior in which both the structure of the organization and interactions and relationships between individuals and groups influence behavior. In this more complex view, it is also assumed that individuals with different experiences and personalities will respond to organizational life in different ways. Organizational politics are also believed to influence behavior, as people seek to obtain and maintain power. Finally, in this view, organizational culture is understood as creating the normative context for our behavior in organizations. In short, for these theorists, people are seen as bringing their social and emotional needs to work. In the sections that follow, we will explore how these issues are dealt with from the perspectives of the Old Public Administration, the New Public Management, and the New Public Service.

The Old Public Administration: Using Control to Achieve Efficiency

The Old Public Administration is based on the ideas that efficiency is the preeminent value and that people won't be productive and work hard unless you make them. In this view, workers will be productive only when they are provided with monetary incentives, and when they believe that management can and will punish them for poor performance. Employee motivation is not considered in a direct way. In the early twentieth century, when the Old Public Administration was the dominant model, people were expected to simply follow orders, and, for the most part, they did. Public employment was considered to be a simple quid pro quo arrangement analogous to employment in the private sector: In exchange for a steady salary, workers would carefully and methodically carry out assigned tasks. The treatment of workers as human beings with emotions and needs, with contributions and insights, with value in their own right, was not part of the equation.

Efficiency, defined as the ratio of costs to outputs, demanded that cost control and productivity were the primary, if not the only, objectives of management. The challenge was to organize and structure the work so as to minimize costs and maximize production. Employees were considered to be costs. Accordingly, the goal was to minimize the cost of labor by obtaining the maximum output from each employee while providing the lowest salary and fewest other monetary incentives possible. The emphasis was on the potential gain in efficiency, not on the long-term well-being of the people who worked in the organization, much less the citizens or the community. It was assumed that the issues of community, citizenship, and democracy fell squarely within the political sphere and completely outside the realm of administration. To the extent that "humanistic" approaches could be accommodated in the Old Public Administration, they were seen merely as vehicles to secure more productivity. For example, in the Hawthorne experiments, it was recommended that managers institute a "suggestion box" for employees, to make them feel more involved and, therefore, potentially more productive. However, there was no consideration of the idea that the suggestions might actually be useful or important in their own right.

The idea was that the organization itself should be the primary concern of management. If it could be structured according to the ideals of bureaucracy, if it could advance the values of neutral competence and expertise, and if management systems could be put into place to control and account for the expenditure of funds, then public organizations would fulfill their intended function.

The New Public Management: Using Incentives to Achieve Productivity

As we saw earlier, public choice theory is based on a number of important assumptions about the behavior of people and how to best manage that behavior to achieve public policy objectives. Principal agent theory applies these assumptions to explain the relationship between executives and the workers in an organization using the metaphor of a contract. This contract is necessary because, although the employee (the agent) acts on behalf of the executive (the principal), their goals and objectives are different. As a result, the principal has to obtain enough information to monitor the agent, determine results, and provide sufficient incentives to consistently obtain them. Because the goal is efficiency, the question then becomes a matter of identifying which least-cost approach the organization can use to keep employees from seeking their own, rather than organizational, goals and to verify that they are doing so.

The New Public Management, with its reliance on public choice and principal agent theory, has made some important contributions to our understanding of human behavior. It is important to note, however, that it relies on economic rationality as the explanation of human behavior, *to the exclusion of other ways of understanding motivation and the human experience*. If that is so, the only way to successfully influence workers' behavior is by altering the decision-making rules or incentives so as to alter their self-interest to be more in line with organizational priorities.

The New Public Service: Respecting Public Service Ideals

The assumptions about the motivations and treatment of people in the New Public Service differ starkly from both the Old Public Administration and the New Public Management. The Old Public Administration assumed people to be as McGregor's Theory X described them: lazy, stupid, lacking in drive, and unwilling to accept responsibility. Accordingly, they had to be controlled and threatened with punishment to secure their performance. The New Public Management has a different, but no more trusting, view of people. It assumes that they are self-interested and will seek to meet their own objectives unless they are monitored and provided with enough incentives to do otherwise. As such, the New Public Management, like Taylor's scientific management, excludes consideration of group norms and values, organizational culture, emotional/social considerations, and psychological and other "irrational" needs. It negates the idea that people act in response to shared values, loyalty, citizenship, and the public interest.

We are not suggesting that people are never lazy or self-interested. Rather, relying on self-interest as the sole explanation of human behavior represents a very narrow, and largely negative, view of people that is neither borne out by experience nor justifiable from a normative standpoint. In other words, people don't typically act that way. More importantly, they shouldn't.

The elements of human behavior that are at the core of the New Public Service, such as human dignity, trust, belongingness, concern for others, service, and citizenship based on shared ideals and the public interests, are deemphasized in the Old Public Administration and the New Public Management. In the New Public Service, ideals such as fairness, equity, responsiveness, respect, empowerment, and commitment do not negate, but often outweigh, the value of efficiency as the sole criterion for the operation of government. As Frederickson states, "Persons who practice public administration must be increasingly familiar with issues of both representational and direct democracy, with citizen participation, with principles of justice and individual freedom" (1982, 503). Frederickson was talking about the relationship between public servants and citizens, but the same principle applies in how public managers ought to treat other public servants.

If you assume that people are capable of other-mindedness, of service, of acting on shared values as citizens, then it is only logically consistent that you assume public employees are capable of these motivations and behaviors. We cannot expect public servants to treat their fellow citizens with respect and dignity if they themselves are not treated with respect and dignity. We cannot expect them to trust and empower others, to listen to their ideas, and to work cooperatively, unless we are willing to do the same for them. In the New Public Service, the enormous challenges and complexities of the work of public administrators are recognized. Service and democratic ideals are applauded. Public servants are not just viewed as employees who crave the security and structure of a bureaucratic job (the Old Public Administration), or as participants in a market (the New Public Management); rather, public servants are people whose motivations and rewards are more than simply a matter of pay or security. They want to make a difference in the lives of others (Coursey et al. 2012; Denhardt 1993; Perry and Buckwalter 2010; Perry and Wise 1990; Vinzant 1998).

Elmer Staats, former comptroller of the United States and a distinguished public servant, once wrote that public service is far more than an occupational category. It is better defined, he said, as "an attitude, a sense of duty—yes even a sense of public morality" (1988, 602). This is consistent with the notion that public service motives are very important and powerful in motivating the behavior of the public servants. Public service motivation is based on an individual's predisposition to respond to motives grounded primarily or uniquely in public institutions and organizations (Perry and Wise 1990). In other words, there are particular motives that are associated with the nature of public service work that revolve around service to others and the public interest. These motives are related to values such as loyalty, duty, citizenship, equity, opportunity, and fairness. Research has shown that these norm-based, affective motives are unique to public service and critical to understanding behavior in public organizations (Balfour and Weschler 1990; Denhardt, Denhardt, and Aristigueta 2002; Frederickson and Hart 1985; Perry and Wise 1990; Vinzant 1998).

As we saw earlier, Frederickson and Hart (1985) argue that, too frequently, we fail to make a distinction between what they call the "moral entailments" of service in the public sector and employment in the private sector. When we do so, we denigrate the ideals of both democratic citizenship and public service. They call for a return to what they call "the patriotism of benevolence," based, first, on the love of and patriotism to democratic values, and second, on benevolence, defined as "extensive and non-instrumental love of others" (1985, 547). This means that we should serve and care for others and work to protect their rights, not because it advances our own interests, but because it is the right thing to do for its own sake. This patriotism of benevolence, they argue, ought to be "the primary motivation of public servants in the United States" (547).

Similarly, Hart points out that the primary obligations of public servants are "to encourage civic autonomy; to govern by persuasion, to transcend the corruptions of power; and to become civic exemplars" (1997, 967). Accordingly, he says, "public servants are obligated to embody those values intentionally in all their actions, *whether with superiors, colleagues, subordinates, or the general public*" (1997, 968; emphasis added). Put simply, in public organizations, we need to treat each other and our fellow citizens in a manner consistent with democratic ideals, trust, and respect. We do so because we believe that people respond to and are motivated by such values, and because we believe that public service plays a special role in advancing and encouraging those aspects of human character.

Practically speaking, then, the values of the New Public Service dictate that we encourage, model, and enact our commitment to democratic ideals and our trust of others. As managers, we can encourage public service motives and values by making them a central part of organizational identity and culture. Because we know and trust that the people we work with want to serve others, we need to treat them as partners in the pursuit of the public interest. This suggests, even demands, a highly inclusive, participative approach to management—not just as an instrumental means to enhance productivity, but as a means to advance the values at the core of public service. Roy Adams puts it succinctly: "Efficiency is not enough" (1992, 18). Participative approaches are needed in order for people in organizations to have "a decent and dignified existence" (18). Moreover, although participation often improves performance, its value should not be dependent upon its contribution to something else. Participation is an important value in and of itself.

Robert Golembiewski (1977), as we saw earlier, has argued that organizational democracy is based on participation by all organization members in decision making, frequent feedback of the results of organizational performance, sharing of management-level information throughout the organization, guarantees for individual rights, the availability of appeal or recourse in cases of intractable disputes, and a set of supporting attitudes or values. He suggested that the closer an organization is to these criteria, the more democratic the organization will be. Edward Lawler (1990) advocates what he calls "high-involvement" management, based on information sharing, training, decision making, and rewards as the four key components of a successful employee participation program. He argues that participation

---

The British Columbia Public Service hosts a Public Service Week (PSW) every year to recognize and celebrate employees with barbecues, picnics, and a variety of other activities. As part of PSW week in 2010, the British Columbia Ministry of the Environment made a video of ministry employees at all levels of the organization lip-synching to the *Glee* television show version of Journey's "Don't Stop Believin'." The video incorporated a variety of educational posters and props to show the ministry's work, goals, and priorities. It was a simple way to reinforce the ministry's commitment to the public service mission, while celebrating its employees. Completed during lunch hours, the video project was a great morale booster and highly successful in engaging a wide variety of employees in doing something both fun and inspirational.

enhances motivation because it helps people understand what is expected and see the relationships between performance and outcomes.

According to Kearney and Hays (1994), public managers are beginning to realize how vitally important it is to use participatory management approaches. These authors argue that participatory approaches should begin with the premise that workers are an organization's most important assets and should be treated accordingly. All employees must be empowered by management to participate in decision making and must be allowed to do so without fear. Based on their review of the research into a participative approach to organizational decision making, they conclude that this approach is an effective way to increase employee satisfaction and productivity. This finding is echoed by other public management scholars (Crevani et al. 2007; Davenport 2001; Schein 2008).

In the New Public Service, the fact that these approaches "work better" to enhance satisfaction, boost productivity, and enhance an organization's capacity for change are important. In fact, it has been shown that, although both quality management and participation in decision making have positive effects on employee performance, participation in decision making has a much greater effect (Stashevsky and Elizur 2000). What is most important from the standpoint of the New Public Service is that participative and inclusive approaches are the only ones that build citizenship, responsibility, and trust, and advance the values of service in the public interest. They are the only approaches that make sense if you begin with the assumption that public servants are, and ought to be, motivated by democratic ideals and service to others. To treat them otherwise discourages this important source of pride and the motivation to be selfless in the pursuit of the public interest. It is this normative core of public service that the nation found so compelling

As part of a brochure issued in Alachua County, Florida, called "Creating Sustainable Workplaces and Organizations," workplace collaboration was named as one of seven areas of concern in a community primer on sustainability for local organizations and businesses. The brochure states in part: "Alachua County has adopted an organizational structure for decisionmaking and policymaking that features deliberately designed opportunities for collaboration between functional groups of departments and encourages opportunities for multilevel, shared and rotational leadership" (http://issuu.com/alachuacounty/docs/sustainable-workplaces).

on watching the police and firefighters, the health care and emergency workers, as well as the citizen volunteers, in the aftermath of the September 11, 2001 attacks on New York and Washington, DC. This devotion to public service represents what is best of, and most important to, the achievement of public values and democractic ideals.

As discussed in Chapter 8, the notion of shared leadership is critical in providing opportunities for employees and citizens to affirm and act upon their public service motives and values. In the New Public Service, shared leadership, collaboration, and empowerment become the norm both inside and outside the organization. Shared leadership focuses on the goals, values, and ideals that the organization and community want to advance. As Burns (1978) would say, leadership exercised by working through and with people transforms the participants and shifts their focus to higher-level values. Through shared (or transformational) leadership, the purposes and ends of organizations, groups, and communities are transformed to another, higher set of goals and values. This process must be characterized by mutual respect, accommodation, and support. The public service motives of citizens and employees alike can be recognized, supported, and rewarded in the process.

Conclusion

Writing about management in the private sector, Plas (1996) states that organizational culture must evolve and find a "place for the heart again" in the workplace. Workers should be permitted, she says, to participate with their labor, with their minds, and with their hearts. Managers should be, and should encourage their employees to be, "authentic." Managers and workers should share their feelings, values, and ethics within the corporate environment. Plas says this requires a new social contract between employees and employers. The old contract assumed that the employee would work hard and the organization would look after the employee. Modern society has shown that these contracts no longer work, if, in fact, they ever did. The new contract is based on the assumption that both the individual and the organization have responsibilities to each other and, accordingly, to creating and maintaining a successful relationship.

Public-sector managers have a special responsibility and a unique opportunity to capitalize on the "heart" of public service. People are attracted to the public service because they are motivated by public service values. These values—to serve others, to make the world better and safer, and to make democracy work—represent the best of what it means to be a citizen in the service of a community. We need to nourish and encourage these higher-level motivations and values, not extinguish them by treating people as if they were cogs in a machine or as if they were only capable of self-serving behavior. How many of us have seen what happens when an idealistic public servant comes to a public organization and is treated as if his or her idealism were naiveté—and is told that what is expected and rewarded is to do what they are told and keep quiet? If we treat people as bureaucrats, as self-serving and self-interested individuals, we encourage them to become just that. Believing in the public service, and our role in serving the public interest, is what allows us to sacrifice, to give our best, to go, as the firefighters and police officers did in the World Trade Center (WTC) disaster, where others would not go.

If we can help others to see that the work they are doing is larger and more important than the individual, if we can help people to understand that public service is honorable and valuable, they will act accordingly. Treating our fellow public servants with the dignity and respect that they deserve in public organizations and empowering them to help find ways to serve their communities allow us to attract and empower those who are willing and able to serve in the public interest. It is the duty, obligation, and privilege of every public manager to do so. As MacKenzie put it, a century ago:

> We must try to see once more, as the wisest of Greeks saw, that there is nothing nobler in human life than politics, in the most comprehensive sense of that term. Few of us can do much to serve humanity in the widest sense: the best thing probably on the whole that most of us can do is serve our country.
>
> (MacKenzie 1901, 22)

Chapter 10

The New Public Service and Citizen Engagement

Cases and Recommendations

In this chapter, we look at specific and practical ways that public agencies committed to the New Public Service can work positively with citizens (broadly defined) and with nongovernmental organizations to achieve a higher level of citizen engagement. The process of citizen engagement has been defined as the "ability and incentive for ordinary people to come together, deliberate, and take action on problems or issues that they themselves have defined as important" (Gibson 2006, 2). Governments at all levels have moved from the federally mandated citizen participation requirements of the 1960s and 1970s to embrace a variety of citizen engagement approaches and goals in multiple policy arenas. In fact, we have now reached a point in contemporary practice that has been termed "the age of citizen engagement." As a result, "citizen engagement is no longer hypothetical: it is very real, and public administrators are central to its evolution" (Roberts 2008, 4).

In many ways, "practice is leading theory" in the area of citizen engagement (Bingham, Nabatchi, and O'Leary 2005, 554). We describe only a few of the many examples of citizen engagement in democratic governments across the United States and around the world. We do not claim that our work provided the catalyst for these initiatives or that the architects of these programs and projects would even necessarily use the term "New Public Service." Indeed, the kinds of activity and practice highlighted in this chapter are what inspired us to write this book, not the other way around.

In other words, the case studies and examples presented here are intended to offer some ideas of the kinds of practice we would include under the mantle of the New Public Service.

A variety of useful materials on citizen engagement and participation practices are available. Sources such as the Civic Practices Network (www. cpn.org), CIVICUS World Alliance for Citizen Participation (www.civicus. org), and *Civic Engagement Magazine*, published by Rutgers University (http://publicservice.newark.rutgers.edu/home/civic-engagement.html), provide information, case studies, and examples of citizen engagement. A search for "citizen participation" on the U.S. government portal (www.usa. gov) yields more than a million results. In the literature, insights into the many facets of public engagement in the governance process can be found in the writings of, for example, Creighton (2005), Fishkin and Laslett (2003), Hambleton (2004), Jacobs et al. (2009), Lukensmeyer and Torres (2006), Roberts (2008), and the contributors to a 2005 symposium in *PAR* organized by Terry Cooper and his colleagues in the University of Southern California's Civic Engagement Initiative (Berry 2005; Bingham et al. 2005; Boyte 2005; Cooper 2005; Kathi and Cooper 2005; Portney 2005).

We begin with a discussion of the practical reasons for using citizen engagement strategies and the differences between participation and engagement. We then describe some cases of successful citizen engagement and conclude with a sampling of different types of approach.

What are the Goals of Citizen Engagement?

How can we increase the likelihood that the goals of citizen engagement can be reached? Of course, determining success depends on what goals are sought. It is necessary to clarify why we are investing time and money in such activities, if we are to have a basis to determine their worth or effectiveness. So, the first question with regard to meeting the challenges of engaging citizens is *why* we want to do so.

There may be many reasons for engaging citizens in governance. Most of these can be categorized as either *normative*, based on the idea that building citizenship and community is important for its own sake, or *instrumental*, aimed at the approval or implementation of a particular policy or project. Or, as Catlaw and Rawlings (2010) express it, citizen engagement can be considered the "right" thing to do as a part of the democratic ideal or the "smart" thing to do in order to gain the information and involvement needed for effective, legitimate government.

From a normative perspective, as we saw earlier, we should facilitate citizen engagement because it is the right thing to do according to democratic ideals and our desire to build a sense of community identity and responsibility. Rather than being a means to an end, engagement *is* the end. It is less about solving a policy or implementation problem than it is about providing a vehicle to help individual community members become "citizens" in the highest sense of the word (Lucio 2009). Citizens are people who have a concern for the larger community in addition to their own interests and are willing to assume personal responsibility for what goes on in their neighborhoods and communities. So, building citizenship is not about legal status or rights; it is about inculcating a way of thinking and acting that is characterized by openness to opposing ideas, collaboration, and a sense of responsibility to others. If promoting these democratic values is the reason for engaging citizens, success would be evaluated based on whether the citizen engagement activities have advanced openness, collaboration, and a sense of shared responsibility.

On the other hand, from an instrumental or "smart" perspective, we should increase citizen involvement because government cannot solve public problems alone. Effective governance increasingly requires active and ongoing citizen participation in planning, policymaking, implementation, and service delivery. The complexity of the problems facing government demands citizen involvement and acceptance, if not active cooperation. Citizens often have information that officials need in order to design a sound program. Further, citizens expect the opportunity to participate and may resist the implementation of plans they have not helped design. In some situations, only citizens can come up with a solution to a problem. An instrumental goal of citizen participation might be to gain support for a particular policy, resolve a conflict, or share information with citizens to achieve their cooperation. Success would be that the policy or project is approved and implemented, the conflict recedes, or citizens cooperate with governmental initiatives.

In the best of all worlds, the "right thing" and the "smart thing" reinforce each other in order to promote shared ownership of problems and a willingness to contribute to their solution. Citizen involvement that achieves extensive participation from persons affected by a decision promotes understanding of the issues involved, grounds the decision in citizen preferences, and builds support for the principle of citizen engagement. What is most important is that government officials spend the time and effort to determine what goals are sought at a particular time or with a particular set of activities. Once the goals are clear, then strategies for achieving them can be effectively designed.

What is Citizen Engagement?

Citizen participation approaches can range along a continuum from one-way communication at one end to dialogue shared and processed among multiple participants at the other (Lukensmeyer and Torres 2006). At one end of the continuum, approaches associated with *exchange* focus on "information processing" and can involve a one-way exchange in either direction between citizens and government officials. As Lukensmeyer and Torres (2006, 7) put it, "to simply inform and to consult are 'thin,' frequently pro forma techniques of participation that often fail to meet the public's expectations for involvement and typically yield little in the way of new knowledge." Although much can be learned from information exchange, it does not necessarily provide an opportunity for participants to hear each other's ideas, and it does not offer the chance for participants to discuss their ideas in a deliberative process.

On the other side of the continuum are citizen *engagement* approaches. A wide array of innovative new approaches foster deliberation between citizens and public officials in order to develop shared understandings and consensus in groups of differing sizes and in face-to-face and electronic settings (Lukensmeyer and Torres 2006; Roberts 2004). Public officials can include and incorporate citizens in the process of making decisions and can collaborate with them in all stages of the decision-making process, including implementation and evaluation of the decision. The final level of involvement is empowerment. The government places final decision-making authority or problem-solving responsibility in the hands of citizens.

An example of local government officials making a similar distinction between levels and types of citizen participation is provided by Ventura, California, in the goals for its Citizen Engagement Division. The city is committed to informing and consulting and to involving and collaborating. Adapting the guidelines of the International Association of Public Participation (IAP2), the city commits itself to these standards for each of these approaches:

- *Inform*: "We will provide the public with balanced and objective information to assist them in understanding a problem, alternatives, opportunities and/or solutions."
- *Consult*: "We will collect public feedback on analysis, alternatives and/or decisions from our community."
- *Involve*: "We will work directly with the public throughout the process to ensure that public concerns and aspirations are consistently understood and considered."
- *Collaborate:* "We will partner with the public in each aspect of the decision including the development of alternatives and identification of the preferred solution" (www.cityofventura.net/cm/civic engagement).

The IAP2 Spectrum of Public Participation includes a fifth dimension, "empower," that entails placing final decision making in the hands of the public and promising to implement what citizens decide.

Listening to the City: The Rebuilding of New York

One of the best-known examples of citizen engagement, and perhaps the most poignant, followed the 9/11 attacks on the WTC in New York. Many strategies—including advisory boards, public meetings, and mailings—were used in New York to elicit participation by citizens and interested groups on the fate of the WTC site (www.renewnyc.com). Among the most innovative, however, was a project called "Listening to the City." On July 20, 2002, more than 4,300 people from very diverse backgrounds met in the Jacob Javits Convention Center to engage in a dialogue about what should be done with the WTC site. This was the largest urban-planning citizen forum to ever take place. A similar but smaller meeting took place two days later with 800 people, followed by an online dialogue that involved more than 800 people and the exchange of approximately 10,000 messages. The process and the results were reported as extraordinary, at least in part for the simple reason that "everyone had a chance to speak and everyone had a chance to listen" (Civic Alliance to Rebuild Downtown New York 2002, 1).

Not only did citizens listen to and learn from one another, but the City of New York also listened and clearly heeded the citizens' advice and counsel. On the first day of the forum, Roland Betts, a member of the Lower Manhattan Development Corporation (LMDC), reassured the group, "Everyone seems to fear that the real meeting is going in some other room. Let me tell you something—this is the real meeting" (3). The result, according to John Whitehead, the chair of the LMDC, was "absolutely beautiful," with 100 percent of the participants in the July 20 forum reporting they were very satisfied or satisfied with the quality of the dialogue (2–3).

The process began when the Civic Alliance to Rebuild Downtown New York, a coalition of business, community, university, labor, and civic groups, was formed shortly after 9/11, to develop strategies for redeveloping Lower Manhattan. The group was convened by the Regional Plan Association in concert with NYU/Wagner, the New School University, and the Pratt Institute Center for Community and Environmental Development (4). The coalition held an initial forum on February 7, which involved 600 people and was designed to gain input on elements of a memorial. Then, in July, the much larger, mediated forum was held to gain citizen reactions to six preliminary alternatives that had been developed by the Port Authority of New York and New Jersey and the LMDC, based on the earlier input.

The July forum used the AmericaSpeaks twenty-first-century Town Meeting model. A group of field organizers developed relationships with various neighborhoods and community organizations and gained their assistance in recruiting and publicizing the event. The field organizers kept track of which groups and geographic areas were underrepresented and ran targeted ads and conducted street outreach so as to be even more representative of the population (Lukensmeyer and Brigham 2002, 357).

The diversity of the participants is credited as one of the major reasons the project worked as well as it did (Civic Alliance to Rebuild Downtown New York 2002, 3). There was diversity in age, racial and ethnic background, geographic location, and economic background, resulting in a group of people who normally might never have met. "Relatives of victims, downtown residents, survivors of 9/11, emergency workers, business leaders, the unemployed and underemployed, interested citizens and community advocates . . . sat side by side and contributed myriad points of view" (2). To facilitate dialogue for this large and diverse group of participants, translators for both the spoken word and sign, facilitators who spoke Chinese and Spanish, as well as hard copies of the discussion materials, in other languages and Braille, were provided. Grief counselors were also available. Most participants reported that their motivation for becoming involved in the forum was a sense of civic responsibility and a desire to ensure that the rebuilding process was guided by many and diverse voices.

The forum participants were divided into 10–12-person discussion groups. By combining face-to-face dialogue with technology, participant ideas not only could be heard by members of a particular group but also could be shared across the forum. A trained facilitator worked with each group, and ideas were recorded on laptop computers. A group of AmericaSpeaks volunteers served as "theme teams" who read and summarized the comments, identified key concepts and ideas, and then immediately reported these back to all the forum participants. The theme team prepared a set of priorities and questions that emerged from the dialogue, which were posted on large screens around the room, giving small-group participants a chance to see other groups' ideas and to gain feedback on their own ideas. Participants then used wireless keypads to vote on various questions, with the results of these polls displayed immediately.

The technology provided an innovative and effective way to ensure that there was widespread participation and feedback. Perhaps even more important to the success of the forum, however, was the response of the planners to the citizens' ideas. Participants urged decision makers not just to build a memorial, but to also revitalize the neighborhood in a way that would address the needs of a wide array of citizens and businesses.

Particularly important were the needs of low-income people and immigrants. Many emphasized the need for affordable housing, as well as a diverse business base. They wanted not only to rebuild buildings, but also to rebuild lives and community by addressing economic development, job creation, culture, transportation, recreation, and other civic amenities. The memorial, they said, should not be an afterthought, but should rather be inspiring—as one participant said, "a place that gives back life" (Civic Alliance to Rebuild Downtown New York 2002, 9). Another said, "I hope that the space will be used in way that promotes peace and understanding and educates people worldwide to prevent future such occurrences" (14).

The participants' reaction to the six alternatives presented to them was that the plans fell short. In fact, "many participants critiqued the plans as mediocre and lacking the vision necessary to reflect the significance of this historic moment" (11), and urged the planners to "Start over!" (12).

So, they did just that—they started over. After the meeting, the governor of New York "reiterated the citizen's directives to go back to the drawing board on site design options, develop mixed-use plans, reduce the density of the site, and find new solutions to the issue of commercial space" (Lukensmeyer and Brigham 2002, 356). A short time later, the LMDC announced that it was opening the planning process to six new design teams and expressed a commitment to fund transportation initiatives, to spread commercial development throughout Lower Manhattan, and to allow for more hotel and retail space in the site plans. In short, "citizens' voices were heard, and their recommendations were heeded" (361).

The concerns and priorities of citizens have continued to guide decision makers as they work to develop and to implement plans for redeveloping Lower Manhattan. In addition to the development of new plans for the site itself, the LMDC has committed to a number of off-site revitalization projects to "address a range of planning, design, and development issues, including: creating usable open spaces, developing residential uses, expanding and diversifying retail, leisure, and cultural uses, improving parks and the public realm, and improving transportation and access conditions" (www.renewnyc. com). For example, in March 2006, Governor George E. Pataki and Mayor Michael Bloomberg announced that the LMDC would award $27.4 million for cultural enhancements to arts organizations in Lower Manhattan (www.renewnyc.com).

Iowa's Citizen-Initiated Performance Assessment

Performance measurement is another area of governance where multiple examples of citizen engagement can be found. Involving citizens in the design of performance measurement systems can enhance the political significance and credibility of the measures, as well as increase the usefulness and relevance of information provided to citizens (Bacova and Maney 2004). For example, in 1991, with support of the Alfred P. Sloan Foundation, nine cities in Iowa embarked on the three-year project titled "Citizen-Initiated Performance Assessment" (CIPA), which engaged citizens in the design and implementation of performance measurement in a wide range of programs. The goals of the CIPA project included: (1) assisting cities to establish a sustainable process for involving citizens in developing credible and useful performance measures; (2) creating a dialogue between citizens and government administrators about the roles, responsibilities, and accountability of local government; and (3) helping cities to integrate performance measurement into the decision-making, budgeting, and management processes (Ho and Coates 2002, 8). The CIPA project was designed to look at performance measurement from a citizen's perspective, to enhance collaboration between citizens and public servants, and to emphasize public dissemination of information to citizens in a manner that is useful and accessible.

Nine cities of varying size chose to participate in the project. In the first phase, each city formed what was called a citizen Performance Team or "PT." The composition of these teams varied from city to city, but the majority of members of each team were citizens and citizen-group representatives, along with various mixtures of city officials and staff (Ho and Coates 2002b, Case Study, 1). One of the first tasks of these newly formed PTs was to identify key groups or neighborhoods that were not represented and to recruit new members as needed, as well as to identify groups that needed to be informed of the team's activities. Evaluators reported that, although concern was initially expressed that city representatives would come to dominate these teams, it did not turn out that way. City officials and staff members were purposefully "very deferential to citizens and . . . served as resources for questions raised by citizens" (7).

Once the teams were finalized, citizen members were given opportunities to learn about city departments and operations, examined information about their cities' characteristics and demographics, and gained information about the purposes and practices of performance measurement (Ho and Coates 2002, 8). Then, each team identified one or two public services for which they would develop performance measures. Because the priorities and concerns of citizens varied from locality to locality, different PTs chose to focus their attention on different programs and services. Then, each Performance Team developed a list of "critical elements" for their selected service area(s). In many cases, the critical elements selected were similar to those identified in the literature, but were different in at least two important respects.

First, in an area that is often overlooked in other performance-measurement systems, citizens expressed strong concerns about the need for the city to better communicate information on performance and results to citizens and wanted to measure how well city departments were doing so. For example, in the area of police and fire, citizens wanted to know what happened after they filed a case, and they wanted progress reports on the department's investigation of their cases (Ho and Coates 2002b, Case Study, 5). Second, although citizens were concerned about the effectiveness of programs, they also cared about the degree to which the individual public servants were "professional, courteous, and non-discriminatory" in their interactions with citizens (5). In other words, they wanted more open communication lines and useful and assessable information on what the city was doing, and they wanted to ensure that city employees treated citizens respectfully, professionally, and without discrimination.

The teams then developed performance measurements based on the critical elements that they had identified. Members were provided with professional assistance to facilitate these discussions. They used a worksheet developed by the CIPA project staff that they found useful as a means for the team to evaluate their own proposed measures. These forms asked members to consider whether the proposed measures were, for example, understandable, measurable, reasonable in terms of cost and time, and useful to citizens (Ho and Coates 2002b, Case Study, Appendix, 2).

Again, the measures in many cases were similar to those identified in professional publications, but evaluators of the project highlighted several important findings that resulted from the process, illustrating the unique contributions of citizens to the design of performance measurement systems. In general, although citizens were concerned about outcomes, they were not singularly focused on outcomes. They also cared about process issues, such as the courtesy of city employees, and input measures, such as training provided to police officers and medical personnel. Equity issues were also more important than might have been expected. For example, citizens expressed the concern that library and recreational services be accessible to low-income and disabled people and a wide range of ages. Surprisingly (at least to advocates of the Old Public Administration and the New Public Management), citizens were relatively uninterested in efficiency. They expressed more concern about the process, outcomes, and equity of services than mere cost measures. In general, "citizens in all nine cities felt a great need to let citizens know what the city government does, how effectively it is done, and what follow-up actions have been taken after citizens voice their opinions and complaints" (Ho and Coates 2002b, Case Study, 6, 7).

In the second stage of the project, citizen PTs helped design a system for data collection and, in some cases, helped collect the data through citizen surveys and other means. The teams then continued to work with the city councils and city staff to integrate performance data into the budget and policymaking processes.

The process was not without challenges. Participating cities have found it challenging to sustain citizen involvement over time. Cities also report that it has been difficult to gain adequate media coverage of the PTs' work. Nonetheless, the experience of the CIPA project has "been positive in all cities" (Ho and Coates 2002b, Case Study, 8). In the *Final Report on the CIPA Project* (2005), evaluators commented on a numbers of "lessons learned" from the experience, including the following observations: (1) Citizens have very little problem understanding performance measurement and different types of measure (i.e., input, output, and outcome). (2) The process of involving citizens along with city elected and appointed officials is very feasible and can lead to good working relationships and joint understanding about what constitutes quality service delivery. (3)The CIPA process is being recognized nationally as a significant contribution to building better public accountability and democratic governance in city government (*Final Report* 2005, 8–9).

Civic Engagement around the World

The ideals and practices associated with the New Public Service are not exclusively American. *The New Public Service* has been translated into Chinese and has been debated and discussed in a wide range of locations around the globe, from the Netherlands to Brazil, from Korea to Italy and Sweden and beyond. Our participation in some of these discussions has reinforced our excitement about, and the possibilities of, civic engagement and democratic values in the governance process. Not surprisingly, efforts to enact New Public Service values differ, not only from jurisdiction to jurisdiction in the United States, but also among different countries around the world. Yet the themes are similar: to try to find new and innovative ways to improve citizen engagement and build communities around a framework of shared values and democratic dialogue. (In the following paragraphs, Lena Langlet from Sweden and Manuella Cocci from Italy discuss efforts to implement the New Public Service in their countries. All quoted material is taken from personal correspondence.)

Our colleague Lena Langlet is the project manager for Participation Democracy–Citizen Consultation of the Swedish Association of Local Authorities and Regions. In Sweden, as in the United States, there is concern about a decrease in public participation and trust. The number of elected officials in local government is large by American standards. Stockholm, for example, has 101 delegates in the Municipal Council. Because of declining participation, in some communities it is difficult for small political parties to find an adequate number of candidates. Langlet writes, "Perhaps in a country like Sweden with a lengthy period of democracy and peace the individual citizen takes for granted somebody else will care for the functioning of democracy." In Sweden, this development has meant that, "Helping every citizen to take responsibility and engage in the democratic process is one of the greatest challenges of municipalities for safeguarding the development of democracy in an ever more globalized society."

Langlet provides the following example of New Public Service in action in Sweden:

> The Sigtuna municipality is situated outside Stockholm along Lake Mälaren. The municipality consists of an older town center, urban as well as rural areas. The Arlanda airport [the international airport serving Stockholm] is situated in the Sigtuna municipality. In 2004, the municipality decided to give the citizens a greater influence in town-planning matters. In 2005 and 2006 the municipality has carried out 10 public meetings devoted to topical urban planning matters. Every one of these was devoted to a specific issue or area. For example: What will the park look like when we start building a new school? Shall we open a new road or continue keeping it closed?
>
> On every matter, concerned citizens in a particular geographic area have been given the chance to vote for alternatives proposed by the municipality. The citizens have been able to vote via the internet or by letters. In the wake of every consultation great efforts have been undertaken through personal letters, daily press, the internet and information meetings on the spot. In order to further illustrate the proposals, efforts have been undertaken visually to illustrate what it is all going to look like. For example, a long cake was baked to show the aspects of a proposed road, and local festival visitors received written information about the proposal. Two balloons were elevated to illustrate the height of a building according to various alternatives. The elected representatives also visited the area during the electoral period to answer questions and receive ideas. According to the municipal commissioner these meetings have yielded much more than information about how the particular question is considered because the citizens have taken the opportunity to give their opinions about several

aspects of their neighborhood. Community members participating in the various neighborhood consultations have ranged from a maximum 64 percent of residents and a minimum of 27 percent.

The political majority in the municipality promised to abide by the consultation results, which they have done. The municipality commissioner says that this job is the most fun she has had during her long period as an active politician and that she has engaged with the citizens in a new way and acquired knowledge about how they look upon living in Sigtuna municipality.

Local governments in Sweden are also working to engage young people in community life and the democratic process. For example, the Stockholm suburb of Botkyrka is one of the most ethnically diverse communities in the country, with some 100 nationalities and ethnicities. A municipal youth council was established in 2003, made up of students aged 13–22, who were asked to consider matters related to education and youth recreation. Langlet reported:

> The youth council is considered very successful both because working with it has provided practice in democratic ways of work for students, but also because it has given young people from different parts of the municipality occasions to encounter and understand each other.

Public servants in Italy are also searching for new ways to engage citizens. Our colleague from the University of Siena, Manuella Cocci, sent us her assessment of the New Public Service in action in her country. She points to the province of Turin's use of deliberative democracy in handling a NIMBY (not in my backyard) problem related to the location of two waste treatment facilities (this case study appears in Bobbio 2005).

She writes:

> In 2000, because of their experience with previous citizen protests, the Department of the Environment of the Province of Turin established the project "Don't refuse to make a choice" to encourage direct citizen involvement in the decision making process concerning the location of an incinerator and a landfill. The first step was the implementation of an information campaign. Over four months, citizens were informed about facts and risks associated with the facilities. Brochures and guides were distributed in cafes and many other public places. An effort was made to ensure that these materials represented a variety of views and opinions.
>
> A commission was then established including representatives from every local community: one representative from the council, and one from

the citizens committee, and one from the provider of garbage collection. The deliberations of the commission were characterized by unconstrained discussion using multiple criteria. All of the alternatives were argued and everyone had the opportunity to propose a solution. In the process, questions of both efficiency and social aspects were considered. The commission accomplished both of its goals: to establish the standards to define the list of locations, and then to propose the name of the locations while respecting the standards and the Territorial Plan of the Province; and to identify the contract guarantees to the communities who will be most disadvantaged by the new facilities.

The experience of the City of Bolzano provides a different approach to citizen engagement. Cocci explains:

> Bolzano is the main city of one of the two bilingual Italian regions; in the past it suffered more than other local governments the lack of political interest. The high rate of conflict in this region is partly related to the presence of different ethnic groups; but the problem is more complex than that. To better understand and deal with this conflict, Bolzano initiated a project to conduct anthropologic territorial research. A work team of practitioners and public administrators involved citizens in defining a map of the conflicts classified by their location. The local government realized that even if the citizen interest and involvement had decreased over the years, members of the local community were willing to explain their interests and their needs. So, the problem was not to gain the attention of citizens. Rather, the challenge was to negotiate and develop synergic relationships within and across neighbourhoods. In the second step of the process in 2004, the pilot neighbourhood—Oltreisarco Asiago—started a participative and integrated process for developing a plan of development. The process had a number of objectives: to define urban space; to identify problems and issues; to give more visibility to the city centre as a meeting place for the citizens; to improve the connection between the neighbourhood and the natural environment; and to facilitate the building of social networks.
>
> On the basis of the citizens' needs and requests, a list of projects was proposed. For example, one project was the construction of the cycle track in the main neighbourhood street. This specific project, and others, provided the opportunity for citizens to work with public servants to discuss specific ideas, but also other relevant changes to the neighbourhood, in a dynamic and integrated process.
>
> In 2005, the Strategic Plan of the City of Bolzano won the Department for Public Administration (Dipartimento della Funzione Pubblica) Prize for being one of the most creative and well-done examples of a local

government planning document in Italy. The strategic planning process was characterized by negotiation and participation. From the first, the town council met with key social actors, institutions, cultural experts, staff from other public local organizations and services. Then, the department established an information centre in the city in order to explain, on the basis of pilot ideas, what kind of changes could be proposed.

Ad hoc work teams (called *cantieri*) were formed by citizens, external experts, and public administrators to identify and solve the problems of the community. A quantitative and qualitative measurement of citizens' desires was conducted: the citizens were asked to define the score of importance of 25 ideas; from those 25 main ideas emerged 8 that were most important for the citizens. Beyond these main ideas, the teams of discussion defined strategic decisions and operational objectives by which to put into practice the general targets. In May 2006, the final strategic plan was approved. The Strategic Plan process improved the interactivity between public administrators and citizens based on a culture of participation and an "active listening democracy."

Although many such efforts, in Italy and elsewhere, are relatively new, Cocci also writes about what she calls "an old Italian experience of citizen engagement" in the city of Grottammare:

Although in the 1990s most European Local Governments were characterized by New Public Management reforms, Grottammare, a small Municipality in the Centre of Italy, distinguished itself from the others by using citizen engagement to develop solutions to the problems they faced. Instead of looking to public sector models and ideas, Grottammare, through the political movement "Solidarity and Participation" (*Solidarietà e Partecipazione*), found a method to listen to the citizens, and set up, for the first time in the city, neighbourhood associations and neighbourhood committees as a means of fostering communication and participation. These neighbourhood associations and committees remain the most important tools of external communication, involving non-profit organizations, service providers and citizens. As a result, the city is able to make public policy supported by shared interests and shared responsibilities.

In the ten years of participation experience, qualitative research on the results found that: (1) the first neighbourhoods to take part [in] the participation process were the ones with most problematic situations; (2) approximately 124 decision processes were developed in ten years of citizen participation; (3) almost 90 percent of the citizens' propositions were realized; (4) in general, opportunistic individual interests were substituted by the public interest; and (5) the city's development is faster than the Local Government decisions taken without citizen involvement.

In 2004, the City of Grottammare won the "Roberto Villirillo—Good Practices in Public Services Award" (Premio Roberto Villirillo–Buone pratiche nei servizi di pubblica utilità) given by CittadinanzaAttiva (www.cittadinanzattiva.it).

Alternative Approaches

In addition to the more detailed cases described above, we want to highlight some of the many different approaches and avenues to enhanced citizen participation and engagement, ranging from surveys to social networking, from collaborative planning to theater. Again, these approaches represent a small sampling of the wide variety of creative approaches being used across the country and around the world.

Using Citizen Surveys

Surveys, citizen panels, and focus groups, singly or together, can be used for a variety of purposes, from measuring preferences and soliciting opinions to engaging citizens in ongoing dialogue. The citizen surveys that were initially used in government in the 1970s and 1980s tended to be non-representative and unsystematic. Since that time, surveys have become increasingly sophisticated and, particularly when coupled with other tools, can be used as an effective method of citizen engagement in their own right.

Stand-alone surveys, which can be written, electronic, or based on telephone polling, are best used to solicit information, ideas, and opinions. They have been used successfully to gather information on, for example, budget priorities, support for particular programs, the evaluation of services, and even preferences with regard to the types of citizen engagement citizens prefer (Glaser, Yeagar, and Parker 2006; Watson, Juster, and Johnson 1991). The strength of surveys is that they can produce quantitative information. However, that is also their potential weakness. If surveys are poorly designed, the information can be misleading or incorrect, while having the appearance of objectivity. Another disadvantage, of course, is that one-time surveys and polls cannot account for what can sometimes be rapid changes in public opinion.

Sharing Information through Small Groups

There are a host of traditional and newly emerging methods for informing the public and inviting its input. Additional ways to share information offer the opportunity for citizens and officials to interact with each other, contribute and listen, and discuss issues that are important to them. What distinguishes engagement from participation in these approaches is that participants do not merely receive information or deliver their message; in addition, they have the chance to learn from each other.

To design a small-group or focus-group discussion as an exchange of information, it is common to structure the interaction with these steps: provide briefing with background information and facts on the issue at hand, ask for questions and comments from the audience, and perhaps get reactions to proposals from the organizers or the participants. Participants may be informed by such discussions, but they often leave the meeting with the same opinions about the issue that they brought with them, and they may be more sharply divided from persons holding differing views than they were before.

Peter Block (2008) urges leaders to approach issues differently in order to increase the possibility for "authentic engagement." This entails creating a context that nurtures an alternative future, one that builds on personal and community assets rather than problems—assets such as generosity, accountability, and mutual commitment (29–30). The leaders, initiating and convening conversations that shift people's experience and perspective, must listen and pay attention to what the participants say. Block stresses the importance of convening conversations in small-group settings: "every large group meeting needs to use small groups to create connection and move the action." The small group is "the unit of transformation," he says, because it creates a sense of intimacy: "The intimacy makes the process personal. It provides the structure where people overcome isolation and where the experience of belonging is created" (96).

Utilizing the Internet and Social Media

Information and communication technology is changing the way people relate to each other, the way that government communicates with citizens, and the way that governmental employees and staff do their work individually and organizationally. These new capabilities have already changed the exchange relationships between government and citizens, for example, by providing new methods of service delivery, and they are opening up new opportunities for engagement as well. Social media are particularly useful for involving younger citizens, as illustrated in a Wikiplanning project in San Jose, California, and include emerging "digital neighborhoods" linked by face-to-face communication as well as new technologies. With social networking, new forms of citizen engagement are emerging as well. Examples of bidirectional interaction and discussion between government officials and citizens include posting comments to blogs and Facebook fan pages.

Online forums to discuss issues in a constructive way are becoming more common. Open City Hall, for example, is operated by Peak Democracy, a nonpartisan company based in the San Francisco Bay area. Peak Democracy helps local governments by setting up electronic forums that feature current issues for public input, monitoring submissions to ensure civil discourse, and providing a variety of formatted summaries for residents and for the host government. Open City Hall offers both information and the opportunity for input, and it provides convenient access for residents to read the ideas of others. Persons responding are encouraged to consider the opinions of others rather than simply taking sides.

These examples show how technology can be used to create a new kind of "public commons" (Gibson 2006). Indeed, methods of "distributed democracy" can draw citizens into the identification, organization, prioritization, and solving of pressing issues. The online venue may be organized by the government as a community forum or an open process for developing a plan for the city's future, or it might be a shared effort such as digital neighborhood channels that blend citizen networking and staff communications.

Nabatchi and Mergel (2010) highlight best practices, including a program called the "Virginia Idea Forum," through which citizens submit, discuss, and collaborate on ideas for improvement. At the local level, Bryer (2010) points to a program called "Manor Labs," in Manor, Texas, where citizens are invited to post proposals for innovation. But, in this instance, citizens are awarded points called "innobucks" for submitting ideas and commenting on others' ideas, with top awards given to those whose ideas are implemented. These points can be spent on "police ride-alongs, meals donated by local restaurants or a chance to serve as a mayor for a day. City officials evaluate the suggestions and every decision is made in plain view on the site" (Bryers 2010).

At the Berkeley, California-based Center for Digital Stories, numerous groups and individuals have created word-and-image stories and used them as the basis for further community discussion. For example, the Department of Education at the University of California at Santa Cruz and local nonprofits in Watsonville, California, used digital stories to invite dialogue among students, parents, teachers, and university faculty about how poverty and oppression impede reform efforts and to develop new ideas for improvements.

Deliberation and Dialogue

As we noted earlier in this chapter, there are also approaches that have as their primary focus making the dialogue and deliberation around the resolution of particular issues more effective and constructive. Deliberation is different from other approaches because it focuses on examining solutions. Rather than information exchange or sharing, deliberation and dialogue emphasize the processing of information in order to come to some resolve about action. As defined by the National Coalition for Dialogue and Deliberation, dialogue involves people sharing perspectives and experiences with regard to complex issues (http://ncdd.org/rc/what-are-dd). The emphasis is on understanding and learning. Deliberation is closely related, with an emphasis on logic and reasoning to make sound decisions. Often, dialogue and the trust, mutual understanding, and relationships it promotes provide the foundation for deliberation. Thus, although particular methods may place greater emphasis on dialogue or deliberation, they can be viewed as interrelated.

There are similar elements in these approaches, but four variations are common: community decision-making dialogues, facilitated and technology-assisted community forums, citizens coming together to solve a problem, and extended interaction in activities such as study circles that enable participants to increase their awareness of the perspectives and life experiences of others. Among these, the citizen jury or panel is a technique that has gained popularity. Citizen panels are a relatively new form of citizen engagement modeled on the jury system used in the courts. The first official use of citizen juries engaged 60 jurors, organized into five juries, to consider the effects of agriculture on water quality in Minnesota (Crosby, Kelly, and Shaefer 1986). According to the nonprofit Jefferson Center for New Democratic Processes website:

> In a Citizens Jury project, a randomly selected and demographically representative panel of citizens meets for four or five days to carefully examine an issue of public significance. The jury of citizens, usually consisting of 18–24 individuals, serves as a microcosm of the public. Jurors are paid a stipend for their time. They hear from a variety of expert witnesses and are able to deliberate together on the issue. On the final day of their moderated hearings, the members of the Citizens Jury present their recommendations to decision-makers and the public. Citizens Jury projects can be enhanced through extensive communication with the public, including a dynamic web presence and significant media contacts.
>
> (http://jefferson-center.org/what-we-do/citizen-juries/)

Service Delivery and Problem Identification

Service delivery can be an important arena for ongoing citizen engagement. As Thomas (2010) argues, citizens can partner with government in coproduction of a service. In addition, citizen engagement in service delivery can be advanced by encouraging volunteer activity and promoting interaction with others in addressing shared concerns, such as citizen-based neighborhood improvement efforts. Coproduction by itself is a form of exchange between the local government and citizens in which the residents take some responsibility for producing a service (Thomas 2010). A common example is separating recyclable material from other trash and placing it in a separate container for collection. The resident is making a contribution, and the action may foster a realization of the shared responsibility for protecting the environment and making better use of resources. Thus, coproduction can enhance the "citizen" rather than "customer" perspective.

Citizens can also be directly involved in the collection of information about local problems as they occur. For example, in Durham, North Carolina, citizens have used cameras and handheld computers to rate local services and record community conditions such as traffic hazards, graffiti, or other problems. The City of Phoenix also encourages citizens to document signs of urban decay by cell-phone cameras, so that the problems might be addressed by the city.

Using the Arts

One of the challenges of citizen engagement is to attract people who are not typically involved in local government activities. Approaches that use the arts involve the whole person and invite citizens to draw on their own experiences and creativity to express thoughts and ideas that might otherwise be too difficult to communicate. A wide variety of tools can be used to create these kinds of opportunity, including art, dance, theater, and storytelling. Approaching citizen engagement through the arts means getting creative:

> Citizens can be reached and engaged if they are offered ways to take part that are interesting and satisfying in themselves, that combine learning and doing, that engage not only their participation, but their creativity. Of all forms of citizen engagement, the most powerful approaches in breaking the participation barrier involve the whole person, which is best done with the methods and techniques of art, where people can put their hands, hearts, hopes and heads into advancing the public good.

(Goldbard 2010)

One advantage of using the arts is that it can engage people who might otherwise shy away from approaches that require prior knowledge of governmental terminology, structures, and processes.

Neighborhood Organizations and Homeowners Associations

Neighborhood organizations, citizen councils, and homeowners associations (HOAs) have emerged in many U.S. cities and towns as tools of citizen engagement and self-governance (Leighninger 2008). McCabe (2010) points out that different organizations play different roles, and the manner in which they interact with local government, and the extent, can create either opportunities or impediments to citizen engagement and community building. The distinction between community and neighborhood can create a double-edged sword in citizen engagement. Communities are based on broad "networks of connection," whereas neighborhoods tend to be place-bound (Chaskin 2001, 2003). This distinction can result in competing interests and values between neighborhoods and the broader community.

Although neighborhoods and neighborhood-based organizations can play an important role in enhancing civic engagement (Leroux 2007), they can also create "civic cocoons" that insulate and isolate residents from the broader community (Benest 1999). How these tensions are balanced depends, in part, on the type of organization and its purpose. Neighborhood

A group of residents in a South Texas community were trained in "Theater of the Oppressed" techniques to assess community knowledge of threats such as lead poisoning and asthma and their prevention. Then, the troupe created dramatic scenes accurately representing ground-level environmental facts and modeling successful grass-roots responses. Finally, the group created a finished show to tour the community, inviting further involvement.

Participatory photography projects can also be an innovative and relatively inexpensive way to use creativity and art to engage citizens. In the People's Portrait Project in Mendocino, in rural northern California, residents, from toddlers to senior citizens, were lent point-and-shoot cameras "to capture images of community life: people, places, problems, signs of promise." A participatory process was used to create a composite portrait that was displayed in community centers and libraries.

organizations, councils, and HOAs can be effective vehicles to engage citizens, but government must actively collaborate and coordinate with these groups to maintain a balance of community and neighborhood goals and interests.

Creating Participatory or Collaborative Organizations

Catlaw and Rawlings (2010, 124) point out that, "the upshot of the research on workplace participation or influence is that 'participation breeds participation.'" When employees have opportunities to contribute meaningfully to the activities of the workplace, they are more likely to be involved in political and community activities outside work. If they are able to shape their work and influence the methods used to achieve objectives, they are more likely to be receptive to interaction with other citizens about what government is doing and how it is performing. The organization can develop the disposition and skills that contribute to citizen engagement and shape attitudes about the openness of the decision-making process. Staff members can enhance their skills in communication, critical thinking, and small-group processes that can be modeled and encouraged in interactions with citizens. If public employees experience group problem solving, consensus-based decision making, and job autonomy in their own work, they are likely to be more receptive to opening up decision making to include citizens.

Interestingly, many of the changes in organizational values and process that have been identified as contributing to recruiting and retaining the "next generation" of local government professionals are relevant to strengthening citizen engagement (Benest 2007; Svara 2010). The service orientation and cross-sectoral perspective of young professionals make them receptive to the methods that promote citizen engagement. It is likely that greater opportunity

> The HOA known as Verrado, in Buckeye, Arizona, has about 30,000 residents, promotes citizen interaction through its physical design (featuring front porches and shaded walks), has its own town manager and community engagement manager, and publishes a monthly newsletter. Nonetheless, although the HOA manager involves himself in the larger community, some Verrado residents sought nominal secession from the traditional, poor municipality of Buckeye, suggesting that at least some residents feel a sense of connection with their HOA community but not their city.

for these staff members to interact with citizens and community organizations will make working in local government more attractive to them. These are people who are looking for the opportunity to participate in the management of the organization and have access to community partnerships and networks. They are also skillful at, and receptive to, social networking with new technologies.

Choosing When and How to Use Citizen Engagement Tools

Here, we have discussed a variety of alternative approaches to citizen engagement. In general, what we have found is that all these approaches and others can be highly effective or largely ineffective. What appears to be most important from a citizen's perspective and from the standpoint of attaining ongoing engagement is not the strategy employed, but the government's response when citizens voice their preferences. For citizens, two questions are paramount: Did the government listen and take action based on what it heard? Was the response worth the citizens' time and effort?

A fundamental point is that citizen engagement must involve actual engagement, rather than simply an exchange of information. The basic test of engagement is whether citizens have the opportunity to discuss ideas or efforts with other citizens and officials in order to better understand each other. A task force in a city recently held sessions in multiple locations that were billed as opportunities for citizen engagement to discuss a sensitive issue involving friction between residents and the police. However, there was no opportunity to talk in small groups or to pose larger questions. It is likely that both the city representatives and the citizens who attended the session went away frustrated and feeling that the city or the residents were not interested in constructive action.

Another guiding principle is that engagement activities should be citizen-centered (Gibson 2006). Governments should move beyond traditional methods and venues, address issues that people perceive to be important, and meet citizens where they are in order to get them engaged. If the citizen participation goal is just to increase turnout at a hearing on the comprehensive plan revision at city hall, the outcome is not likely to be successful in attracting participants or particularly productive. On the other hand, a well-publicized series of roundtable discussions on significant local issues in Decatur, Georgia, held in multiple locations, drew over 700 citizens.

Governments should incorporate other places and organizations in which people are already interacting. Government officials should look for others to be the conveners, rather than organizing all activities themselves. For example, getting residents to become more involved in improving their neighborhood must start with the concerns that residents express at meetings convened by a person or group already known to residents. Meetings can then be organized in ways that encourage participants to look at an issue more broadly and learn from each other and officials how to address it.

A major choice is whether to undertake or seek to foster a large, deliberative decision-making project and to give citizens a significant role in making a major policy choice. The first factor is the degree to which the problem is structured or unstructured. A structured problem is one for which information is available and alternatives and expected outcomes are known. In these situations, not only may there be less need to engage the public in the decision-making process, but citizen involvement may be shallow and ineffectual in helping citizens learn from each other and form attachments to the community.

If, however, the problem is unstructured, information is lacking, there is conflict or controversy, and/or citizen acceptance is needed for legitimacy and effective action, citizen engagement efforts are more often appropriate, necessary, and effectual (see Thomas 1995, 2010; Walters, Aydelotte, and Miller 2000). As Roberts (2008) points out, "wicked" or intractable problems require trade-off and value choices, and the only way to successfully address them is through more rather than less participation and through greater opportunity for deliberation.

The complexity of the issue can also be related to another factor: time constraints. If an issue, even a complex one, must be decided in a very short time, it may not be well suited to a broad-based public engagement process. However, the degree to which an issue is time limited can easily be overestimated. Time constraints on public policy decisions are often more flexible than first assumed, and the public may object if they think a decision has been made too quickly (Thomas 1995). Further, "although citizen engagement takes time, it also affords time for meaningful dialogue and deliberations" (Roberts 2008, 494). Besides, time constraints on both decision making and implementation may be inversely related—time saved on the decision-making process by limiting involvement may slow implementation.

Perhaps the most important factor to be considered is whether decision makers are willing to listen and take into account the result of citizen engagement in decision making. A guide to citizen engagement prepared by the Swedish Association of Local Authorities and Regions (2010) states that, "citizen dialogue must be meaningful . . . people must know that they are being listened to, and get feedback on how their views have been taken into account." To ensure that this is the case, before a citizen engagement initiative is embarked upon, there must be commitment and "honest intent" by both politicians and public officials within the locality to use the information and preferences expressed by the community. It is also important to then be clear and specific with participants about their role in the decision-making process. Further, determining who will be involved and how the process will be managed should itself be an open process.

The relationship between the ideas generated in the process of engagement and the decisions taken by officials is complex. Citizen engagement is not an alternative to representative government. Empowerment of citizens is not the top rung in a contest of control, but rather one of the optional ways that citizens can be involved that will be appropriate to some situations but not to others. If active citizen engagement occurs, the jurisdiction does not have to be divided into camps of officials and citizens. The views of officials will be affected through dialogue with citizens and vice versa when there is ongoing interaction, rather than isolated instances of citizen review and advice.

Conclusion

In this chapter, we have discussed specific and practical ways in which the New Public Service might be implemented in conjunction with new approaches to citizen engagement. We conclude with the following summary:

- Consistent with the New Public Service, citizen engagement is both the "smart" and the "right" thing to do to achieve effective democratic governance.
- Creating an engaged and connected community can involve both citizen "exchange" activities, to inform, collect information, invite input, and consult, as well as citizen "engagement" activities, to encourage collaboration between citizens and officials, create dialogue around key questions and issues, build relationships, and empower citizens to make decisions and take responsibility for their community.
- Citizen engagement involves decisions about policies and priorities, as well as service delivery.
- There are a wide range of strategies and approaches for generating and sharing information, deliberating on issues and policies, delivering services, and building a sense of community. These approaches can be used effectively in combination with each other.
- To increase the likelihood of success, it is important to match the methods used to the intended purpose, to make clear what the role and potential impact of citizens will be, and to listen to citizens and honestly explain how their views have been taken into account.

- Citizen engagement must "belong" to citizens and government alike. The government or government agency has a special obligation and opportunity to view the process holistically, build attachment to the broader community, and seek to fill gaps through its own actions or those of other actors. It must also be receptive to, and supportive of, initiatives from citizens.

The following is a preliminary set of specific and practical recommendations:

- Citizens and officials should undertake a dialogue on citizen engagement to identify how citizens wish to be involved in shaping community life and how the government or government agency can contribute to meeting citizens' aspirations.
- Public agencies should honestly assess what they are trying to accomplish through citizen engagement and consider whether they are willing and able to listen to, and act on, what they hear.
- Governments and public agencies should examine what they are doing to involve citizens through exchange and engagement activities and how these activities can be expanded and refocused:
  - How can exchanges be expanded to create greater public awareness and transparency and to expand citizen input?
  - Are there opportunities to engage citizens in a dialogue about issues and problems that are currently handled with one-way exchanges?
  - What new activities should the local government pursue to advance the goals of citizen engagement and community building?
- Governments should expand capacity for engagement by:
  - supporting efforts to educate and enable citizens to act;
  - developing the skills of their staff members; and
  - encouraging participation and shared responsibility among staff members in their internal operations in order to foster a positive climate and develop skills for citizen engagement.
- Public agencies should examine ways to connect participants in various citizen engagement activities to each other, link separate engagement activities, and build new ventures on previous ones.
- Public officials should seek to expand the diversity of participants in engagement activities and to broaden participation by persons who differ in background, age, location, and other characteristics.

- Governments and their community partners should work to broaden the scope of issues they address by using citizen engagement approaches—for example, moving beyond community goal setting to examine ways to alleviate persistent social and economic problems.
- Public officials should develop measures of the outcomes of engagement approaches, the number and range of participants, the quality of participation, the change in public attitudes, and the extent to which people have come together to resolve important community issues.

The New Public Service is and will continue to be realized in both small moments and large activities, in conversations and public pronouncements, in formal rules and informal behavior. The cases and examples presented in this chapter hopefully offer a glimpse into the kinds of effort that organizations and individuals in towns and cities and states, and at the national level, are experimenting with to try to enhance citizen engagement and service in the public interest.

Portions of this chapter are based on a 2010 white paper, "Connected Communities," prepared by James Svara and Janet Denhardt for the Alliance for Innovation (http://transformgov.org/en/home). The alliance is an international network of progressive governments working in partnership with the International City/County Management Association and Arizona State University to transform local government and promote excellence by accelerating the development and dissemination of innovations.

Chapter 11

Fifteen Years Later

Are We Rowing, Steering, or Serving?

Since the New Public Service first appeared as a *PAR* article in 2000, there have been major shifts in how we understand the challenges we face in a variety of public policy arenas, such as health and the environment, safety and security, technology and information, governance and global interdependence. Over the past 15 years, we have seen doctors map the human genome and achieve medical advances, giving us a foothold with some of the world's most intractable diseases. Technology has utterly transformed society, business, and government, with the launch of Facebook in 2004 ushering in an era of social media and virtual community. The first black president of the United States was inaugurated in 2008. During this same 15-year period, we faced both natural disasters and terrorist attacks that tested the resilience of the public sector and highlighted instances of both heroism and weakness. Global economic collapse challenged governments around the world to provide more services with less money. In light of these and other dramatic changes, we now ask: How have the values of the New Public Service fared over the past 15 years?

One way to evaluate the impact of the New Public Service is by looking at its presence in the academic literature. As Bryson, Crosby and Bloomberg note in their 2014 analysis of competing value-based frameworks represented in the literature in the field of public administration, there may not be a clear consensus, but, "New Public Service certainly appears to be the leading contender" (2014).

Certainly, a great deal of important work has been published that addresses the key questions raised by the New Public Service. This research has moved the discussion forward, outward, and beyond to consider new conceptual frameworks and issues. Consider, for example, works that have built on the foundations laid by the New Public Service, including Zeemering (2008) on the importance of cross-boundary cooperation among constituencies affected by service delivery; Nabatchi and Mergel (2010) on the necessity for administrators to view governance in terms of networks of public–private arrangements that present opportunities for citizen participation; Meijer (2011) on the ways in which Dutch citizens have helped each other and reduced government workloads by taking advantage of online forums for government benefit recipients; Terry (2005) on the weakening of administrative institutions; Fung (2013) on the importance of transparency in enabling citizens to hold institutions accountable; Nalbandian (2008) on the heightened need for citizen engagement in increasingly complex local governance contexts; and Durant and Ali (2013) on continuing citizen estrangement despite administrative reforms. These are but a few examples of the wealth of critical analysis that continues to test and add to the tenets of the New Public Service.

It appears that the field of public administration's ardor for the New Public Management—popularized by Osborne and Gaebler (1992), Ferlie (1996), and Pollitt (1993), among others—has noticeably cooled over the last decade. According to Raadschnelders and Lee's 2011 evaluation of *PAR* articles from 2000 to 2009, the New Public Management "dominated the study and practice of public administration over the past three decades." They also point out, however, that, "During the past decade . . . NPM increasingly met with criticism of its limitations and disadvantages" (2011, 25). Similarly, Bryson et al. observe, "Just as traditional public administration was overshadowed as the dominant view in the 1980s and 1990s by the New Public Management, we believe that a new movement is underway that is likely to eclipse New Public Management" (2014).

Many in the field of public administration have voiced skepticism about the usefulness and application of the New Public Management and the use of business practices and models. Raadschelders and Lee, for example, observe that various researchers and theorists have found that the success of New Public Management is, somewhat paradoxically, based on the administrative capacity of government (Brown and Potoski 2003; Yang, Hsieh, and Lie 2009), and that it hasn't paid adequate attention to politics, law, and culture (Haruna 2003; Kassel 2008; Riccuci and Thompson 2008). Raadschelders and Lee note additionally that some scholars maintain that legislative and judicial constraints have been overlooked (Reed and Meyer

2004), and that the New Public Management has eroded accountability to citizens and civil society (Eikenberry and Kluver 2004; Kelly 2005; Romzek and Johnston 2005).

This doesn't necessarily mean, however, that the New Public Management hasn't retained much of its hold over the day-to-day work of public administration practitioners, who may remain more impressed by the promise of increased efficiency and effectiveness than their academic counterparts. In other words, scholarly critiques of theory may not immediately equate to changes in practice. Further, there is little question that the use of New Public Management techniques and approaches has had a significant and often positive effect on government practices over the past two decades. Although it may not have lived up to the expectations of those who argued that it would "fix" the problems of government, its mark on the public sector remains clearly visible. Governments are still using business models to contract services, city officials still frequently refer to their "customers" rather than citizens, and, as always, efficiency remains a hallmark of public administration practice (Callahan 2010; Rho 2013; Terry 2005).

Researchers are increasingly finding, however, that, in practice, New Public Management is less efficient and effective than expected (Leland and Smirnova 2009; Lenkowsky and Perry 2000; Moynihan 2006; Thompson 2000), and that there remains a disconnect between theory and practice (Van Slyke 2003; Williams 2000). The dominance of the New Public Management that we found in 2000 is not borne out in research and practice in 2015. In this chapter, we present the empirical evidence relevant to the application of the New Public Service in practice, as well as analyzing the manner in which core value conflicts between politics and administration, bureaucracy and democracy, and even fact and value, continue.

We ask four questions in order to present an update on the development of related theory and practice since our original publication in 2000: (1) Does citizen engagement work? (2) How have the values of the public interest and collaborative leadership fared in relation to models based on self-interest? (3) Has the reliance on market models of entrepreneurship and privatization decreased? (4) Are we rowing, steering, or serving? We conclude with an assessment of possible future directions for the field of public administration as it struggles to match its practices and its ideals.

Does Citizen Engagement Work?

Evidence shows that, when deliberative processes are used to create two-way communications and agencies are responsive to what they hear, there are positive gains in terms of citizenship, trust, and the quality of decisions. For example, Beierle and Cayford analyzed the results of 239 cases of public engagement in environmental policymaking, based on the extent to which: (1) public values were incorporated into decisions, (2) the substantive quality of decisions was improved, (3) conflict was resolved, (4) trust was built in the lead agency, and (5) the public became better educated and informed. Overall, they found that the results "paint an encouraging picture," and that such participation "frequently produce(s) decisions that are responsive to public values and substantively robust, but it also helps to resolve conflict, build trust, and educate and inform the public" (2002, 74). They further found that the process used makes all the difference: "Processes in which agencies are responsive, participants are motivated, the quality of deliberation is high, and participants have at least a moderate degree of control over the process are more successful" (74).

In examining citizen engagement practices around the world, Innes and Booher found that, when collaborative processes were used, the benefits became clear. There are numerous examples of collaborative dialogue in budgeting that have resulted in "agreements that were otherwise politically impossible." Dialogue has also been shown to defuse racial tensions, build social capital, and enhance civic capacity (2004, 427).

Along the same lines, Brainard and McNutt (2011) studied the use of online citizen discussion groups by the Washington, DC, Police Department. They found that most of these discussions could not be characterized as collaborative. Instead, the bulk of the activity was focused on giving or exchanging information. Importantly, however, in those instances when "police did take on a more facilitative, collaborative approach, residents responded positively and collaborative problem solving did occur ... This holds true even for District 7," which had one of the highest crime and poverty rates in the city (853, 844).

The reverse argument also seems to be confirmed: If citizen engagement is done in an *inauthentic* manner, based on a mistrust of citizens and one-way communication, with restricted access and little follow-through, it not only will not "work," but it may damage citizenship and trust and reduce the capacity of the governance system (Innes and Booher 2004). It has become increasingly clear that, not only do the more traditional methods of participation not work, they can actually be harmful. Legally mandated public hearings and comment periods do "not achieve genuine participation," fail to make people feel heard, seldom improve decisions, and do not involve a broad cross-section of the public. Worse, these approaches antagonize the public and create greater polarization (Innes and Booher 2004, 419).

Unfortunately, most of what is called citizen participation is not the sort of deliberative dialogue and engagement that is advocated by the New Public Service. So, in a sense, those who claim that citizen participation doesn't work are absolutely correct if they are referring to the traditional mechanisms. Conversely, when done well, citizen dialogue and engagement have the opposite effect: they build citizenship, trust, and capacity.

This makes it very difficult to interpret the findings of studies that purport to measure the effects of public "participation," when participation is defined as everything from a public hearing to filling out a survey and/or attending a series of neighborhood meetings. When all of those approaches are included (e.g. Wang 2001), it is not surprising that the results are mixed.

Of course, although evidence shows the effectiveness of citizen engagement, the arguments behind the New Public Service are clearly normative. How important are these values in the decisions about how to use citizen engagement strategies? Are citizen engagement initiatives used for management or political expediency, or because they are the right thing to do? Yang and Callahan (2007) suggest that there are three possible drivers: (1) the presence of pressure to do so from external stakeholders; (2) the nature of managerial attitudes regarding the value of participation; and (3) perceived obstacles, including resources, capacity, and structural barriers. Based on a survey of local governments, these researchers found that citizen involvement efforts do reflect all three of these drivers, but that public managers' attitudes had the greatest explanatory power: "the most important factor in citizen involvement decisions is the attitude public managers hold towards the value of participation." On the other hand, when public participation is done grudgingly or as a marginal addition, "the most that can be hoped for . . . is that they do no harm" (Beierle and Cayford 2002, 75).

Coursey et al. (2012) looked at data from the National Administrative Studies Project and found that a manager's public service motivation and perceived commitment to citizen participation "affect managerial attitudes towards participation in both direct and indirect ways." In other words, recruiting and retaining public servants who have high levels of public service motivation, particularly when they perceive a high level of organizational support for participation, are likely to lead to desirable participation outcomes. Although, on one level, this may appear almost self-evident, given the similarity of the constructs, it also speaks to the importance of democratic values. In the absence of these values, citizen participation is more likely to be marginal and inauthentic, and more likely to "not work." If you believe the idea that people are only self-interested, almost by definition, you are unlikely to engage in politics and governmental concerns beyond what is legally required.

This suggests that the normative component of the New Public Service has important implications for practice. If public managers question traditional assumptions and methods of citizen participation, and they instead value citizen engagement and dialogue as essential to democratic governance, they may be more likely to (1) use approaches that are more intensive, and (2) be more responsive to what citizens say. Research suggests that doing so will likely have positive effects on decision making, citizenship, and governance.

Although a review of the research on the effectiveness of various approaches to citizen participation points to mixed results, it is equally apparent that the vast majority of researchers conclude that we should not abandon the citizen engagement experiment. Rather, agencies should do more to ensure that the approaches they use are well planned, authentic, and include two-way citizen dialogue (Lukensmeyer, Goldman, and Stern 2011),

The fact that online technologies and social media have transformed citizen engagement in the last decade should also be highlighted. There has been a growing recognition that, in order for citizen engagement to be effective, citizens need access to information. New forms of transparency have emerged in the United States and in other countries in the past decade, in part as a result of expanding information technology. In 2011, the United States and seven other governments (United Kingdom, Brazil, Indonesia, Mexico, Norway, Philippines, and South Africa) initiated "Open Government Partnership" programs to provide their citizens with access to government data that had not been readily accessed previously (Fung 2013). In the United States, President Obama's commitment to open government ushered in a new era of citizen access through the Internet.

A 2011 assessment of public participation in federal agencies under the Open Government Directive included examples from the U.S. Departments of Labor, Defense, Homeland Security, Energy, Interior, Justice, Treasury, and others using online technologies. Federal departments are using crowdsourcing, online contests, online town halls, wikis, and a wide variety of social media to solicit input, build relationships, and encourage collaboration (Lukensmeyer et al. 2011, 17–18). Although there is much work still to be done, many federal agencies "are taking important initial steps to embed a culture of participation in their organizations."

In short, citizen engagement that does not rely on traditional, legally mandated participation mechanisms, but instead embraces authentic dialogue, has been shown to produce positive effects on decision making, citizenship, and governance. Citizen engagement has become increasingly important in governance at all levels, providing a significant and growing counterpoint to models based solely on "customer service" and the market.

How Have the Values of the Public Interest, Shared Leadership, and Collaboration Fared?

New Public Management advocates claimed that the public interest is either irrelevant or nonexistent, favoring instead a reliance on individual choice as it is exercised in a market. The aggregation of individual choices based on self-interest was assumed to the best means to determine and achieve policy objectives. Public servants were encouraged to act as entrepreneurs and to take action to ensure marketlike efficiency.

In the New Public Service, on the other hand, the search for a shared view of the public interest, based on an open, inclusive, and informed discussion of values and tradeoffs, should be a guiding principle in the public service. Over the last decade, the ideal of the public interest—defined by Perry and Wise (1990) as "an individual's predisposition to respond to motives primarily or uniquely in public institutions and organizations"—has been explored in a variety of ways, including as a component of public service motivation. Perry (1996) suggested that there are four dimensions to measuring public service motivation: (1) attraction to policymaking, (2) commitment to the public interest, (3) compassion, and (4) self-sacrifice.

This framework served as a catalyst for extensive subsequent research on public service motivation. In 2010, Perry, Hondegon, and Wise reviewed 20 years of research and concluded that, although there were methodological and other issues, there was general support for the idea that public service motivation leads people to choose public service work, and that it is positively related to performance. They contrast public service motivation's reliance on the idea that behavior is motivated by a desire to do good for others and serve the public interest with the self-interest motivations assumed by public choice and New Public Management perspectives and find that the former is more significant.

The ideal of the public interest has also played an interesting role in arguments about privatization and contracting out, which will be discussed more fully in the section that follows. A key tenet of New Public Management is the idea that business can deliver services much more cheaply and efficiently than government, and, therefore, governments should privatize or "contract out" public services when possible, to take advantage of private-sector competition and freedom from governmental red tape. On the other hand, one of the primary conceptual arguments against privatization is that private, for-profit interests might devalue the public interest and values such as equity, representativeness, and fairness.

Advocates of the New Public Service contend that the concept of the public interest is central to public administration and related work. Or, as Bozeman put it, in working to create a collective, shared notion of the public interest, public administrators should seek, not quick fixes to problems derived from individual choices, but rather to provide help in creating shared interests and responsibility (2007).

As already noted, early public choice theorists actually seem to agree with the New Public Service on this point. These theorists were much more resistant to dismissing the role of the public interest in arrangements involving privatization and coproduction. For example, Ostrom, Tiebout, and Warren stated, in 1961, that cooperative arrangements work when they "produce a greater return to all parties concerned, *if the appropriate set of public interests is adequately represented among the negotiators*" (1961, 833; emphasis added). Moreover, because of the wide range of stakeholders and perspectives involved in the many public issues, it is most effective and responsible to use collective, collaborative approaches to operate programs targeting public needs. Collaboration and shared leadership that are grounded in respect for all people have been proven to be crucial in predicting long-term success for public organizations and the networks to which they belong.

There is no question that collaboration and shared leadership are significant trends in public administration scholarship and practice. One indicator of this trend is the publication of a special issue of the *PAR* (2006) on "Collaborative Public Management." For the purposes of the symposium, the editors defined collaborative public management as the process of facilitating and operating in multi-organizational arrangements to solve problems that cannot be solved or easily solved by single organizations. "Collaborative means to *co-labor*, to cooperate to achieve common goals, working across boundaries in multi-sector relationships. Cooperation is based on the value of reciprocity" (O'Leary, Gerard, and Bingham 2006, 7).

Thomson and Perry (2006) suggest five dimensions of collaboration that we might interpret as *challenges* facing any potential leader of a governance network. The first is what Thomson and Perry (2006) call the *governance dimension*, the requirement that parties must come together to jointly make decisions about the rules to govern their activities and develop structures through which power can be shared. Lacking the traditional hierarchical authority structures for policy development and implementation, all parties must recognize the legitimate interests of other parties in the relationship. Obviously, the traditional conceptions of leadership make this difficult to accommodate. The second, the *administration dimension*, is necessary to put ideas into action and, in the best cases, requires "clear roles and responsibilities, the capacity to set boundaries, the presence of concrete achievable goals, and good communication" (Thomson and Perry 2006, 25). Again, leadership strategies that might operate successfully in such an environment must be considerably more open and flexible than is typically the case.

Third is the *autonomy dimension*, that is, the process of reconciling individual and collective interests. Parties to a collaboration or network retain their own distinct identities and allegiances to their "home" organizations, but must simultaneously contribute to the achievement of collective goals and objectives. Many scholars point to this circumstance as perhaps the most challenging to the maintenance of effective governance networks (Tschirhart, Christensen, and Perry 2005; Vigoda-Gadot 2003; Wood and Gray 1991). When individual goals or self-interest conflict with the goals of the collective, holding the network or collaborative together becomes quite difficult. For this reason, one of the requisite skills of leaders in networks is that of arriving at agreement around a set of shared goals or directions (Crevani et al. 2007; Durant and Ali 2008). There is certainly no room for the leader to impose a vision, or control efforts to achieve that vision.

The fourth is the *mutuality dimension*, the idea that, unless all parties receive mutual benefits from the collaboration, either in terms of differing interests or shared interests, the collaboration will not likely be maintained. In contrast to negotiation, which begins from differences, Thomson and Perry (2006) stress the importance of "jointly identifying commonalities among organizations such as similarity of mission, commitment to the target population, or professional orientation and culture" (27). Fifth is the *trust and reciprocity dimension*, which refers to the necessity of establishing conditions of mutual trust among partners to the collaboration and building of both short-term and long-term reciprocity, a willingness to contribute, assuming that others will contribute as well. We argue that trust building is a central leadership skill, especially in governance networks.

McGuire (2006) suggests four such skills: activation, framing, mobilizing, and synthesizing. *Activation* is the process of identifying and bringing into the network the right people and the right resources needed to meet mutually-agreed-upon program goals and objectives. *Framing* has to do with facilitating agreement around leadership and administrative roles and structures, even though those may change and evolve rapidly over time. *Mobilizing* is concerned with gaining commitment to the joint undertaking and building support from those who are participating in the network, as well as those outside. Finally, *synthesizing* involves engendering productive and purposeful interaction among all actors. This again includes facilitating relationships in order to build trust and promote information exchange.

Obviously, traditional leadership models emphasizing hierarchical power, authority based on position, and strict managerial control are ill suited for the modern governance system. And, not surprisingly, these same models are being called into question in other sectors as well. A recent IBM study of public and private CEOs from around the world pointed to the turbulence and complexity of the newly globalized world in which we live. Such circumstances themselves demand something other than command-and-control leadership—something more like flexible, adaptive, and shared leadership. But they also suggest that, rather than turning out repetitive products or services, organizations of the future are going to need to become more creative and innovative. Again, organizations of the past were designed for efficiency in the production of uniform products or services; organizations of the future will need to foster new ideas and creative solutions to ever-changing problems (Feldman 2010).

Has the Reliance on Market Models of Entrepreneurship and Privatization Decreased?

Looking at the history of privatization and contracting paints a picture of less-successful privatization and contracting than the New Public Management predicted. Every five years since 1982, the International City County Management Association has conducted a survey on alternative service-delivery arrangements in local government in the US. Since the survey began, the most common form of service delivery has been through public organizations. In 1992, when Osborne and Gaebler's book was published, 50 percent of services were provided by public employees. By 2002, the percentage of directly provided public services had increased to 59 percent. Five years later, in 2007, 52 percent of services were publically provided. So, with the exception of a modest decrease in contracting in 2002, the level of contracting has remained fairly constant over the past three decades.

This does not tell the whole story, however. What has changed is whom government is contracting with, the nature of those contracts, and the fact that contracting includes both contracting out and contracting back in. From 1992 to 1997, for instance, "on average, governments newly contract out six services and contract back in four services" (Hefetz and Warner 2004, 172). In an analysis of 26 case studies of contracting back in, Ballard and Warner (2000) found that, in most cases, poor service quality, difficulties with contract specifications, and the challenges of monitoring were the reasons for bringing services back in-house. In summarizing the results of their research, Hefetz and Warner state that the data "support the new public service that argues public managers do more than steer a market process; they balance technical and political concerns to secure public value" (171).

It is not just local government managers in the US who are reversing the trend towards privatization. The UK and New Zealand were among the first adherents to New Public Management and market-based approaches to government. Both enacted legislation requiring compulsory competitive contracting in an effort to promote extensive privatization. New Zealand, in particular, served as an exemplar for the New Public Management in the United States (Osborne and Gaebler 1992). Since that time, the UK and Australia have both abolished the requirement for competitive bidding on service contracts, and New Zealand's prime minister is focused on rebuilding the capacity of government for service delivery. The idea behind privatization was that it would give consumer citizens more voice through market choice. The problem is that, in practice, governments typically contract with only one or two providers. In the case of the former, choice is neither increased nor decreased. As a result, "the citizen consumer does not see a choice of providers" and thus has no more choices than when the service is publically provided (Warner 2008, 167). Warner concludes that the experiment to "increase the role of markets in local government service delivery . . . has failed to deliver adequately on efficiency, equity or voice." This does not indicate a return to what we call "old public administration." Rather, "it heralds the emergence of a new balanced position which combines use of markets, democracy, and planning to reach decisions which may be both efficient and more socially optimal" (Warner 2008, 171).

The government's use of full contracts and mixed contracts has also shifted. Full contracts are arrangements where the service is completely contracted out to a nongovernmental entity. Mixed contracts use a combination of public and private employees. "Mixed delivery has been a source of consternation for market advocates, who view such redundancy as potentially inefficient and unnecessary" (163). As Warner and Hefetz found in their analysis of the International City/County Management Association (ICMA) data, in 1992, there were twice as many fully privatized contracts as there were mixed contracts. By 1997, the situation was reversed. There were one and one-half times as many mixed contracts as full contracts. During this time period, full contracts dropped from 33 percent to 18 percent of service delivery. Mixed contracts, on the other hand, went from 18 percent in 1992 to 24 percent five years later. That meant that, by 2002, public services were less likely to be provided by purely outside contracts than in 1992, and that there had been a "dramatic rise in mixed public–private delivery" (2008, 155).

In analyzing these data, Warner and Hefetz arrived at some interesting conclusions. "By remaining directly engaged in service delivery, governments can assure that contractors maintain efficient processes, high quality, competitive costs, and citizen satisfaction" (162). Their review of the empirical evidence suggests that private delivery does not save money over time. Part of the reason for this is the cost of monitoring. As Rho found in studying contracting in public education, "the results using the data over the 12-year period repeatedly confirmed that more contracting generates greater bureaucracy, because of the demands to monitor contracts" (Rho 2013). They suggest that, although privatization remains a "political project," city managers recognize the need to balance efficiency concerns with citizen satisfaction and the costs and challenges of monitoring private contractors.

Are We Rowing, Steering, or Serving?

New Public Management advocates Osborne and Gaebler recommended that government move increasingly away from a service-delivery role (which they call "rowing") toward policy development instead (which they call "steering"). In the New Public Service, we argued that an increasingly important role of the public servant is to serve citizens and communities by helping citizens articulate and meet their shared goals, rather than attempting to control or steer society in new directions. We noted, however, that ensuring accountability for those goals is anything but simple. In our view, public servants need to pay close attention, not only to the market, but also to a long list of other concerns, including local, state, and federal laws, professional standards, and the political climate, as well as community values and citizen interests. Further, public administrators must participate in new governance mechanisms, in which steering and rowing are mixed in convoluted ways. In these situations, administrators are increasingly called on to adopt a new approach to public leadership, one based on serving, facilitating, and collaborating around shared values.

Certainly, since we first wrote about the New Public Service, the design and implementation of public policy has moved even further away from a single governmental unit acting alone or in close concert with one or two others to a complex system featuring governance networks comprised of a plurality of public, private, and nonprofit actors, each bringing their own special interests, resources, and sets of expertise. This circumstance has profound implications for leadership in the public service (and elsewhere), especially as these networks typically rely on nonhierarchical patterns of governance. Sorensen and Torfing (2008) define a governance network as:

> (1) a relatively stable horizontal articulation of interdependent, but operationally autonomous actors; (2) who interact through negotiations; (3) which take place within a . . . normative, cognitive and imaginary framework; (4) that is self-regulating within limits set by external agencies; and (5) which contributes to the production of public purpose.

(9)

Similarly, in the same volume, Börzel and Panke (2006) define network governance as "the formulation and implementation of collectively binding decisions by the systematic involvement of private actors with whom public actors coordinate their preferences and resources on the voluntary (nonhierarchical) basis" (156).

Network governance, by definition, depends on the interaction of many independent voluntary participants, any one of whom may withdraw at any time. For this reason, leadership approaches emphasizing trust and collaboration are essential. Additionally, leadership must be seen as a process shifting from player to player, rather than the "property" of any single individual or group. Nevertheless, effective leadership and service in the public interest will be essential to the success of the network.

Effective leadership also involves measuring the impact of programs and policies operated on behalf of the public, in order to determine effectiveness and other issues. Public administrators have long struggled with how to measure outcomes of public programs and policies in the context of a complex, networked governance system, the pursuit of multiple and sometimes conflicting goals, and the increasingly intractable and "wicked" nature of public problems. Especially pertinent to the discussion here, performance measurement tools have traditionally neglected the potential role of citizens in developing performance measures that are meaningful and useful, as well as the need to measure the impact of public programs on citizenship.

In considering performance measurement programs in the US, Callahan (2010) suggested that the best programs seek ongoing community input, present data by theme or issue area rather than department, use plain language, use measures to learn and improve, and make appropriate use of forums and web technologies to share information. Others have not only emphasized the importance of involving citizens in developing performance measurement strategies, but also suggest measuring the impact of public programs on citizenship. Drawing from policy feedback theory, Wichowsky and Moynihan state that there is "empirical evidence that certain policies have measurable effects on political participation, social capital, sense of civic belonging, and political efficacy" (2008, 908). They make a compelling argument that performance measurement systems should incorporate measures of how public policies and programs influence citizenship outcomes such as political efficacy, social trust, and civic engagement.

In short, although public servants sometimes "row" in providing direct service, they "steer" in terms of creating the parameters and processes of decision making, and increasingly their role is one of serving citizens and networks of governance. They are accountable, not only for direct service delivery and rule making, but also for helping broad networks of organizations and individuals find the common ground from which to take public action.

Conclusion

As much as advocates of the New Public Management and the New Public Service both might want to stake claim to "the answer," government and governance have been and will always be complicated. If there were easy answers to the problems and challenges we face, someone would have developed the solutions to them already. Still, it is our contention that there is much more room in the New Public Service for the lessons of New Public Management than the other way around.

It is probably fair to conclude that neither the principles of the New Public Service nor the principles of the New Public Management have become a dominant paradigm, but the New Public Service and the ideas and practices consistent with its ideals have become increasingly evident in public administration scholarship and practice. The present state of theory and practice might be best characterized as a more nuanced view of public administration, responsive to both democratic and market-based values. In the first edition of our book, we argued that one set of values—either the New Public Management or the New Public Service—ultimately had to take precedence, and that, in our view, *the practices of the New Public Management should fit within the ideals of the New Public Service.* At this point, however, we see more of a blending, with scholars and practitioners subscribing to some aspects of both. However, the direction is toward increasing civic engagement and involvement in the governance process.

The pursuit of New Public Service values is not without barriers and potential problems. Not all expressions of the public interest that emerge from political process and dialogue are "equally morally compelling" (Moore 2014, 495). Moreover, public dialogue can be dominated by well-financed special interests and partisan activists who are skilled at framing issues (Jacobs 2014). Nonetheless, we continue to question whether individuals making judgments about their own interests are the best or only arbiters of public value. There is no denying the "challenges of a networked, multi-sector, no-one-wholly-in-charge world" and the need to "embrace values beyond efficiency and effectiveness—and especially democratic values" (Bryson et al. 2014, 445). Although the market is efficient, "the correct arbiter of *public* value has to be a *collective* public—imperfectly formed by the processes of democratic governance" (Moore 2014, 475). And there is reason for optimism about the realization of those democratic values: "recent research demonstrates a surprising degree of public participation in deliberation regarding public policy"; two-thirds report engaging in "public talk" about public issues, and "an impressive 25 percent attend organized forums to participate in face-to-face deliberation" (Jacobs 2014, 492).

Particularly to the extent that New Public Management relies on public choice and "a relentless focus on the importance of efficiency" (McGinness and Ostrom 2012, 19), value-based models such as the New Public Service will continue to provide a needed counterpoint. Public servants operate in the context of competing values in a complex and ever-changing environment. We agree with Salminen and Mäntysalo (2013) that a professional public service ethos can begin to bridge the gap between bureaucratic and democratic values, "by creating a logic of appropriateness . . . pertaining to quality and performance" (2013, 169). A professional ethos is not purely objective, but rather recognizes that judgments about values and how they should be balanced, advocated, and reconciled are necessary and should be guided both by personal values and the values and ethics of the profession as a whole. These judgments necessitate both an ongoing dialogue and a strong framework of public service values and ethics. We consider these debates part of an ongoing dynamic that animates theory and practice and defines the current challenges and opportunities for the public service.

This chapter is based on a 2014 manuscript submitted to the *PAR*, "The New Public Service Revisited." This manuscript was commissioned by *PAR* in recognition of the original New Public Service article (2000) being named as one of the 75 most influential articles published in the journal since its inception.

Chapter 12

Conclusion

In the preceding chapters, we have presented a theoretical framework that gives full priority to democracy, citizenship, and service in the public interest. We have called this framework the New Public Service. We have argued that the New Public Service offers an important and viable alternative to both the traditional and the managerialist models of public management. It is an alternative that has been built on the basis of theoretical explorations and practical innovations in public agencies, many of which we examined, especially in Chapter 10. In this chapter, we want to return to the normative model that inspires the New Public Service and invite your participation in building and expanding that model.

We began with a description of what we called the Old Public Administration, or the orthodoxy of the field. We suggested that, under the Old Public Administration, the purpose of government was simply to deliver services efficiently, and that problems were to be addressed primarily by changing the organization's structure and control systems. Although some in the field called for greater attention to democratic values, the voices calling for hierarchy and control, little citizen involvement, and neutral expertise largely prevailed.

More recently, the New Public Management came to dominate thought and action in the field of public administration. The New Public Management, as we have seen, is grounded in the idea that the best way to understand human behavior is to assume that governmental and other actors make choices and undertake action based on their own self-interest. In this view, the role of government is to unleash market forces so as to facilitate individual choice and to achieve efficiency. Citizens are seen as customers, and problems are addressed by manipulating incentives. Public servants are expected to be entrepreneurial risk-takers who get the "best deals" and reduce costs.

In contrast, we have made an argument for what we call the New Public Service. We have suggested that public administrators should begin with the recognition that an engaged and enlightened citizenship is critical to democratic governance. We assert that this "high" citizenship is both important and achievable, because human behavior is not only a matter of self-interest, but also involves values, beliefs, and a concern for others. Citizens are seen as the owners of government and as capable of acting together in pursuit of the greater good. Accordingly, we have argued that the public interest transcends the aggregation of individual self-interests. The New Public Service seeks shared values and common interests through widespread dialogue and citizen engagement. It fosters deliberative democracy. Public service itself is seen as an extension of citizenship, motivated by desire to serve others and to achieve public objectives.

From this perspective, the role of public administrator is to bring people "to the table" and to serve citizens in a manner that recognizes the multiple and complex layers of responsibility, ethics, and accountability in a democratic system. The responsible administrator should work to engage citizens, not only in planning, but also in implementing programs to achieve public objectives. This is done, not only because it makes government work better, but also because it is consistent with our values. The job of the public administrator is not primarily control, nor the manipulation of incentives; it is service. In this model, democratic ideals and respect for others, not only permeate our interactions with citizens, but also are modeled within public organizations.

In short, we have argued for a model of New Public Service, based on citizenship, democracy, and service in the public interest, as an alternative to the now-dominant model based on economic theory and self-interest. Although debates among theorists will continue and although administrative practitioners will test and explore new possibilities, it is important to acknowledge that this is not just an abstract debate. The actions that public administrators take and have taken will differ markedly, depending on the types of assumption and principle upon which those actions are based. If we assume that the responsibility of government is to facilitate individual self-interest, we will take one set of actions. If, on the other hand, we assume that the responsibility of government is to promote citizenship, public discourse, and the public interest, we will take an entirely different set of actions. As stated in *Street-Level Leadership*:

One of the most potent and effective ways to influence practice is to change the theory and language used to understand that practice. . . . From this perspective, it is not an overstatement to suggest that the capacity of the governance system and efficacy of public administration as a component of that system are products of the acceptance of a particular set of theories which undergird them.

(Vinzant and Crothers 1998, 143–144)

Put simply, the theories to which we ascribe *matter*. Theories, values, and beliefs are what facilitate or constrain, encourage or discourage particular kinds of action. Consider, for example, the implications for action of the following two statements: (1) "The customers are waiting to see us" and (2) "The owners are waiting to see us." In the first instance, we may respond to the preferences of each individual, in the order that they appear, in the most efficient manner possible. We respond as politely and as quickly as possible to their demands. When we have completed the transaction, the relationship is over until the next demand is made. The customer is satisfied and goes away. In the second case, the people we serve are the owners. In responding to owners, we recognize that each owner has a stake in what we do, and that the guidance and involvement of all owners are both needed and appropriate. They are allowed to keep their dignity and are treated with respect in the context of a long-term relationship. We recognize that, instead of responding only to the self-interest of each, we must engage in an extended conversation about the larger public interest. In short, there are clear practical and behavioral implications in the ways we see, understand, and talk about the people we serve. As we change how we think and how we talk, we will change what we do.

It is also important to note that, although changing a single word can have important implications for how we think and behave, realizing the values of the New Public Service will require simultaneous attention to all the factors and principles discussed in this book. The New Public Service is a call for, not only a redefinition of how we see the citizens we serve, but also a change in how we see ourselves and our responsibilities—how we treat each other, how we define our purpose and goals, how we evaluate ourselves and others, how we make decisions, how we view success and failure, and how we think about the legitimacy of our actions. It refocuses our attention on the ideals of democracy and the public interest, of citizenship and human dignity, of service and commitment as the foundation of *everything* we do.

So, the lessons and principles of New Public Service are not sequential steps or a linear process; all rely on and are expressions of the same core principles. They form the interdependent threads of the whole fabric of public service. Without each other, they are simply frayed pieces of the newest management fashion. They become "looks" or styles of management without the substance—briefly tried and then abandoned when the desired results cannot be consistently and continually shown.

In Chapter 11, we found that, since 2000, both theory and practice have moved away from the then-dominant model of New Public Management and have begun to embrace and reflect the values of the New Public Service outlined here. This is indicative of the always-present commitment to democratic values and public service that we observed even when New Public Management was at its peak of popularity. That commitment has grown to the point that, in both research and practice, the ideals of the New Public Service are increasingly evident. At this point, probably neither the principles of the New Public Service nor the principles of the New Public Management dominate. As we already noted, the present state of theory and practice might be best characterized as a more nuanced view of public administration, responsive to both democratic and market-based values.

The values of the New Public Service pose a constant and critically important challenge to practitioners and academics alike. It requires that we rethink organizational processes, structures, and rules to open access and participation to those we serve in all phases of the governance process. It is not a blueprint for a structure or a quantifiable objective to be met. It is an ideal, based on the immeasurable but critical values of democracy, citizenship, and the public interest. Although we have given action recommendations, examples, and cases of the New Public Service in action, the process of striving for the ideals of service in the public interest is the heart of the matter. The point is to always do a better job than we have before.

In one sense, the future of the New Public Service will be determined by all of us. Whether we are students or teachers, public servants or private-sector employees, American or Italian or Brazilian, each of us can make a difference in our communities, in our organizations, and in our world. The questions we face are at once both simple and enormously complex: How will we treat our neighbors? Will we take responsibility for our role in democratic governance? Are we willing to listen to and try to understand views that are different from our own? Are we willing to forgo our personal interests for the sake of others? Are we willing to change our minds?

At the core of this tension between the business models of New Public Management and the governance model outlined here is the idea of self-interest. As Denhardt argued in *The Pursuit of Significance* (1993), the central and most basic concept in traditional views of management was the idea of self-interest. He pointed out that standard approaches to management flow from the assumption of self-interest, whether pay and performance, motivation and control, or communication and conflict. He then asked:

> What if we turned the whole thing upside down and suggested that what is central to the operation . . . of public organizations is not a concern for self-interest but the pursuit of significance? This would change the way we think about public organizations in some very interesting ways. Using this new assumption, for example, wouldn't we want to state more clearly what is significant about the work of the organization so that people could focus their energy and excitement? Wouldn't we want to place the needs of clients and citizens at the forefront of all our activities? Wouldn't we want to give persons throughout our organizations the strength and power and responsibility to be significant? And wouldn't we want everything we do to be touched, indeed propelled by a commitment to public service? In other words, wouldn't we be doing all of those things that the best public managers already seem to be doing?
>
> (Denhardt 1993, 276)

Nonetheless, the 1990s were clearly a celebration of economic self-interest, as evidenced by the dominance of economics as the primary explanation for human behavoir. However, the call to service and significance was not lost, and it seems that the balance is slowly being restored. The New Public Service is not a new management technique; it is a definition of who we are and why we serve others. It is a fundamental reordering of values. We don't embrace these values because they increase satisfaction, motivation, retention, effectiveness, and service and improve decision making (although we would argue that they do). Rather, we simply act on them because we believe they are, and always have been, integral components of American democracy.

Decades ago, Herbert Kaufman (1956) suggested that, although administrative institutions are organized and operated in pursuit of different values at different times, during the period in which one idea is dominant, others are never totally neglected. Building on this idea, it makes sense to think of one normative model as prevailing at any point in time, with the other (or others) playing a somewhat lesser role *within* the context of the prevailing view. Currently, the New Public Management and its surrogates have been established as the dominant paradigm in the field of governance and public administration. In this process, a concern for democratic citizenship and the public interest has not been fully lost, but it has been subordinated.

We would argue, however, that, in a democratic society, a concern for democratic values should be paramount in the way we think about systems of governance. Values such as efficiency and productivity should not be lost, but should be placed in the larger context of democracy, community, and the public interest. In terms of the normative models we have examined here, the New Public Service clearly seems most consistent with the basic foundations of democracy in this country and, therefore, provides a framework *within which* other valuable techniques and values, including the best elements of the Old Public Administration and the New Public Management, might be played out. The New Public Service provides a rallying point around which we might envision a public service based on, and fully integrated with, civic discourse and the public interest.

How do we realize these ideals? As individual public servants, each of us has the opportunity and responsibility to serve others in the public interest, though, at present, many of us wouldn't, or couldn't, express it this way. Rather, we might say that we have the responsibility to process claims, investigate cases, process paperwork, teach classes, supervise workers, or answer the phone. However, if we think about how we can contribute to service in the public interest and to building active citizenship, it changes, not only how we feel about our work, but also how we approach our daily tasks. As Louis Gawthrop suggests:

> To labor in the service of democracy is to recognize that all of us are called, in varying degrees of responsibility, to be watchmen, sentinels, or prophets for others—any others—as well as for one another, in attempting to attain the common good.
>
> (1998, 100)

Perhaps we should each start with ourselves. Think about what brought *you* to the public service. What gives *your* work meaning? Do you remember feeling, when you started your public service career, that you were about to become part of something important? How can you do your job in a way that affirms these larger purposes? What can you do to reawaken in yourself that feeling of purpose, of calling, or of service? Through this process of self-reflection, we can begin to rediscover our desire to serve our fellow citizens and to think about our public service work in a way that celebrates its "soul" and meaning.

We are often struck by how our students, many of whom are midcareer public servants, react to classroom discussions about the values and meaning of the public service and their role in enacting those values. Their attention is captured; they listen more carefully to each other, and the conversation is more charged with emotion. Reticent students become engaged and involved. Many seem excited and almost grateful to have the chance to talk about what public service means to them. Some confess that they had never thought about the larger meaning and societal value of their work. Perhaps most telling is the frequency of such comments as, "I wish my supervisor/employees felt this way (and talked this way) about the public service."

Most of us probably do value the significance, the meaning, the "soul" of public service. We just don't think or talk about it very much. Or, worst of all, we think it applies to someone other than ourselves. In our efforts to improve productivity and efficiency, we seem to have lost the ability to speak with passion about each other and about what we do. Perhaps our speech and our professional self-identity have instead become overrun with words and concepts such as efficiency, deadlines, productivity, measures, objectives, analysis, performance, alignment, structure, customers, and procedures. Consider how we talk about our work to other people. If we fail to talk about the public service in a way that reflects its inherent value and societal meaning, we contribute to the loss of the soul of the field—a loss that robs us of our own excitement and satisfaction, and robs citizens of our caring and commitment. If we fail to infuse our own professional identity, as well as our conversations with others, with words and phrases such as public service, citizenship, public interest, meaning, values, ethics, community, and democracy, to name just a few, we miss opportunities to enhance and advance the heart of public service.

Self-reflection is both important and difficult. It is only through self-reflection that we can develop our capacity to serve others and recapture the pride we are missing as public servants. Through the process, we can strive to be proud, without being arrogant; to be strong, without being morally insensitive; to be respectful, without being timid; to be vigilant, without being oppressive; to be cautious, without letting fear control us; and to be caring, without being patronizing. Finding this balance through honest self-reflection is hard work, but it can make each of us a better person, a better citizen, and a better public servant.

We are convinced that, at the core, public servants want to do something that matters and has value. If that is true, it is critical that we find a voice in ourselves that applauds, recognizes, and advances these ideas. We need to find and use the words. The next time you talk to an employee, a student, a colleague, or even a friend, ask yourself how your speech reflects the soul of public administration. Think about the specific words and phrases you use. Do they motivate and inspire? As public servants, we would be well served if each of us consciously, deliberately, and frequently reminded ourselves and others that what we do profoundly matters.

As we said earlier, if we change how we think and talk, we also change how we behave. What do we think about the people we serve? Are they simply cases to be dispensed with as quickly as possible? Are they, fundamentally, unlike us? Do we treat the people we serve in a way that reflects both our self-respect and our respect for them? Do we look them in the eye and honestly try to help, serve, respond, and/or engage them? Are they treated as the citizen–owners of our organization? Do they feel valued as people? Do they leave our interactions feeling better or worse about their government? Do our interactions create a good foundation for continued involvement and participation, or will the people we serve dread their next interaction with government? We can begin by treating citizens as citizens, remembering that, in a democracy, these people are not just our clients or customers, they are our "bosses," and as such they deserve no less than sincere respect and full and complete involvement in the work of government.

What can we do as citizens and members of communities to contribute to the creation of a civil society and the ideals of democracy? The short answer is that we can do what comes naturally—we can act on our desire to belong and to join with others. Again, this begins with how we think about our role in democratic governance. In a sense, our rightful role will always be challenged, not because of evil intent or an elitist plot, but as a natural outgrowth of approaches to governance and management that begin and end with the assumption that we are incapable of anything other than self-interest. However, for us as citizens, it is important to recognize that making our country and our communities better requires at the very least our cooperation, and ideally, our active involvement. By definition, our government belongs to us and is our responsibility. We can and should have high expectations for government, but, for government to work well, it needs active citizenship. We can expect that our fellow citizens, who work for government, will treat us with respect and invite our active participation in their work. It is our right, duty, and privilege to do so. In return, we can honor and respect their contribution, not just during times of turmoil and disaster, but in everyday service to others.

Finally, we can ask ourselves whether we would perhaps find more meaning, higher purpose, and greater significance in our lives if we were to make public service our life's work. There are great opportunities and tremendous satisfactions to be gained in working toward making the world and our communities better, serving others, and pursuing something larger and more important than ourselves. As individuals, as public servants, and as a nation, we must have the integrity, the strength, and the commitment to be honest with ourselves and to work continually to be true to our shared values. Whether we express our citizenship by becoming more involved in our community dialogue, participating directly in democratic processes and institutions, or renewing our commitment, or by becoming public servants ourselves—whatever form it takes—an expansion of democratic citizenship will not only benefit citizens in their work together but also help build the spirit of public service throughout society, to the benefit of all.

Recall Portia's characterization of mercy in the Shakespearean play *The Merchant of Venice*: "The quality of mercy is not strained. It droppeth as the gentle rain from heaven upon the place beneath. It is twice blest: It blesseth him that gives and him that receives." The same is true of public service. We invite you to join in building the New Public Service.

References

Adams, G.B., and D.L. Balfour. 2009. *Unmasking Administrative Evil*. 3rd ed. Armonk, NY: M.E. Sharpe.

Adams, J.S. 1963. "Toward an Understanding of Inequity." *Journal of Abnormal Social Psychology* 67(1): 422–436.

Adams, R.J. 1992. "Efficiency is Not Enough." *Labor Studies Journal* 17(1): 18–29.

Agranoff, R. 2007. *Managing Within Networks*. Washington, DC: Georgetown University Press.

Albretch, K., and R. Zemke. 1985. *Service America*. Homewood, IL: Dow Jones–Irwin.

Alford, J. 2000. "A Public Management Road Less Traveled: Clients as Co-Producers of Public Service." *Australian Journal of Public Administration* 57(4): 128–137.

American Heritage Dictionary. 2000. Boston, MA: Houghton Mifflin.

American Society for Public Administration (ASPA). 2013. *Code of Ethics*. Available at: www.aspanet.org/public/ASPA/About_ASPA/Code_of_Ethics/ASPA/Resources/Code_of_Ethics/Code_of_Ethics1.aspx?hkey=222cd7a5-3997-425a-8a12-5284f81046a8

Appleby, P. 1945. *Big Democracy*. New York: Knopf.

———. 1949. *Policy and Administration*. Tuscaloosa, AL: University of Alabama Press.

———. 1950. *Morality and Administration in Democratic Government*. Baton Rouge, LA: Louisana State University Press.

Argyris, C. 1957. *Personality and Organization*. New York: Harper & Row.

———. 1962. *Interpersonal Competence and Organizational Effectiveness*. Homewood, IL: Dorsey Press.

———. 1973. "Some Limits of Rational Man Organization Theory." *Public Administration Review* 33(3): 253–267.

Asch, S. 1951. "Effects of Group Pressure upon the Modification and Distortion of Judgments." In *Groups, Leadership, and Men*, Ed. Harold Guetzkow, 222–236. Pittsburgh, PA: Carnegie Press.

Bacova, M., and A. Maney. 2004. "Strengthening Policymaking and Community Economic Development through Citizen Participation." Paper presented to 12th annual conference of the Network of Institutes and Schools of Public Administration in Central and Eastern Europe, Vilnius, Lithuania, May.

Bailey, S.K. 1966. "Ethics and the Public Service." In *Public Administration: Readings in Institutions, Processes, Behavior*, Eds. R.T. Golembiewski, F. Gibson, and G. Cornog, 22–31. Chicago, IL: Rand McNally.

Balfour, D., and B. Weschler. 1990. "Organizational Commitment: A Reconceptualization and Empirical Test of Public–Private Differences." *Review of Public Personnel Administration* 10(3): 23–40.

Ballard, M.J., and M.E. Warner. 2000. "Taking the High Road: Local Government Restructuring and the Quest for Quality" (white paper). In *Power Tools for Fighting Privatization*. Washington, DC: American Federation of State, County and Municipal Employees.

Barber, B. 1984. *Strong Democracy: Participatory Politics for a New Age*. Berkeley, CA: University of California Press.

———. 1998. *A Passion for Democracy*. Princeton, NJ: Princeton University Press.

Barnard, C. 1948. *The Function of the Executive*. Cambridge, MA: Harvard University Press.

Barzelay, M. 1992. *Breaking Through Bureaucracy*. Berkeley, CA: University of California Press.

———. 2001a. *The New Public Management*. Berkeley, CA: University of California Press.

———. 2001b. *Rethinking Democratic Accountability*. Washington, DC: Brookings Institution.

Beierle, T., and J. Cayford. 2002. *Democracy in Practice: Public Participation in Environmental Decisions*. Washington, DC: RFF Press.

Bell, D., and I. Kristol. 1965. "What is the Public Interest?" *Public Interest* 1 (Autumn): 3–5.

Bellah, R., R. Madsen,W. Sullivan, A. Swidler, and S. Tipton. 1985. *Habits of the Heart*. Berkeley, CA: University of California Press.

———. 1991. *The Good Society*. New York: Knopf.

Benest, F. 1999. "Reconnecting Citizens with Citizens: What is the Role of Local Government?" *PM* (January): 6–11.

———. 2007. "A Demographic Tsunami." In *Local Governments Preparing the Next Generation: Successful Case Studies*, 2–6. Sacramento, CA: Cal-ICMA.

Benhabib, S. 1996. "Toward a Deliberative Model of Democratic Legitimacy." In *Democracy and Difference*, Ed. S. Benhabib, 67–94. Princeton, NJ: Princeton University Press.

Bennett, W., Ed. 1993. *The Book of Virtues*. New York: Simon & Schuster.

Bennis, W. 1992. "The Artform of Leadership." In *Public Administration in Action*, Eds. R.B. Denhardt and B.S. Hammond, 311–315. Pacific Grove, CA: Brooks-Cole.

Berry, J.M. 2005. "Nonprofits and Civic Engagement." *Public Administration Review* 65(5): 568–578.

Berry, J.M., K. Portney, and K. Thomson. 1993. *The Rebirth of Urban Democracy*. Washington, DC: Brookings Institution.

Bevir, M. 2009. *Key Concepts in Governance*. Los Angeles, CA: Sage.

Bingham, L.B., T. Nabatchi, and R. O'Leary. 2005. "The New Governance: Practices and Processes for Stakeholder and Citizen Participation in the Work of Government." *Public Administration Review* 65(5): 547–558.

Block, P. 2008. *Community: The Structure of Belonging*. San Francisco, CA: Berrett Koehler.

Bobbio, L., Ed. 2005. *A più voci [To More Voices]*. Rome: Edizioni Scientifiche Italiane. (As translated by Manuella Cocci in her personal correspondence.)

Bolman, L.G. and T.E. Deal. 2008. *Reframing Organizations: Artistry, Choice, and Leadership*. San Francisco, CA: Jossey-Bass.

Borins, S. 2013. "Leadership and Innovation in the Public Sector." In *The Jossey-Bass Reader on Nonprofit and Public Leadership*, Ed. J. Perry, 502–521. San Francisco, CA: Wiley.

Börzel, T.A., and D. Panke. 2006. "Network Governance. Effective and Legitimate?" In *Theories of Democratic Network Governance*, Eds. J. Torfing and E. Sørensen, 153–166. Basingstoke, UK: Palgrave.

Boston, J. 1991. "The Theoretical Underpinnings of Public Sector Restructuring in New Zealand." In *Reshaping the State*, Eds. J. Boston, J. Martin, J. Pallot, and P. Walsh, 1–24. Oxford, UK: Oxford University Press.

Boston, J., J. Martin, J. Pallot, and P. Walsh. 1996. *Public Management: The New Zealand Model*. New York: Oxford University Press.

Box, R. 1998. *Citizen Governance*. Thousand Oaks, CA: Sage.

———. 2008. *Making a Difference*. Armonk, NY: M.E. Sharpe.

Box, R.C., G.S. Marshall, B.J. Reed, and C.M. Reed. 2001. "New Public Management and Substantive Democracy." *Public Administration Review* 61(5): 608–619.

Boyte, H.C. 2005. "Reframing Democracy: Governance, Civic Agency, and Politics." *Public Administration Review* 65(5): 536–546.

Boyte, H.C., and N.N. Kari. 1996. *Building America*. Philadelphia, PA: Temple University Press.

Bozeman, B. 2007. *Public Values and Public Interest*. Washington, DC: Georgetown University Press.

Brainard, L.A. and J.G. McNutt. 2010. "Virtual Government–Citizen Relations: Informational, Transactional, or Collaborative?" *Administration & Society November* 42(7): 836–858.

Brown, T.L., and M. Potoski. 2003. "Contract-Management Capacity in Municipal and County Governments." *Public Administration Review* 63(2): 153–164.

Brudney, J.L., and R.E. England. 1983. "Toward a Definition of the Coproduction Concept." *Public Administration Review* 43(1): 59–65.

Bryer, T. 2010. "Across the Great Divide: Social Media and Networking for Citizen Engagement." In *Connected Communities*, Eds. J. Svara and J.V. Denhardt, 73–79. Phoenix, AZ: Alliance for Innovation.

Bryson, J.M., and R. Einsweiler. 1991. "Introduction." In *Shared Power*, Eds. J.M. Bryson and R. Einsweiler, 1–24. Minneapolis, MN: Humphrey Institute of Public Affairs.

Bryson, J.M., and B. Crosby. 1992. *Leadership for the Common Good*. San Francisco, CA: Jossey-Bass.

Bryson, J.M., B.C. Crosby, and L. Bloomberg. 2014. "Public Value Governance: Moving Beyond Traditional Public Administration and the New Public Management." *Public Administration Review* 74: 445–456.

Bumgarner, J., and C. Newswander. 2009. "The Irony of NPM: The Inevitable Extension of the Role of the American State." *American Review of Public Administration* 39(2): 189–207.

Burke, J. 1986. *Bureaucratic Responsibility*. Baltimore, MD: Johns Hopkins Press.

——. 1987. "A Prescriptive View of the Implementation Process: When Should Bureaucrats Exercise Discretion?" *Policy Studies Review* 7(1): 217–231.

Burns, J.M. 1978. *Leadership*. New York: Harper & Row.

Callahan, K. 2010. "Next Wave of Performance Measurement: Citizen Engagement." In *Connected Communities*, Eds. J. Svara and J.V. Denhardt, 95–101. Phoenix, AZ: Alliance for Innovation.

Carlson, M.S., and R. Schwarz. 1995. "What Do Citizens Really Want?" *Popular Government* (Spring): 26–33.

Carnavale, D. 1995. *Trustworthy Government*. San Francisco, CA: Jossey-Bass.

Carroll, J., and D.B. Lynn. 1996. "The Future of Federal Reinvention: Congressional Perspectives." *Public Administration Review* 56(3): 299–304.

Cassinelli, C.W. 1962. "The Public Interest in Political Ethics." In *Nomos V: The Public Interest*, Ed. C.J. Friedrich, 44–53. New York: Atherton Press.

Catlaw, T. 2007. *Fabricating the People*. Tuscaloosa, AL: University of Alabama Press.

Catlaw, T., and K.C. Rawlings. 2010. "Promoting Participation from the Inside Out: Workplace Democracy and Public Engagement." In *Connected Communities*, Eds. J. Svara and J.V. Denhardt, 115–119. Phoenix, AZ: Alliance for Innovation.

Cayer, N.J. 1986. *Public Personnel in the United States*. 2nd ed. New York: St. Martin's Press.

Chapin, L.W., and R.B. Denhardt. 1995. "Putting 'Citizens First!' in Orange County, Florida." *National Civic Review* 84(3): 210–215.

Chaskin, R.J. 2001. "Building Community Capacity: A Definitional Framework and Case Studies from a Comprehensive Community Initiative." *Urban Affairs Review* 36(3): 291–323.

——. 2003. "Fostering Neighborhood Democracy: Legitimacy, Accountability Within Loosely Coupled Systems." *Nonprofit and Voluntary Sector Quarterly* 32(2): 161–189.

Civic Alliance to Rebuild Downtown New York. 2002. Listening to the City: Report of Proceedings. New York.

Cleveland, F.A. 1920. *The Budget and Responsible Government*. New York: Macmillan.

Cleveland, H. 1985. "The Twilight of Hierarchy." *Public Administration Review* 45(2): 185–195.

Cline, K.D. 2000. "Defining the Implementation Problem: Organizational Management versus Cooperation." *Journal of Public Administration Research and Theory* 10(3): 551–571.

Cochran, C. 1974. "Political Science and 'The Public Interest.'" *Journal of Politics* 36(2): 327–355.

Cook, B.J. 1996. *Bureaucracy and Self-Government*. Baltimore, MD: Johns Hopkins University Press.

Cook, T., and L.D. Dobson. 1982. "Reaction to Reexamination: More on Type III Error in Program Evaluation." *Evaluation and Program Planning* 5(1): 119–121.

Cooper, T.L. 1991. *An Ethic of Citizenship for Public Administration*. Englewood Cliffs, NJ: Prentice-Hall.

——. 1998. *The Responsible Administrator*. 4th ed. San Francisco, CA: Jossey-Bass.

——. 2005. "Civic Engagement in the Twenty-First Century: Toward a Scholarly and Practical Agenda." *Public Administration Review* 65(5): 534–535.

Cope, G. 1997. "Bureaucratic Reform and Issues of Political Responsiveness." *Journal of Public Administration Research and Theory* 7(3): 461–471.

Coursey, D.D., K. Yang, and S.K. Pandey. 2012. "Public Service Motivation (PSM) and Support for Citizen Participation: A Test of Perry and Vandenabeele's Reformulation of PSM Theory." *Public Administration Review* 72(4): 572–582.

Creighton, J. 2005. *The Public Participation Handbook.* San Francisco, CA: Jossey-Bass.

Crevani, L., M. Lindgren, and J. Packendorff. 2007. "Shared Leadership: A Postheroic Perspective on Leadership as a Collective Construction." *International Journal of Leadership Studies* 3(2): 40–67.

Cronin, T.E., and M.A. Genovese. 2012. *The Paradoxes of the American Presidency.* New York: Oxford University Press.

Crosby, B. 2010. "Leading in the Shared Power World of 2020." *Public Administration Review* 70(S1): 69–77.

Crosby, N., J. Kelly, and P. Schaefer. 1986. "Citizen Panels: A New Approach to Citizen Participation." *Public Administration Review* 46(2): 170–178.

Dagger, R. 1997. *Civic Virtues.* New York: Oxford University Press.

Dahl, R.A. 1947. "The Science of Public Administration." *Public Administration Review* 7(Winter): 1–11.

———. 1956. *A Preface to Democratic Theory.* Chicago, IL: University of Chicago Press.

———. 1961. *Who Governs?* New Haven, CT: Yale University Press.

Davenport, T.H. 2001. "Knowledge Work and the Future of Management." In *The Future of Leadership,* Eds. W. Bennis, G.M. Spreitzer, and T.G. Cummings, 41–58. San Francisco, CA: Jossey Bass.

The Declaration of Independence. [1776]1970. Worcester, MA: A.J. St. Onge.

deLeon, L., and R.B. Denhardt. 2000. "The Political Theory of Reinvention." *Public Administration Review* 60(2): 89–97.

deLeon, P. 1997. *Democracy and the Policy Sciences.* Albany, NY: State University of New York Press.

———. 1999. "The Missing Link Revisited: Contemporary Implementation Research." *Policy Studies Review* 16(3/4): 311–338.

Denhardt, R.B. 1981. *In the Shadow of Organization.* Lawrence, KS: Regents Press of Kansas.

———. 1993. *The Pursuit of Significance.* Pacific Grove, CA: Wadsworth.

———. 1999. *Public Administration: An Action Orientation.* 3rd ed. Fort Worth, TX: Harcourt Brace.

———. 2000. *Theories of Public Organization,* 3rd ed. San Diego, CA: Harcourt Brace.

———. 2008. *Theories of Public Organizations.* Belmont, CA: Wadsworth.

Denhardt, R.B., and J.E. Gray. 1998. "Targeting Community Development in Orange County, Florida." *National Civic Review* 87(3): 227–235.

Denhardt, R.B., and J.V. Denhardt. 1999. *Leadership for Change: Case Studies in American Local Government.* Arlington, VA: PricewaterhouseCoopers Endowment for the Business of Government.

———. 2001a. "The Power of Public Service." Available at: http://64.91.242.87/publications/COLUMNS/archives/2001/Sep/denhardts0913.html

———. 2001b. "Citizenship and Public Service." Available at: http://64.91.242.87/publications/COLUMNS/archives/2001/Nov/denhardts1109.html

——. 2006. *The Dance of Leadership*. Armonk, NY: M.E. Sharpe.

Denhardt, R.B., J.V. Denhardt, and M. Aristigueta. 2002. *Managing Human Behavior in Public and Nonprofit Organizations*. Thousand Oaks, CA: Sage.

Dent, M., J. Chandler, and J. Barry. 2004. *Questioning the New Public Management*. Aldershot, UK: Ashgate.

Dimock, M.E. 1936. "Criteria and Objectives of Public Administration." In *The Frontiers of Public Administration*, Eds. J.M. Gaus, L.D. White, and M.E. Dimock, 116–134. Chicago, IL: University of Chicago Press.

Dimock, M.E., and G.O. Dimock. 1969. *Public Administration*. 4th ed. Hinsdale, IL: Dryden Press.

Dobel, P. 1990. "Integrity in the Public Service." *Public Administration Review* 50(3): 354–367.

——. 1999. *Deliberative Democracy and Beyond*. Oxford, UK: Oxford University Press.

Dunleavy, P. 1991. *Democracy, Bureaucracy and Public Choice*. New York: Harvester Wheatsheaf.

Dunn, D.D., and J.S. Legge, Jr. 2000. "U.S. Local Government Managers and the Complexity of Responsibility and Accountability in Democratic Governance." *Journal of Public Administration Research and Theory* 11(1): 73–88.

Durant, R.F., and S.B. Ali. 2013. "Repositioning American Public Administration? Citizen Estrangement, Administrative Reform, and the Disarticulated State." *Public Administration Review* 73(2): 278–289.

Dwivedi, O.P. 1985. "Ethics and Values of Public Responsibility and Accountability." *International Journal of Administrative Sciences* 51(1): 61–66.

Eikenberry, A.M. and J.D. Kluver. 2004. "The Marketization of the Nonprofit Sector: Civil Society at Risk?" *Public Administration Review* 64(2): 132–140.

Etzioni, A. 1988. *The Moral Dimension*. New York: Free Press.

——. 1995. *The New Communitarian Thinking*. Charlottesville, VA: University of Virginia Press.

Evans, S.M., and H.C. Boyte. 1986. *Free Spaces*. New York: Harper & Row.

Everett, E. 2009. "Community Building: How to Do It, Why It Matters." *ICMA IQ Report* 41(4): 1–14.

Farmer, J.D. 1995. *The Language of Public Administration*. Tuscaloosa, AL: University of Alabama Press.

——. 2005. *To Kill the King*. Armonk, NY: M.E. Sharpe.

Feldman, M.S. 2010. "Managing the Organization of the Future." *Public Administration Review* 70(S1): 159–163.

Ferlie, E. 1996. *The New Public Management in Action*. Oxford, UK: Oxford University Press.

Final Report on the Iowa Citizen Initiated Performance Assessment Project (CIPA). 2005. Submitted to the Alfred P. Sloan Foundation.

Finer, H. 1941. "Administrative Responsibility in Democratic Government." *Public Administration Review* 1: 335–350.

Fisher, F. 2009. *Democracy and Expertise: Reorienting Policy Inquiry*. New York: Oxford University Press.

Fishkin, J.S. 1991. *Democracy and Deliberation.* New Haven, CT: Yale University Press.

———. 1995. *The Voice of the People.* New Haven, CT: Yale University Press.

Fishkin, J.S., and P. Laslett, Eds. 2003. *Debating Deliberative Democracy.* Malden, MA: Wiley Blackwell.

Follett, M.P. 1926. "The Giving of Order." In *Scientific Foundations of Business Administration.* Baltimore, MD: Williams & Wilkins.

Fox, C. 1987. "Biases in Public Policy Implementation." *Policy Studies Review* 7(1): 128–141.

———. 1996. "Reinventing Government as Postmodern Symbolic Politics." *Public Administration Review* 56(3): 256–261.

Fox, C., and H. Miller. 1995. *Postmodern Public Administration.* Thousand Oaks, CA: Sage.

———. 1997. "The Depreciating Public Policy Discourse." *American Behavioral Scientist* 41(1): 64–120.

Fox, H. 2002. *Postmodern Public Policy.* Albany, NY: State University of New York Press.

Frederickson, H.G. 1980. *New Public Administration.* Tuscaloosa, AL: University of Alabama Press.

———. 1982. "The Recovery of Civism in Public Administration." *Public Administration Review* 43(6): 501–508.

———. 1991. "Toward a Theory of the Public for Public Administration." *Administration and Society* 22(4): 395–417.

———. 1992. "Painting Bulls-Eyes around Bullet Holes." *Governing* 6(1): 13.

———. 1996. "Comparing the Reinventing Government Movement with the New Public Administration." *Public Administration Review* 56(3): 263–269.

———. 1997. *The Spirit of Public Administration.* San Francisco, CA: Jossey-Bass.

Frederickson, H.G., and R.C. Chandler, Eds. 1984. "A Symposium on Citizenship and Public Administration." *Public Administration Review* 44 (Special Issue): 99–206.

Frederickson, H.G., and D.K. Hart. 1985. "The Public Service and Patriotism of Benevolence." *Public Administration Review* 45(5): 547–553.

French, J.R., Jr., and B. Raven. 1959. "The Bases of Social Power." In *Studies in Social Power*, Ed. D. Cartwright, 189–202. Ann Arbor, MI: Institute for Social Research.

Friedrich, C.J. 1940. "Public Policy and the Nature of Administrative Responsibility." *Public Policy* 1: 1–20.

———. 1960. "The Dilemma of Administrative Responsibility." In *Responsibility*, Ed. C.J. Friedrich, 189–202. New York: Liberal Arts Press.

Fung, A. 2013. "Infotopia: Unleashing the Democratic Power of Transparency." *Politics & Society* 41(2): 183–212.

Gardner, J. 1987. "Remarks to the NASPAA Conference." *Enterprise: The Newsletter of NASPAA* (October 23): 1.

———. 1991. *Building Community.* Washington, DC: Independent Sector.

Gawthrop, L.C. 1998. *Public Service and Democracy.* New York: Chandler.

Gergen, D., and B. Kellerman. 2003. "Public Leaders: Riding a New Tiger." In *For the People: Can We Fix Public Service?*, Eds. J.D. Donahue and J.S. Nye Jr., 13–28. Washington, DC: Brookings Institution Press.

Gerth, H.H., and C.W. Mills. 1946. *From Max Weber: Essays in Sociology*. New York: Oxford University Press.

Gibson, C. 2006. *Citizens at the Center: A New Approach to Citizen Engagement*. Washington, DC: The Case Foundation.

Gilley, A., P. Dixon, and J.W. Gilley. 2013. "Characteristics of Leadership Effectiveness: Implementing Change and Driving Innovation in Organizations." In *The Jossey-Bass Reader on Nonprofit and Public Leadership*, Ed. J. Perry, 479–501. San Francisco, CA: Wiley.

Gilmore, R.S., and L.S. Jensen. 1998. "Reinventing Government Accountability: Public Functions, Privatization, and the Meaning of State Action." *Public Administration Review* 58(3): 247–258.

Glaser, M., L. Parker, and S. Payton. 2001. "The Paradox Between Community and Self-Interest: Local Government, Neighborhoods, and the Media." *Journal of Urban Affairs* 23(1): 87–102.

Glaser, M., J.V. Denhardt, and L. Hamilton. 2002. "Community v. Self-Interest: Citizen Perceptions of Schools as Civic Investments." *Journal of Public Administration Theory and Practice* 12(1): 103–127.

Glaser, M., S. Yeagar, and L. Parker. 2006. "Involving Citizens in the Decisions of Government and Community." *Public Administration Quarterly* 30: 177–217.

Goggin, M., A. Bowman, L. O'Toole, and J. Lester. 1990. *Implementation Theory and Practice: Toward a Third Generation*. Glenwood, IL: Scott Foresman/Little, Brown.

Goldbard, A. 2010. "The Art of Engagement: Creativity in the Service of Citizenship." In *Connected Communities*, Eds. J. Svara and J.V. Denhardt, 106–111. Phoenix, AZ: Alliance for Innovation.

Goleman, D., R. Boyatis, and A. McKee. 2002. *Primal Leadership*. Cambridge, MA: Harvard Business School Press.

Golembiewski, R.T. 1967. *Men, Management, and Morality*. New York: McGraw-Hill.

———. 1977. "A Critique of 'Democratic Administration' and its Supporting Ideation." *American Political Science Review* 71(December): 1488–1507.

Goodnow, F. 1987. "Politics and Administration." In *Classics of Public Administration*. 2nd ed., Eds. J. Shafritz and A. Hyde, 26–29. Chicago, IL: Dorsey Press.

Goodsell, C.T. 1994. *The Case for Bureaucracy*. Chatham, NJ: Chatham House.

Gore, A. 1993. *From Red Tape to Results*. Washington, DC: The Review.

Gray, J., and L. Chapin. 1998. "Targeted Community Initiative." In *Government is Us*, Eds. C.S. King and C. Stivers, 175–194. Thousand Oaks, CA: Sage.

Gulick, L. 1933. "Politics, Administration, and the New Deal." *Annals of the Academy of Political and Social Science* 169 (September): 545–566.

———. 1937. "Notes on the Theory of Organization." In *Papers on the Science of Administration*, Eds. L. Gulick and L. Urwick, 1–46. New York: Institute of Government.

Gutman, A., and D. Thompson. 1996. *Democracy and Disagreement*. Cambridge, MA: Harvard University Press.

———. 2004. *Why Deliberative Democracy?* Princeton, NJ: Princeton University Press.

Habermas, J. 1996. *Between Facts and Norms*. Boston, MA: MIT Press.

Hall, J.S. 2002. "Reconsidering the Connection Between Capacity and Governance." *Public Organization Review* 2(1): 5–22.

Hall, T.E., and L.J. O'Toole, Jr. 2000. "Structures for Policy Implementation." *Administration and Society* 31(6): 667–687.

Hambleton, R. 2004. "Beyond New Public Management—City Leadership, Democratic Renewal and the Politics of Change." Paper presented to the City Futures International Conference, Chicago, July 8–19.

Haque, M.S. 1994. "The Emerging Challenges to Bureaucratic Accountability: A Critical Perspective." In *Handbook of Bureaucracy*, Ed. A. Farazmand, 265–286. New York: Marcel Dekker.

Harmon, M. 1981. *Action Theory for Public Administration*. New York: Longman.

———. 1995. *Responsibility as Paradox*. Thousand Oaks, CA: Sage.

———. 2006. *Public Administration's Final Exam*. Tuscaloosa, AL: University of Alabama Press.

Hart, D.K. 1984. "The Virtuous Citizen, the Honorable Bureaucrat, and 'Public' Administration." *Public Administration Review* 44 (Special Issue): 111–120.

———. 1997. "'A Partnership in Virtue Among All Citizens': The Public Service and the Civic Humanist Tradition." *International Journal of Public Administration* 20(4–5): 967–980.

Haruna, P.F. 2003. "Reforming Ghana's Public Service: Issues and Experiences in Comparative Perspective." *Public Administration Review* 63(3): 343–354.

Hefetz, A., and M. Warner. 2004. "Privatization and Its Reverse: Explaining the Dynamics of the Government Contracting Process." *Journal of Public Administration Research and Theory* 14(2): 171–190.

Heifetz, R.A. 1994. *Leadership Without Easy Answers*. Cambridge, MA: Harvard University Press.

Herring, E.P. 1936. *Public Administration and the Public Interest*. New York: Russell & Russell.

Herzberg, F. 1968. "One More Time: How Do You Motivate Employees?" *Harvard Business Review* 46 (January–February): 53–62.

Ho, A.T.-K., and P. Coates. 2002. "Citizen Participation: Legitimizing Performance Measurement as a Decision Tool." *Government Finance Review* (April): 8–10.

———. 2004. "Citizen-Initiated Performance Assessment." *Public Performance & Management Review* 27(3): 29–50.

Homans, G. 1954. *The Human Group*. New York: McGraw-Hill.

Hood, C. 1991. "A Public Administration for All Seasons." *Public Administration* 69(1): 3–19.

———. 1995. "The 'New Public Management' in the Eighties." *Accounting, Organization and Society* 20(2–3): 93–109.

Hood, C., and M. Jackson. 1991. *Administrative Argument*. Aldershot, UK: Dartmouth Press.

Hummel, R. 1994. *The Bureaucratic Experience*. 4th ed. New York: St. Martin's Press.

Ignatieff, M. 1995. "The Myth of Citizenship." In *Theorizing Citizenship*, Ed. R. Beiner, 53–78. Albany, NY: State University of New York Press.

Ingraham, P.W., and C. Ban. 1988. "Politics and Merit: Can They Meet in a Public Service Model?" *Review of Public Personnel Administration* 8(2): 1–19.

Ingraham, P.W., and D.H. Rosenbloom. 1989. "The New Public Personnel and the New Public Service." *Public Administration Review* 49(2): 116–125.

Ingraham, P.W., and L.E. Lynn, Jr., Eds. 2004. *The Art of Governance*. Washington, DC: Georgetown University Press.

Ingraham, P.W., B.S. Romzek, and Associates. 1994. *New Paradigms for Government.* San Francisco, CA: Jossey-Bass.

Innes, E.J., and E.D. Booher. 2004. "Reframing Public Participation: Strategies for the 21st Century." *Planning Theory and Practice* 5(4): 419–436.

Jacobs, L.R. 2014. "The Contested Politics of Public Value." *Public Administration Review* 74(4): 480–494.

Jacobs, L.R., F. Cook, and M. Carpini. 2009. *Talking Together: Public Deliberation in America.* Chicago, IL: University of Chicago Press.

Jefferson, T. 1903. *The Writings of Thomas Jefferson.* Memorial ed. Washington, DC: Thomas Jefferson Memorial Association.

Jun, J.S. 2006. *The Social Construction of Public Administration.* Albany, NY: State University of New York Press.

Kaboolian, L. 1998. "The New Public Management." *Public Administration Review* 58(3): 189–193.

Kamensky, J.M. 1996. "The Role of the Reinventing Government Movement in Federal Management Reform." *Public Administration Review* 56(3): 247–255.

Kantor, R.M. 1972. *Commitment and Community.* Cambridge, MA: Harvard University Press.

Kass, H. 1990. "Stewardship as Fundamental Element in Images of Public Administration." In *Images and Identities in Public Administration*, Eds. H. Kass and B. Catron, 112–130. Newbury Park, CA: Sage.

Kassel, D.S. 2008. "Performance, Accountability, and the Debate over Rules." *Public Administration Review* 68(2): 241–252.

Kathi, P.C., and T. Cooper. 2005. "Democratizing the Administrative State: Connecting Neighborhood Councils and City Agencies." *Public Administration Review* 65(5): 559–567.

Kaufman, H. 1956. "Emerging Conflicts in the Doctrines of Public Administration." *American Political Science Review* 50(4): 1057–1073.

Kearney, R.C., and S. Hays. 1994. "Labor Management Relations and Participative Decision Making: Toward a New Paradigm." *Public Administration Review* 54(1): 44–51.

Kearns, K.P. 1994. "The Strategic Management of Accountability in Nonprofit Organizations: An Analytical Framework." *Public Administration Review* 54(2): 185–192.

Kelly, J.M. 2005. "The Dilemma of the Unsatisfied Customer in a Market Model of Public Administration." *Public Administration Review* 65(1): 76–84.

Kettl, D.F. 1998. *Reinventing Government: A Fifth-Year Report Card.* Washington, DC: Brookings Institute.

———. 2000a. *The Global Public Management Revolution.* Washington, DC: Brookings Institution.

———. 2000b. "The Transformation of Governance." *Public Administration Review* 60(6): 488–497.

———. 2005. *The Global Public Management Revolution.* Washington, DC: Brookings Institution.

———. 2009. *The Next Government of the United States.* New York: Norton.

Kettl, D.F., and H.B. Milward, Eds. 1996. *The State of Public Management.* Baltimore, MD: Johns Hopkins University Press.

King, C.S., and C. Stivers. 1998. *Government is Us: Public Administration in an Anti-Government Era*. Thousand Oaks, CA: Sage.

King, C.S., and L. Zanetti. 2005. *Transformational Public Service*. Armonk, NY: M.E. Sharpe.

King, C.S., K.M. Feltey, and B. O'Neill. 1998. "The Question of Participation: Toward Authentic Public Participation in Public Administration." *Public Administration Review* 58(4): 317–326.

Kirlin, J.J. 1996. "What Government Must Do Well: Creating Value for Society." *Journal of Public Administration Research and Theory* 6 (January): 161–186.

Knickerbocker, I., and D. McGregor. 1942. "Union Management Cooperation: A Psychological Analysis." *Personnel* 19(3): 520–539.

Kotter, J.P. 1977. "Power, Dependence, and Effective Management." *Harvard Business Review* 55 (July–August): 125–136.

Krause, S. 2008. *Civil Passions: Moral Sentiment and Democratic Deliberation*. Princeton, NJ: Princeton University Press.

Landy, M. 1993. "Public Policy and Citizenship." In *Public Policy for Democracy*, Eds. H. Ingram and S.R. Smith, 19–44. Washington, DC: Brookings Institution.

Lappé, F.M., and P.M. Du Bois. 1994. *The Quickening of America: Rebuilding Our Nation, Remaking Our Lives*. San Francisco, CA: Jossey-Bass.

Lawler, E. 1990. *High Involvement Management*. San Francisco, CA: Jossey-Bass.

Leazes, F.J., Jr. 1997. "Public Accountability: Is it a Private Responsibility?" *Administration & Society* 29(4): 395–412.

Lee, Y.S. 2005. *A Reasonable Public Servant*. Armonk, NY: M.E. Sharpe.

Leighninger, M. 2008. *The Promise and Challenge of Neighborhood Democracy: Lessons from the Intersection of Government and Community*. Washington, DC: Grassroots Grantmakers, the Deliberative Democracy Consortium, with assistance from the National League of Cities and Neighbor Works America.

Leland, S., and O. Smirnova. 2009. "Reassessing Privatization Strategies 25 Years Later: Revisiting Perry and Babitsky's Comparative Performance Study of Urban Bus Transit Services." *Public Administration Review* 69: 855–867.

Lenkowsky, L., and J.L. Perry. 2000. "Reinventing Government: The Case of National Service." *Public Administration Review* 60(4): 298–307.

Leroux, K. 2007. "Nonprofits as Civic Intermediaries: The Role of Community-Based Organizations in Promoting Political Participation." *Urban Affairs Review* 42: 410–422.

Levine, C. 1984. "Citizenship and Service Delivery: The Promise of Coproduction." *Public Administration Review* 44 (Special Issue): 178–187.

Levitan, D. 1943. "Political Ends and Administrative Means." *Public Administration Review* 4(4): 353–359.

Levy, R. 2010. "New Public Management: End of an Era?" *Public Policy and Administration* 25(2): 234–240.

Lewin, K. 1951. *Field Theory in Social Science*. New York: Harper & Row.

Lewis, E. 1980. *Public Entrepreneurship*. Bloomington, IN: Indiana University Press.

Lægreid, P., and T. Christensen, Eds. 2007. *Transcending New Public Management*. Hampshire, UK: Ashgate.

Light, P. 1997. *The Tides of Reform*. New Haven, CT: Yale University Press.

———. 2008. *A Government Ill Executed*. Cambridge, MA: Harvard University Press.

Linder, S., and B.G. Peters. 1986. "A Design Perspective on Policy Implementation: The Fallacies of Misplaced Prescriptions." *Policy Studies Review* 6(3): 459–475.

———. 1987. "Relativism, Contingency, and the Definition of Success in Implementation Research." *Policy Studies Review* 7(1): 102–127.

Lippmann, W. 1955. *Essays in the Public Philosophy*. Boston, MA: Little, Brown.

Locke, E. 1978. "The Ubiquity of the Technique of Goal Setting in Theories of and Approaches to Employee Motivation." *Academy of Management Review* (July): 594–601.

Love, J., and P. Sederberg. 1987. "Euphony and Cacophony in Policy Implementation: SCF and the Somali Refugee Problem." *Policy Studies Review* 7(1): 155–173.

Lucio, J. 2009. "Customers, Citizens, and Residents: The Semantics of Public Service Recipients." *Administration & Society* 41: 878–899.

Luke, J. 1998. *Catalytic Leadership*. San Francisco, CA: Jossey-Bass.

Lukensmeyer, C.J., and S. Brigham. 2002. "Taking Democracy to Scale: Creating a Town Hall Meeting for the Twenty-First Century." *National Civic Review* 91(4): 351–366.

Lukensmeyer, C.J., and L.H. Torres. 2006. *Public Deliberation: A Manager's Guide to Citizen Engagement*. Washington, DC: IBM Center for the Business of Government.

Lukensmeyer, C.J., J. Goldman, and D. Stern. 2011. *Assessing Public Participation in an Open Government Era: A Review of Federal Agency Plans*. Washington, DC: IBM Center for The Business of Government.

Lynn, L.E. 1996. *Public Management as Art, Science, and Profession*. Chatham, NJ: Chatham House.

———. 2006. *Public Management: Old and New*. New York: Routledge.

Lynn, L.E., C. Heinrich, and C. Hill. 2000. "Studying Governance and Public Management: Challenges and Prospects." *Journal of Public Administration Research and Theory* 10(2): 233–262.

Maass, A.A., and L.I. Radaway. 1959. "Gauging Administrative Responsibility." In *Democracy, Bureaucracy, and the Study of Administration*, Ed. C. Stivers, 163–181. Boulder, CO: Westview Press.

McCabe, B. 2010. "Neighborhood and Homeowner Associations." In *Connected Communities*, Eds. J. Svara and J.V. Denhardt, 119–122. Phoenix, AZ: Alliance for Innovation.

McCabe, B., and J. Vinzant. 1999. "Governance Lessons: The Case of Charter Schools." *Administration and Society* 31(3): 361–377.

McClelland, D. 1985. *Human Motivation*. Glenview, IL: Scott, Foresman.

Macedo, S., Ed. 1999. *Deliberative Politics*. New York: Oxford University Press.

McGinnis, M.D., and E. Ostrom. 2012. "Reflections on Vincent Ostrom, Public Administration, and Polycentricity." *Public Administration Review* 72: 15–25.

McGregor, D. 1957. "The Human Side of the Enterprise." *Management Review* 46(November): 22–28.

McGuire, M. 2006. "Collaborative Public Management: Assessing What We Know and How We Know It." *Public Administration Review* 66(6): 33–43.

MacKenzie, J.S. 1901. "The Use of Moral Ideas in Politics." *International Journal of Politics* 12(1): 1–23.

McSwite, O.C. 1997. *Legitimacy in Public Administration*. Thousand Oaks, CA: Sage.

——. 2000. "On the Discourse Movement: A Self-Interview." *Administrative Theory and Praxis* 22(1): 49–65.

Madison, J., A. Hamilton, and J. Jay. [1787]1987. *The Federalist Papers*, Ed. Isaac Kramnick. Harmondsworth, UK: Penguin.

Mansbridge, J., Ed. 1990. *Beyond Self-Interest*. Chicago, IL: University of Chicago Press.

—— 1994. "Public Spirit in Political Systems." In *Values and Public Policy*, Eds. H.J. Aaron, T. Mann, and T. Taylor, 146–172. Washington, DC: Brookings Institution.

Marsh, M. 2013. "Leadership and Leading: Leadership Challenges." In *The Jossey-Bass Reader on Nonprofit and Public Leadership*, Ed. J. Perry. San Francisco, CA: Wiley.

Maslow, A. 1943. "A Theory of Human Motivation." *Psychological Review* 50: 370–396.

Mathews, D. 1994. *Politics for People*. Urbana, IL: University of Illinois Press.

Meier, K.J., and L.J. O'Toole. 2006. *Bureaucracy in a Democratic State*. Baltimore, MD: Johns Hopkins University Press.

——. 2009. "The Proverbs of New Public Management." *American Review of Public Administration* 39(1): 4–22.

Meijer, A.J. 2011. "Networked Coproduction of Public Services in Virtual Communities: From a Government-Centric to a Community Approach to Public Service Support." *Public Administration Review* 71(4): 598–607.

Menzel, D. 1981. "Implementation of the Federal Surface Mining Control and Reclamation Act of 1977." *Public Administration Review* 51(2): 212–219.

Mill, J.S. 1862. *Considerations on Representative Government*, II. New York: Harper.

Miller, H., and C. Fox. 1997. *Postmodern "Reality" and Public Administration*. Burke, VA: Chatelaine Press.

Miller, T. 1989. "The Operation of Democratic Institutions." *Public Administration Review* 49(6): 511–521.

Milward, H.B. 1991. "Current Institutional Arrangements that Create or Require Shared Power." In *Shared Power*, Eds. J.M. Bryson and R.C. Einsweiler, 51–77. Minneapolis, MN: Humphrey Institute of Public Affairs.

Mintzberg, H. 1996. "Managing Government, Governing Management." *Harvard Business Review* 74 (May–June): 75–83.

Mommsen, W. 1974. *The Age of Bureaucracy*. New York: Harper & Row.

Monypenny, P. 1953. "A Code of Ethics as a Means of Controlling Administrative Conduct." *Public Administration Review* 13(3): 184–187.

Mooney, J., and A.C. Reiley. 1939. *The Principles of Organization*. New York: Harper & Row.

Moore, M.H. 2014. "Public Value Accounting: Establishing the Philosophical Basis." *Public Administration Review* 74(4): 465–477.

Mosher, F. 1968. *Democracy and the Public Service*. New York: Oxford University Press.

Moynihan, D.P. 2006. "Managing for Results in State Government: Evaluating a Decade of Reform." *Public Administration Review* 66: 77–89.

——. 2008. *The Dynamics of Performance Management*. Washington, DC: Georgetown University Press.

Mulgan, R. 2000. "Comparing Accountability in the Public and Private Sectors." *Australian Journal of Public Administration* 59(1): 87–98.

Munsterberg, H. 1913. *Psychology and Industrial Efficiency*. Boston, MA: Houghton Mifflin.

Myers, R., and R. Lacey. 1996. "Consumer Satisfaction, Performance and Accountability in the Public Sector." *International Review of Administrative Sciences* 62(2): 331–350.

Nabatchi, T, and I. Mergel. 2010. "Participation 2.0: Using Internet and Social Media Technologies to Promote Distributed Democracy and Create Digital Neighborhoods." In *Connected Communities*, Eds. J. Svara and J.V. Denhardt, 80–87. Phoenix, AZ: Alliance for Innovation.

Nakamura, R. 1987. "The Textbook Policy Process and Implementation Research." *Policy Studies Review* 7(1): 142–154.

Nalbandian, J. 1999. "Facilitating Community, Enabling Democracy: New Roles of Local Government Managers." *Public Administration Review* 59(3): 187–198.

Nalbandian, J. 2008. "Predicting the Future: Why Citizen Engagement No Longer is Optional." *Public Management* 90(11): 35–37.

Nelissen, N. 2002. "The Administrative Capacity of New Types of Governance." *Public Organization Review* 2(1): 23–43.

Nelissen, N., M.L.B. Videc, A. Godfroij, and P. de Goede. 1999. *Renewing Government*. Utrecht, NL: International Books.

Northouse, P.G. 2013. *Leadership: Theory and Practice*. Thousand Oaks, CA: Sage.

Nye, J.S., Jr. 2013. "New Models of Public Leadership." In *The Jossey-Bass Reader on Nonprofit and Public Leadership*, Ed. J. Perry, 586–593. San Francisco, CA: Wiley.

O'Leary, R. 2006. *The Ethics of Dissent*. Washington, DC: CQ Press.

O'Leary, R., C. Gerard, and L.B. Bingham. 2006. "Introduction to the Symposium on Collaborative Public Management." *Public Administration Review* 66(6): 6–9.

Organization for Economic Cooperation and Development (OECD). 2001. *Citizens as Partners: Information, Consultation, and Public Participation in Policy Making*. Paris: OECD.

Osborne, D., and T. Gaebler. 1992. *Reinventing Government: How the Entrepreneurial Spirit is Transforming the Public Sector*. Reading, MA: Addison-Wesley.

Osborne, D., with P. Plastrik. 1997. *Banishing Bureaucracy*. Reading, MA: Addison-Wesley.

Ostrom, V., and E. Ostrom. 1971. "Public Choice: A Different Approach to the Study of Public Administration." *Public Administration Review* 31 (March–April): 203–216.

Ostrom, V., C.M. Tiebout, and R. Warren. 1961. "The Organization of Government in Metropolitan Areas: A Theoretical Inquiry." *American Political Science Review* 55(4): 831–842.

O'Toole, L. 2000. "Research on Policy Implementation: Assessment and Prospects." *Journal of Public Administration Research and Theory* 10(2): 263–288.

O'Toole, L., and R. Montjoy. 1984. "Intergovernmental Policy Implementation: A Theoretical Perspective." *Public Administration Review* 54(6): 491–503.

Ott, J.S., Ed. 1989. *Classic Readings in Organizational Behavior*. Belmont, CA: Brooks/Cole.

——. 1996. *Classic Readings in Organizational Behavior*. 2nd ed. Fort Worth, TX: Harcourt Brace.

Ott, J.S., S. Parks, and R. Simpson. 2007. *Classic Readings in Organizational Behavior*. 4th ed. Belmont, CA: Cengage.

Palumbo, D. 1987. "What Have We Learned and Still Need to Know?" *Policy Studies Review* 7(1): 91–102.

Pateman, C. 1970. *Participation and Democratic Theory*. Cambridge, UK: Cambridge University Press.

Percy, S. 1984. "Citizen Participation in the Coproduction of Urban Services." *Urban Affairs Quarterly* 19(4): 431–446.

Perry, J.L., Ed. 1996. *Handbook of Public Administration*. 2nd ed. San Francisco, CA: Jossey-Bass.

Perry, J.L., and L. Wise. 1990. "The Motivational Bases of Public Service." *Public Administration Review* 50(3): 367–373.

Perry, J.L., and N.D. Buckwalter. 2010. "The Public Service of the Future." *Public Administration Review* 70(S1): 238–245.

Perry, J.L., A. Hondeghem, and L.R. Wise. 2010. "Revisiting the Motivational Bases of Public Service: Twenty Years of Research and an Agenda for the Future." *Public Administration Review* 70(5): 681–690.

Peters, B. Guy, and D. Savoie. 1996. "Managing Incoherence: The Coordination and Empowerment Conundrum." *Public Administration Review* 56(3): 281–289.

Peters, T., and R. Waterman. 1982. *In Search of Excellence*. New York: HarperCollins.

Pfeffer, J. 1981. *Power in Organizations*. Cambridge, MA: Ballinger.

Plas, J.M. 1996. *Person-Centered Leadership: An American Approach to Participatory Management*. London: Sage.

Pocock, J.G.A. 1995. "The Ideal of Citizenship Since Classical Times." In *Theorizing Citizenship*, Ed. Ronald Beiner, 29–52. Albany, NY: State University of New York Press.

Pollitt, C. 1988. "Bring Consumers into Performance Measurement." *Policy and Politics* 16(2): 77–88.

———. 1993. *Managerialism and the Public Service*. 2nd ed. Cambridge, UK: Basil Blackwell.

Pollitt, C., and G. Bouckaert. 2000. *Public Management Reform*. Oxford, UK: Oxford University Press.

Pollitt, C., S. Van Thiel, and V. Homberg, Eds. 2007. *The New Public Management in Europe*. Houndsmill, UK: Palgrave Macmillan.

Portney, K. 2005. "Civic Engagement and Sustainable Cities in the United States." *Public Administration Review* 65(5): 579–591.

Potter, J. 1988. "Consumerism and the Public Sector." *Public Administration* 66(Summer): 149–164.

Pranger, R.J. 1968. *The Eclipse of Citizenship*. New York: Holt, Rinehart & Winston.

Pressman, J., and A. Wildavsky. 1973. *Implementation*. Berkeley, CA: University of California Press.

———. 1979. *Implementation*. 2nd ed. Berkeley, CA: University of California Press.

Pusey, M. 1991. *Economic Rationalism in Canberra*. New York: Cambridge University Press.

Putnam, R. 2000. *Bowling Alone*. New York: Simon & Schuster.

Rabin, J., W. Bartley Hildreth, and G.J. Miller, Eds. 1998. *Handbook of Public Administration*. 2nd ed. New York: Marcel Dekker.

Raadschelders, J.C., and K.-H. Lee. 2011. "Trends in the Study of Public Administration: Empirical and Qualitative Observations from Public Administration Review, 2000–2009." *Public Administration Review* 71(1): 19–33.

Ramesh, M., E. Araral, and X. Wu, Eds. 2010. *Reasserting the Public in Public Services*. New York: Routledge Studies in Governance and Public Policy.

Redford, E. 1954. "The Protection of the Public Interest with Special Reference to Administrative Regulation." *American Political Science Review* 48: 1103–1108.

———. 1969. *Democracy in the Administrative State*. New York: Oxford University Press.

Reed, C.M., and K.P. Meyer. 2004. "Medicaid Managed Care for Children with Special Health Care Needs: Examining Legislative and Judicial Constraints on Privatization." *Public Administration Review* 64(2): 234–242.

Reich, R.B. 1988. "Policy Making in a Democracy." In *The Power of Public Ideas*, Ed. R.B. Reich, 119–145. Cambridge, MA: Ballinger.

Rezmovic, E. 1982. "Program Implementation and Evaluation Results." *Evaluation and Program Planning* 5(1): 111–118.

Rho, E. 2013. "Contracting Revisited: Determinants and Consequences of Contracting Out for Public Education Services." *Public Administration Review* 73(2): 327–337.

Riccucci, N.M., and F.J. Thompson. 2008. "New Public Management, Homeland Security, and the Politics of Civil Service Reform." *Public Administration Review* 68(5): 877–890.

Roberts, N. 2004. "Public Deliberation in an Age of Direct Citizen Participation." *American Review of Public Administration* 34(4): 315–353.

———. 2008. *The Age of Direct Citizen Participation*. Armonk, NY: M.E. Sharpe.

Roethlisberger, F.J., and W. Dickson. 1939. *Management and the Worker*. Cambridge, MA: Harvard University Press.

Rohr, J.A. 1986. *To Run a Constitution: The Legitimacy of the Administrative State*. Lawrence, KS: University Press of Kansas, Studies in Government and Public Policy.

———. 1998. *Public Service, Ethics and Constitutional Practice*. Lawrence, KS: University Press of Kansas.

Romzek, B.S., and P. Ingraham. 2000. "Cross Pressures of Accountability: Initiative, Command, and Failure in the Ron Brown Plane Crash." *Public Administration Review* 60(3): 240–253.

Romzek, B.S., and J.M. Johnston. 2005. "State Social Services Contracting: Exploring the Determinants of Effective Contract Accountability." *Public Administration Review* 65(4): 436–449.

Rosen, B. 1989. *Holding Government Bureaucracies Accountable*. 2nd ed. New York: Praeger.

Ruscio, K. 1996. "Trust, Democracy, and Public Management: A Theoretical Argument." *Journal of Public Administration Research and Theory* 6(3): 461–477.

Salminen, A., and V. Mäntysalo. 2013. "Exploring the Public Service Ethos." *Public Integrity* 15(2): 167–186.

Sandel, M. 1996. *Democracy's Discontent*. Cambridge, MA: Belknap Press of Harvard University Press.

Schachter, H.L. 1997. *Reinventing Government or Reinventing Ourselves*. Albany, NY: State University of New York Press.

Schattschneider, E.E. 1952. "Political Parties and the Public Interest." *Annals of the American Academy of Political and Social Science* 280: 13–31.

Schein, E. 1987. *Organizational Culture and Leadership*. San Francisco, CA: Jossey-Bass.

Schein, E.H. 2008. "The Learning Leader as Culture Manager." In *Classic Readings in Organizational Behavior*, Eds. S.J. Ott, S.J. Parkes, and R.B. Simpson, 74–81. Belmont, CA: Thomson Wadsworth.

Schmidt, F., with T. Strickland. 1998. *Client Satisfaction Surveying*. Ottawa, ON: Canadian Centre for Management Development, Citizen-Centered Service Network.

Schneider, A.L., and H. Ingram. 1997. *Policy Design for Democracy*. Lawrence, KS: University Press of Kansas.

Schott, R. 1986. "The Psychological Development of Adults: Implications of Public Administration." *Public Administration Review* 46(6): 657–667.

Schubert, G. 1957. "'The Public Interest' in Administrative Decision-Making: Theorem, Theosophy, or Theory." *American Political Science Review* 51(2): 346–368.

———. 1960. *The Public Interest: A Critique of the Theory of a Political Concept*. Glencoe, IL: Free Press.

———. 1962. "Is There a Public Interest Theory?" In *The Public Interest*, Ed. Carl Friedrich, 162–176. New York: Atherton Press.

Selznick, P. 1992. *The Moral Commonwealth*. Berkeley, CA: University of California Press.

Shafritz, J., and A. Hyde. 1997. *Classics of Public Administration*. 2nd ed. Fort Worth, TX: Harcourt Brace.

Shamsul, H. 2007. "Revisiting the New Public Management." *Public Administration Review* 67(1): 19–182.

Sharpe, E. 1980. "Toward a New Understanding of Urban Services and Citizen Participation." *Midwest Review of Public Administration* 14(2): 105–118.

Sherif, M. 1936. *The Psychology of Social Norms*. New York: Harper.

Simon, H.A. 1957. *Administrative Behavior*. 2nd ed. New York: Free Press.

Simon, H.A., D.W. Smithburg, and V.A. Thompson. 1950. *Public Administration*. New York: Knopf.

Sirianni, C., and L. Friedland. 2001. *Civic Innovation in America*. Berkeley, CA: University of California Press.

Smith, H. 1960. *Democracy and the Public Interest*. Athens, GA: University of Georgia Press.

Sorauf, F. 1957. "The Public Interest Reconsidered." *Journal of Politics* 19(4): 616–639.

Sorensen, E., and J. Torfing, Eds. 2008. *Theories of Democratic Network Governance*. New York: Palgrave Macmillan.

Spiro, H.J. 1969. *Responsibility in Government: Theory and Practice*. New York: Van Nostrand Reinhold.

Staats, E. 1988. "Public Service and the Public Interest." *Public Administration Review* (March–April): 601–605.

Stashevsky, S., and D. Elizur. 2000. "The Effect of Quality Management and Participation in Decision-Making on Individual Performance." *Journal of Quality Management* 5: 53.

Stivers, C. 1990. "The Public Agency as Polis: Active Citizenship in the Administrative State." *Administration & Society* 22(1): 86–105.

———. 1993. *Gender Images in Public Administration*. Newbury Park, CA: Sage.

———. 1994a. "Citizenship Ethics in Public Administration." In *Handbook of Administrative Ethics*, Ed. T. Cooper, 583–602. New York: Marcel Dekker.

——. 1994b. "The Listening Bureaucrat." *Public Administration Review* 54(4): 364–369.

Stone, D. 1988. *Policy Paradox and Political Reason.* New York: HarperCollins.

——. 1997. *Policy Paradox: The Art of Political Decision Making.* New York: Norton.

Sundeen, R. 1985. "Coproduction and Communities." *Administration & Society* 16(4): 387–402.

Svara, J. 2007. *The Ethics Primer for Public Administrators in Government and Nonprofit Organizations.* Sudbury, MA: Jones & Bartlett.

——. 2010. "The Next Generation Challenge: Finding and Incorporating the Local Government Managers of the Future." *Journal of Public Administration Education* 16(3): 361–377.

Swedish Association of Local Authorities and Regions. 2010. *11 Thoughts About Citizen Dialogue in Local Government.* Stockholm: Author.

Taylor, F.W. 1923. *Scientific Management.* New York: Harper & Row.

Terry, L.D. 1993. "Why We Should Abandon the Misconceived Quest to Reconcile Public Entrepreneurship with Democracy." *Public Administration Review* 53(4): 393–395.

——. 1995. *Leadership of Public Bureaucracies.* Thousand Oaks, CA: Sage.

——. 1998. "Administrative Leadership, Neo-Managerialism, and the Public Management Movement." *Public Administration Review* 58(3): 194–200.

——. 2005. "The Thinning of Administrative Institutions in the Hollow State." *Administration & Society* 37(4): 426–444.

Thomas, J.C. 1995. *Public Participation in Public Decisions.* San Francisco, CA: Jossey-Bass.

——. 2010. "Citizen, Customer, Partner: Thinking about Local Governance with and for the Public." In *Connected Communities*, Eds. J. Svara and J.V. Denhardt, 57–61. Phoenix, AZ: Alliance for Innovation.

Thompson, D. 1970. *The Democratic Citizen.* Cambridge, UK: Cambridge University Press.

Thompson, J.R. 2000. "Reinvention as Reform: Assessing the National Performance Review." *Public Administration Review* 60(6): 508–521.

Thomson, A.M. and J.L. Perry. 2006. "Collaboration Processes: Inside the Black Box." *Public Administration Review* 66(6): 20–32.

de Tocqueville, Alexis. [1835]1969. *Democracy in America*, trans. G. Lawrence, Ed. J.P. Mayer. Garden City, NY: Doubleday.

Tornatzky, L., and E. Johnson. 1982. "Research on Implementation: Implications for Evaluation Practice and Evaluation Policy." *Evaluation and Program Planning* 5(1): 193–198.

Trajanowicz, R., V. Kappeler, L. Gaines, and B. Bucqueroux. 1998. *Community Policing: A Contemporary Perspective.* Cincinnati, OH: Anderson.

Tschirhart, M., R.K. Christensen, and J.L. Perry. 2005. "The Paradox of Branding and Collaboration." *Public Performance & Management* 29(1): 67–84.

Turner, B.S., Ed. 1993. *Citizenship and Social Theory.* London: Sage.

Van der Wal, Z., and L. Huberts. 2008. "Value Solidarity in Government and Business: Results of an Empirical Study on Public and Private Sector Organizational Values." *The American Review of Public Administration* 38(3): 264–285.

Van Meter, D.S., and C.E. Van Horn. 1975. "The Policy Implementation Process: A Conceptual Framework." *Administration & Society* 6(4): 445–488.

Van Slyke, D.M. 2003. "The Mythology of Privatization in Contracting for Social Services." *Public Administration Review* 63(3): 296–315.

Van Wart, M. 2005. *Dynamics of Leadership in Public Service.* Armonk, NY: M.E. Sharpe.

Vigoda-Gadot, E. 2004. "Collaborative Public Administration: Some Lessons from the Israeli Experience." *Managerial Auditing Journal* 19(6): 700–711.

Vinzant, J. 1998. "Where Values Collide: Motivation and Role Conflict in Child and Adult Protective Services." *American Review of Public Administration* 28(4): 347–366.

Vinzant, J., and L. Crothers. 1998. *Street-Level Leadership: Discretion and Legitimacy in Front-Line Public Service.* Washington, DC: Georgetown University Press.

Vroom, V. 1964. *Work and Motivation.* New York: John Wiley.

Wagenaar, H. 2007. "Governance, Complexity, and Democratic Participation: How Citizens and Public Officials Harness the Complexities of Neighborhood Decline." *American Review of Public Administration* 37(1): 17–50.

Waldo, D. 1948. *The Administrative State.* New York: Ronald Press.

———. 1952. "The Development of a Theory of Democratic Administration." *American Political Science Review* 46 (March): 81–103.

Walters, L.C., J. Aydelotte, and J. Miller. 2000. "Putting More Public in Policy Analysis." *Public Administration Review* 60: 349–359.

Walzer, M. 1995. "The Civil Society Argument." In *Theorizing Citizenship*, Ed. R. Beiner, 153–174. Albany, NY: State University of New York Press.

Wamsley, G., and J. Wolf. 1996. *Refounding Democratic Public Administration.* Thousand Oaks, CA: Sage.

Wamsley, G., R. Bacher, C. Goodsell, P. Kronenberg, J. Rohr, C. Stivers, O. White, and J. Wolf. 1990. *Refounding Public Administration.* Newbury Park, CA: Sage.

Wang, X. 2001. "Assessing Public Participation in U.S. Cities." *Public Performance & Management Review* 24(4): 322–336.

Warner, M.E. 2008. "Reversing Privatization, Rebalancing Government Reform: Markets, Deliberation and Planning." *Policy and Society* 27: 163–174.

Warner, M.E., and A. Hefetz. 2008. "Managing Markets for Public Service: The Role of Mixed Public–Private Delivery of City Services." *Public Administration Review* 68(1): 155–166.

Watson, D., R. Juster, and G. Johnson. 1991. "Institutional Use of Citizen Surveys in the Budgetary and Policy-Making Processes." *Public Administration Review* 51(3): 232–239.

Weale, A. 2007. *Democracy.* Houndsmill, UK: Palgrave Macmillan.

Weber, E.P. 1999. "The Question of Accountability in Historical Perspective." *Administration & Society* 31(4): 451–495.

Weeks, E.C. 2000. "The Practice of Deliberative Democracy." *Public Administration Review* 60(4): 360–372.

Weimer, D. 1980. "CMIS Implementation: A Demonstration of Predictive Analysis." *Public Administration Review* 50(3): 231–240.

White, J. 2002. *Taking Language Seriously: The Narrative Foundations of Public Administration Research.* Washington, DC: Georgetown University Press.

White, L.D. 1926. *Introduction to the Study of Public Administration.* New York: Macmillan.

Whyte, W.F. 1943. *Street Corner Society*. Chicago, IL: University of Chicago Press.

Wichowsky, A., and D.P. Moynihan. 2008. "Measuring How Administration Shapes Citizenship: A Policy Feedback Perspective on Performance Management." *Public Administration Review* 68(5): 908–920.

Williams, D.W. 2000. "Reinventing the Proverbs of Government." *Public Administration Review* 60(6): 522–534.

Willoughby, W.F. 1927. *Principles of Public Administration*. Baltimore, MD: Johns Hopkins University Press.

Wilson, Woodrow. [1887]1987. "The Study of Administration." *Political Science Quarterly* 2 (June). Reprinted, 1997, in *Classics of Public Administration*, 2nd ed., Eds. J. Shafritz and A. Hyde, 10–25. Chicago, IL: Dorsey Press.

Wolfe, A. 1989. *Whose Keeper? Social Science and Moral Obligation*. Berkeley, CA: University of California Press.

Wood, D.J., and B. Gray. 1991. "Toward a Comprehensive Theory of Collaboration." *The Journal of Applied Behavioral Science* 27(2), 139–162.

Woolum, J. 2000. "Social Capital as a Community Resource: Implications for Public Administration." Unpublished manuscript.

———. 2010. "Citizen–Government Dialogue in Performance Measurement Cycle: Cases from Local Government." In *Connected Communities*, Eds. J. Svara and J.V. Denhardt, 102–105. Phoenix, AZ: Alliance for Innovation.

Wolin, S. 1960. *Politics and Vision*. Boston, MA: Little, Brown.

Yang, K., and K. Callahan. 2007. "Citizen Involvement Efforts and Bureaucratic Responsiveness: Participatory Values, Stakeholder Pressures, and Administrative Practicality." *Public Administration Review* 67(2): 249–264.

Yang, K., J.Y. Hsieh, and S.T. Li. 2009. "Contracting Capacity and Perceived Contracting Performance: Nonlinear Effects and the Role of Time." *Public Administration Review* 69(4): 681–696.

Yankelovich, D. 1991. *Coming to Public Judgment*. Syracuse, NY: Syracuse University Press.

———. 1999. *The Magic of Dialogue*. New York: Simon & Schuster.

Yeatman, A. 1987. "The Concept of Public Management and the Australian State." *Australian Journal of Public Administration* 46(4): 339–353.

Zeemering, E.S. 2008. "Governing Interlocal Cooperation: City Council Interests and the Implications for Public Management." *Public Administration Review* 68(4): 731–741.

Index

About the Authors

Janet V. Denhardt is the Chester A. Newland Professor of Public Administration, Director of the University of Southern California (USC) Price School of Public Policy Sacramento Center, and fellow of the National Academy of Public Administration. Her teaching and research interests focus on governance, organizational theory, organization behavior, and leadership. Her books include *Organizational Behavior* (with A. Nahavandi, R. Denhardt, and M. Aristegueta), *The Dance of Leadership* (with R. Denhardt), *Managing Human Behavior in Public and Nonprofit Organizations* (with R. Denhardt and M. Aristigueta), *Public Administration: An Action Orientation* (with R. Denhardt and T. Blanc), and *Street-Level Leadership: Discretion and Legitimacy in Front-Line Service* (with L. Crothers). She has also published numerous articles in journals such as *Public Administration Review*, *Administration & Society*, *American Review of Public Administration*, and *Journal of Public Administration Research and Theory*. Prior to joining the faculty at USC, she taught at Arizona State University and Eastern Washington University. Earlier in her career, she served in a variety of administrative positions for the State of Washington and the U.S. Department of Health and Human Services. Her doctorate is from the University of Southern California.

Robert B. Denhardt is a Professor and the Director of Leadership Programs in the USC Price School of Public Policy. He also holds the title of Regents Professor Emeritus at Arizona State University and Distinguished Visiting Scholar at the University of Delaware. He is past president of the ASPA and a fellow of the National Academy of Public Adminnistration. He has published more than 20 books, including *Organizational Behavior* (with A. Nahavandi, J. Denhardt, and M. Aristegueta), *The Dance of Leadership* (with J. Denhardt), *Theories of Public Organization, Public Administration:*

An Action Orientation (with J. Denhardt and T. Blanc), *In the Shadow of Organization*, *The Pursuit of Significance*, and *Managing Human Behavior in Public and Nonprofit Organizations* (with J. Denhardt and M. Aristigueta). He has published more than 100 articles in professional journals, primarily in the areas of leadership, management, and organizational change. His doctorate is from the University of Kentucky.